Escaping The Hostility Trap

ESCAPING THE HOSTILITY TRAP

Milton Layden, M.D.

Prentice-Hall, Inc., Englewood Cliffs, New Jersey

Escaping the Hostility Trap
by Milton Layden, M.D.
Copyright © 1977 by Milton Layden, M.D.

Printed in the United States of America
Prentice-Hall International, Inc., London
Prentice-Hall of Australia, Pty. Ltd., Sydney
Prentice-Hall of Canada, Ltd., Toronto
Prentice-Hall of India Private Ltd., New Delhi
Prentice-Hall of Japan, Inc., Tokyo
Prentice-Hall of Southeast Asia Pte. Ltd.
Whitehall Books Limited, Wellington, New Zealand
10 9 8 7 6 5 4

Library of Congress Cataloging in Publication Data

Layden, Milton
    Escaping the hostility trap.

    Includes index.
    1. Hostility (Psychology)   2. Inferiority complex.
3. Medicine, Psychosomatic.   I. Title.
BF575.H6L39   152.4'2   76-54672
ISBN 0-13-283580-0

Contents

Escaping The Hostility Trap

Introduction:
A Single, Simplified Approach to Personal Problems

When I began my residency in psychiatry at Johns Hopkins Hospital in 1945, one of the very first patients I was permitted to treat was a gentle, quiet-spoken man of fifty-two. He had fainted several times at work and for over a year had been unable to work due to physical exhaustion. Since fainting and exhaustion are often emotionally caused, he was hospitalized in the psychiatric department.

When I questioned him about his marriage, he proudly declared that he and his wife got along very well; in fact, they never argued. But suddenly, in the next interview, he erupted into a torrent of rage against his wife, accompanied by violent spasms from head to foot. Unprepared for such an outburst, I almost took to my heels; since in four years of medical school and two years of internship, I had never been taught how to treat rage.

I soon learned that for the past twenty-six years this friendly chap had been trying to conceal his bitter resentment toward a wife who, after only a few months of marriage, had refused sexual relations; they had not shared a bed since.

"I've never let her know how bitter I've felt about this," he said. It had not occurred to him that she could perceive the resentment he strove to conceal. Yet he had been silently condemning *her* for doing the very same thing: striving to conceal her resentment for him.

Only after I explained that he had been infecting her with his own hostility was he able to begin freeing himself of those feelings. From this point on, he made rapid progress. The physical exhaustion which had kept him from working disappeared. When he re-

1

turned home, his wife soon responded to his hostile-free state with affection instead of resentment, and desire instead of frigidity.

Observing the elimination in a matter of weeks of hostility that had taken years to accumulate excited me as nothing ever had before. Convinced that this case was no fluke, I set out to perfect a method of overcoming hostility that would work for others as it had for this man.

I soon realized, however, that hostility wasn't limited to patients; much of it was present in the learned professors who were teaching us how to treat psychiatric illnesses and, for the first time, I became aware of my own abundant hostility.

Twelve years later, my first patient dropped in for a visit. He wanted to let me know that he had been applying my method of getting rid of hostility in all his relationships ever since he had learned it at Johns Hopkins. The result was a happy marriage, successful career, and excellent health.

His evidence—and that of many others in the next 30 years—has led me to believe that the best approach to the solution of our personal problems is through an understanding of a relatively few basic principles governing human behavior. In treating common personal problems (such as those between marriage partners, parents and children, teachers and students, and co-workers in industrial and other organizations); illnesses such as headache (including migraine), high blood pressure, and stomach ulcer; addictions to such things as alcohol, drugs, food, and gambling; and emotional illnesses such as neurosis and depression, I have found that hostility is at the heart of each and every one of them.

Hostility—anger, resentment, hurt feelings—is the chief saboteur of the mind. It wrecks all varieties of interpersonal relationship. When habitually suppressed, it becomes a significant factor in the formation of many serious diseases such as high blood pressure, coronary heart attack, and stomach ulcer.

On the job, it is the leading cause of misery, depression, inefficiency, sickness, accidents, loss of work time and financial loss to industry. The spread of hostility from the head of a firm to the rest of the work team is incalculable. No matter what the problem —marital conflict, alcoholism, a wife's frigidity, a child's defiance, nervous or physical disease—elimination of hostility is a key factor in its solution.

Is the treatment of all these conditions *simply* a matter of getting rid of hostility? Definitely not. In any given problem, a number of other complex factors are involved. Nevertheless, all emotional determinants of behavior arise from the same source in the brain as hostility and are intimately connected with one another. For this reason, as one overcomes hostility, one necessarily overcomes other harmful determinants of behavior.

ANTI-HOSTILITY THERAPY

"What system of treatment do you employ?"

Sooner or later, every patient in individual or group therapy asks me this question. Many people expect therapy to be brand-new, mystical and exotic, involving perhaps a special kind of electrical stimulation, hypnotism, a new drug or diet, rather than a simple commonsense procedure. Those who have been treated before invariably comment on the difference from their previous treatment. The difference, however, is in the method of arriving at the goal of treatment, not in the goal itself. My goal is the same as that of any other therapist: to make the patient well and to equip him so that he can stay well. Understanding the basis of such traits as the superiority complex and obsession with oneself is essential, but successful therapy is always based on learning to rid oneself of hostility.

I have taught my technique in the wards and clinics of Johns Hopkins Hospital, in private therapy in my office, and in groups consisting of married couples, business executives, parents, teachers, and pupils.

No one can be *constantly* and *totally* free of hostility, of course. But even when it doesn't totally eliminate hostility, my method enables you to reduce this emotion to a harmless level. Most failures have occurred in individuals who were either unwilling to acknowledge their own hostility or who did not put in the study and practice required to apply the technique successfully.

I intend to show here that an understanding of a few underlying emotional principles will furnish the basic tools you need to overcome:

1. personal conflicts with loved ones, friends, and co-workers
2. the physical symptoms and illnesses in which emotional disturbance is a prime factor
3. anxiety, tension, depression, alcoholism, drug addiction, and gambling

When you're trained in anti-hostility, you not only aren't hurt by formerly aggravating encounters, but can regularly turn them to your own advantage. No matter whom you're dealing with, you're always mindful of any hostility that may be present. Whether it's the repair man or your child, you'll stand the best chance of getting his cooperation by aggressively applying your knowledge of Anti-H.

And when you realize the widespread destructive mental and physical consequences of hostility, you'll want to apply this knowledge to keep yourself and your family well and to spread its benefits to your friends and fellow-workers.

Let's begin with some basic facts about the origin, nature, and emotional connections of hostility.

1.

The I→H Reaction

"Why is my husband so selfish?"

"Why does my wife complain so much?"

"How could a man with his intelligence do such a stupid thing?" said a senator about the ex-President of the United States. "He must have taken leave of his senses."

These questions are typical of those asked by intelligent persons attempting to make some kind of sense out of someone else's behavior. Such questions can't be answered correctly unless one learns how the mind operates.

Prior to the advent of modern science, the greatest geniuses of the ages were unable to fathom the basis of fire, chemical reactions, or illness. The understanding of these phenomena came only after many thousands of skilled and dedicated investigators corrected, bit by bit, the misapprehensions of their predecessors and patiently put together our present treasure house of scientific knowledge.

You don't have to be an animal behavior scientist to recognize the striking similarities in the behavior patterns of animals and man. Like most of us, your dog has a need for a territory of his own. If you dislodge him from the easy chair he's taken over, he'll react with a primitive form of the reaction you might display under similar circumstances. Is there any dog owner who doesn't recognize the hurt pride in his pet's face and posture after a scolding by his master?

In his classic book, *On Aggression*, the renowned animal behavior scientist Dr. Konrad Lorenz draws on a lifetime of observation and research to present convincing evidence for the evolutionary development of man's aggression from his animal ancestry. He shows us the intimate relationship between aggression and love in fish, birds, and a variety of other animals.

Lorenz's genius for careful observation of animal behavior points to the animal origin of man's superiority complex. The meeting of two previously unacquainted stickleback fish begins with a mutual "showing-off," a swaggering act of self-display in which every luminous color spot and brilliant ray of the shapely fins is brought into maximum play—attitudes which bear a striking resemblance to those of the human "show-off."

When the stickleback's territory is threatened, the fish opens its jaws so wide that all its teeth are directed forward and, in this attitude, it rams them, with all the force of its muscular body, into the side of the threatening invader.

Why do animals react with hostility when someone encroaches on their territory? Territorial acquisition is an essential activity—for obtaining food, in mating, in providing a nest for the young—and is the primitive forerunner of the self-respect associated with material possessions. When a biological need of an animal is threatened, it reacts instinctively with fear, as is also the case with man. The threat of physical harm, or the loss of one's family, territory, or self-respect, invariably produces an immediate response of fear—simply because the deprivation threatens the creature with the loss of an essential requirement that would relegate him to an inferior status.

In the course of evolution, hostility came into existence as a self-preservation device. Prior to its development, animals had to rely on fear alone to protect themselves from threatening danger. Fear produces an overwhelming impulse to escape—by flight or other forms of avoidance. However, you can see why animals equipped with the fear-flight mechanism *alone* would often lose out to those with greater hostility in the struggle for survival. For example, the stickleback with a small capacity for hostility could react only with fear and flight to a fish who would fight because it was equipped with more hostility. The fish with little hostility would thus lose his opportunities for mating.

The source of hostility in any creature is the same as in the stickleback: *Hostility is generated only in reaction to depletion of status.* A simple way of expressing this is:

I → H
I (Inferiority) generates H (Hostility).

This pattern of reaction in animals appears to be a primitive forerunner of the same reaction in man. The I → H Reaction holds true all the way up the evolutionary ladder. Konrad Lorenz relates how, as a youngster, he acquired his first bird, a jackdaw who developed increasing affection for him and followed him constantly until Lorenz acquired some baby jackdaws. No sooner did he touch one of them than he heard a sharp, metallic, grating cry of rage. His "pet" swooped down from above like an arrow, and Lorenz found himself staring in astonishment at a round, bleeding, deeply-pecked wound in the back of his hand. Isn't this akin to the hostile component in the jealousy of humans?

THE EVOLUTIONARY ORIGIN OF SUPERIORITY

Another example of a primitive form of superiority or pride is when a fish who is ready to mate changes to a gorgeous, iridescent color for the purpose of attracting a female. Or when a male bird, wishing to attract a prospective mate proudly rears his head and neck, emits his mating call and seeks to impress his loved one with his possession of a nifty-looking nest.

Dr. Lorenz also describes the response of the female cichlid fish when frightened by the aggressive actions of a male: she darts away from his territory, only to return soon manifesting a variety of submissive and coy gestures. If she fails to show him this respect, he continues his hostile actions. But if she humbly acknowledges his superiority, he becomes sexually activated. This reminds us of a man who loses his sex desire because of a hostile reaction to a woman's disrespectful attitude, but is sexually stimulated by an admiring woman.

The need for superiority is clearly seen in the pecking order of birds, fowl, rodents, dogs, and apes. When this need is threatened, a contest for superiority is set in motion, with hostility the inevitable result. An invader must be expelled from one's territory. A female bird will be furiously attacked if she is caught trying to snare another female's mate.

When I was writing this book, I would go over the material with my typist several nights a week at her home. We would sit side by side at the dining room table with our papers in front of us. Totally absorbed in discussing the work with me, my typist was, of course, oblivious to her dog. This collie could not long endure being cast in this inferior, left-out position. After a while she would insinuate her long body between our chairs and try to put her forelegs around her mistress' neck. The dog's stance and the expression in her eyes quite clearly conveyed, "You belong to me, not to that lug sitting beside you." That her need for superiority was also accompanied by hostility was manifested by her barking angrily at me—something she would not do as long as I didn't sit next to her mistress.

Proceeding up the evolutionary scale, an analogous display of superiority is seen in the chimpanzee, in frustrating situations that arouse something akin to human inferiority feelings. After showing signs of whimpering, the chimp suddenly charges off and, in a spectacular manner, assumes the erect position, stamps and slaps, drags or waves branches and hurls rocks. He may leap up at a buttressed tree and drum on it with his feet. Ethologists believe this charging display is a big bluff to make the chimp look larger and fiercer.

It is a mistake, however, to think that the wild beasts of the jungle are basically hostile creatures. *Aggressive* yes; *hostile* no. Repeated careful observation by animal behavior scientists reveals that these animals do not appear hostile when they kill for food.

"From many excellent photographs," says Lorenz, "it can be seen that the lion, in the dramatic moment before he springs, is in no way angry. A dog about to catch a rabbit has the same kind of excitedly happy expression as when he greets his master or awaits some longed-for treat. Growling, laying the ears back, and other well-known expression movements of fighting behavior are seen in predatory animals only when they are very afraid of a wildly resisting prey." It is fear that motivates the greatest violence in the animal, just as in man, as expressed in "fighting like a cornered rat."

Human hostility also occurs in reaction to depletion of any of our biological needs—for example, when someone tries to take over our food, our house, or our money. But because man is a "civilized," social animal, such occurrences are few. In fact, an attractive home, a beautiful wife, and a large salary are not always ends in themselves, but may be sought after for what we know as "status." Far more important than owning status symbols is the respect we get from people who admire them. Emotional problems and the resulting illnesses are almost always the consequence of the hostility arising from a deficiency of respect—experienced as a feeling of inferiority.

Because we need to feel liked and appreciated by our associates, we automatically compare ourselves to those around us throughout life. Like the contestants in a tournament, we interpret our position on the ladder of respect by comparison. Mother follows this approach when she tells the younger child, "Now eat your cereal, so you'll grow big and strong like your brother." Such stimulation of a child's faculty of comparison is often strong enough to induce him to eat some of mother's most tasteless concoctions!

THE EMOTIONAL BALANCING MECHANISM

When at rest, we breathe at the normal, unhurried rate. With extra muscular effort, however, proportionally more oxygen is required, and the breathing rate automatically speeds up.

We don't decide to increase our breathing rate; it increases as the result of an involuntary, automatic balancing mechanism called *homeostasis*. This mechanism acts not only to restore the oxygen to its normal level in the body, but to maintain the balance of all of our essential needs. For example, when your sugar level is low, it brings about a sense of hunger, pleasurable anticipation, and visions of food for the obvious purpose of getting you to eat.

Every system of the body is subject to this mechanism —including the emotional system. Thus, when your self-respect drops below the normal level (of equality with your associates) the balancing mechanism is automatically activated.

Suppose, for example, that your neighbor has done you a good turn. Later on, when you're tired, he asks for some help. The thought of turning him down gives rise to a feeling of disrespect for yourself. This inferiority feeling is automatically corrected; you feel pressured into helping the neighbor despite your fatigue, thus restoring your self-respect.

HOW AND WHY WE BECOME HOSTILE

Healthy behavior is based on the belief that we are the equal of our peers. This does not refer to equality in specific fields, such as mathematics or golf, but in the sense of being liked, appreciated and respected as a worthwhile person. When we do not feel respected by others, our opinion of our own worth is lowered. Since it is an essential human characteristic to compare ourselves constantly with those around us, we experience lack of respect as a relative feeling of inferiority. Since we interpret our hostility as, "It's his fault, not mine," it gives us, among other things, a feeling of pleasurable satisfaction.

Hostility is as normal a physiological response as shivering. Just as we shiver in response to sufficient lowering of our temperature, so we become hostile in response to lowering of our self-respect, via any kind of provocation which we interpret as disrespectful. Such provocations may arise from our own thoughts or from the attitudes and feelings of others; they are so frequent that we rarely get through a day without them.

Because of our natural tendency to sympathize with those who appear to be having the same troubles as ourselves, we readily react with hostility to incidents in which *others* are disrespected. This accounts for our repugnance toward those who belittle and blame people for the personal traits and viewpoints with which we identify ourselves. For example, a person who regularly votes for the Democratic candidate is likely to become hostile when an acquaintance remarks, "The Democrats are ruining this country." Heroes and villains, saints and sinners, the beautiful and the ugly, the loud-mouth and the meek, the intelligent and the stupid—all of us are natural producers of hostility.

The degree of hostility produced is determined by the degree of inferiority we feel at any given time. Note how kind, sympathetic, and unselfish you're apt to become after a successful accomplishment and how irritable-prone you are after a failure. After a man's self-respect is lowered by something that happened at work, he's apt to blow his top when his child spills his milk. But when the same thing occurs after a successful day, he can murmur with admirable tolerance, "Don't worry, Daddy'll get you another glass of milk."

Although the function of the balancing mechanism is to maintain health, this system doesn't work well under certain conditions. For example, if a man who has neglected to keep himself physically fit tries to shovel snow, he may suffer a heart attack. Homeostasis cannot overcome poorly maintained equipment, such as a sluggish circulation. Similarly, you can restore self-respect only when your emotional system is in a healthy state. Like the physically unfit person who hasn't the strength to shovel snow, an emotionally unfit person, one with a poor self-image, finds it difficult to withstand even a trivial slight, and suffers a sharp drop in self-respect. The person who *feels* inferior is not inferior at all: he simply has arrived at this self-concept as a result of the repetition of belittling experiences. The more inferior he feels, the more intense his reaction to any slight.

An example of this is an engineer who despite high technical competence has marked feelings of inferiority. While he was complaining about a problem with his office staff, his wife interrupted to suggest how he could remedy the problem. He became angry and told her it was his job to run his office, not hers.

It was because of his deficient level of respect that he reacted so strongly. Unfortunately, her angry response lowered his Respect Level even more.

Physical homeostasis also acts to induce hoarding. Thus, when the body is short of water, the sweat and salivary glands and kidneys are inhibited, enabling the body to hoard its reduced supply of water. When we are starved for any of our essentials, the balancing mechanism prods us into *exceeding* the required balance and we consume more than we need. A starving man must be restrained, lest he overeat to the point of becoming ill. Similarly, when the Respect Level is too low, the balancing mechanism doesn't merely restore it to normal. Instead, it overreacts, provoking far more hostility than we need, goading us into conflicts that cause us to lose the very things we seek to protect. Besides "hoarding" and "overconsumption," a low Respect Level produces a number of other reactions that you'll find regrettably familiar.

1. *Anxiety*

The first reaction to a deficiency of respect is fear. As the deficiency of respect increases, fear increases. It is a signal designed to alert the individual to a state of biological deficiency.

The fear that one is insufficiently respected is termed "anxiety" in order to distinguish it from other fears such as the fear of imminent starvation or injury. The nervous system can withstand transient fears, such as when a person is within an inch of being run over, since the fear is only momentary. But since anxiety is a reaction to a concept, it stays with us continually. Just as pain signals a threat to our physical well-being, anxiety signals the presence of a threat to our emotional well-being. Its intended message is, "Look, something's wrong with you, so you'd better stop whatever you're thinking about or doing and tend to it." But while this advice is well intentioned, it leaves us in utter ignorance of what we should do since it doesn't tell us *what's* wrong. Anxiety doesn't identify the underlying conflict any more than pain provides the individual with a diagnosis of his ailment.

Since the victim of anxiety doesn't know its cause, he is at a loss to combat it. This feeling of helplessness in the face of an unknown oppressor is what makes anxiety so much harder to bear than other forms of fear. Because of its distracting effect, anxiety interferes with attention and concentration and therefore is a frequent cause of confusion, mistakes, and accidents. Since the anxiety-ridden individual doesn't know what the danger is, the urge to escape is overwhelming. This leads to behavior such as pacing the floor, going outside to get away from confined quarters, keeping obsessively busy, or escaping by smoking, using drugs, alcohol, or tranquilizers. These expedients have no more effect in removing the cause of the anxiety than do other forms of escape. In fact, the temporary relief provided by tranquilizers or alcohol lulls the anxiety-ridden person into a false sense of well-being in which he fails to come to grips with the disturbing underlying problems causing the anxiety.

2. *The Superiority Complex: A Mirage Trap*

A starving person may actually believe that he sees food and water before him—even though they aren't present. And even the most intelligent persons are rarely aware that a deficiency in self-respect sets off a similar Mirage in which one conceives of himself as superior to others. Suppose a fellow breaks a date with a girl who has a poor opinion of her rating with boys. When asked about what happened, she's apt to say, "That creep, I wouldn't be caught dead with him." Her immediate stance of superiority is an overreaction to the lowering of her Respect Level.

This is the mechanism that causes us to believe anything that flatters us and disbelieve anything that appears to reflect discredit on us. But this isn't mere wishful thinking—the individual actually *believes* he is superior. The balancing mechanism (homeostasis) has provided this Mirage of Superiority to relieve him of the miserable concept of inferiority. Of course, he isn't superior at all; he is the victim of his distortion of reality. As a result, he bites off more than he can chew and makes self-defeating mistakes. A typical example is that of the hungry person on a diet. Wishful thinking leads to a Mirage in which he mistakenly believes that he can have that piece of pie and still maintain his diet.

Many of our more serious blunders are also due to Mirages that victimize the brainy as well as those of lesser intelligence. An example is that of a former Secretary of Defense, a man of proven brilliance and dedication to his country. As a result of numerous mistaken predictions of approaching success in the Vietnam War and the growing hostility of the public about them, his respect had taken a severe beating. Finally in 1965 he declared that the United States involvement in the war should come to an end and our boys should be home by Christmas of that year. They did come home —eight years later.

The Mirage resulting from deficiency in respect all too often leads a person into unreal beliefs of how he can solve his problems. It causes him to become convinced that he is right when he is actually mistaken, and that the other fellow is wrong even though he is dead right. Acting on his erroneous belief, he manifests know-it-all, holier-than-thou, can't-be-wrong, exalted, and arrogant attitudes. Unaware that his blame of the other person is based on a Mirage, he believes he is justified in his hostile feeling.

An example is the supervisor who knows she is physically

unattractive. Her Respect Level is not upset by the fourteen homely women who work under her supervision. The balance *is* upset, however, by a more attractive addition to the crew. Her comparison with the new girl tips the balance, so that the supervisor finds herself in the inferior position. Because of the superiority complex this produces, she visualizes many forms of superiority to the new girl and, on one occasion, she sneeringly remarks to her nemesis, "My, what big feet you have." This remark relegates her to an inferior position and thus provokes the immediate snappy retort, "My big feet are only surpassed by your big mouth."

The formation of a Mirage is always most pronounced in that aspect of one's life in which he feels the most inferior. For example, Herman, a man who felt very inferior in his relationships with women, was constantly boring his friends with tales of his female conquests. One woman who had been trapped into listening to him finally remarked, "If you ever stop talking about your love life, we'll know you really have one."

The inevitable reaction to your Mirage of superiority is failure in the problem you're trying to solve and a loss of the cooperation and respect of the other person. Their dislike lowers your Respect Level more and therefore intensifies your Mirage. A case in point is that of Tom N., a thirty-eight-year-old man who had become very anxious and depressed following his recent divorce. He had repeatedly beseeched his wife not to go through with the divorce, but to no avail. In his first therapy hour he said, "The next time I marry, I'll be more discriminating."

This statement revealed that he pictured himself as a great catch and that it was his wife's fault the marriage had failed. According to his thinking, all he needed to do was to exert more care in his next selection of a wife. What he didn't perceive, however, was that *he* had caused the marriage's failure.

He had entered marriage with a depleted level of self-respect. As a result of the Mirage of superiority, Tom had adamantly insisted that he was right on most of the issues in the marriage. His wife had reacted as any normal person would to such an attitude. Instead of increasing her respect, his superiority Mirage made her lose respect for him, thus lowering his Respect Level further. This rapid return of inferiority automatically caused a reappearance of Tom's Mirage of superiority and hostility. Therefore, you can see that the Mirage in which Tom conceived that his wife was to blame for the failure of the marriage would doom him to fail in his next try.

3. Obsession With Oneself—Me-ism
When an animal is deprived of a biological need, it becomes obsessed with it—the more the deprivation, the more the obsession. Suppose,

for example, a dog's master returns from a trying day at work looking forward to his dog's welcome. When he arrives home he sets out a bowl of food. Since the dog hasn't eaten all day, he wastes no time in tackling it.

Meanwhile his master, yearning for some token of affection, throws a ball across the room. Since the dog is obsessed with his need for food, he ignores all pleas to retrieve the ball. "The ungrateful cur," his master thinks, "after all the loving care I've given him." Well, he'll just have to wait until his pet overcomes his food deficit.

Human beings react similarly to deprivation of essential needs. When deprived of status, a person becomes so totally absorbed in his own need for it that he loses sight of this need in his associates. He bores and antagonizes them by harping on his own activities, while excluding them from sneaking in a word edgewise.

A commanding officer repeatedly manifested this trait at the Officers' Club, elaborating on his own exploits and drowning out any attempts of his junior officers to express their opinions. One of the offended junior officers later commented, "You know, the colonel is shot in the ass with himself."

Convinced by his Mirage that he is right about any topic under discussion, such a person is intolerant of any views opposite to his own. For example, he's so anxious to have you believe in his superiority that he'll rave about some restaurant or movie. If you fail to detect that his opinion is based on his Mirage, you may become the victim of an unappetizing dinner and wonder what he could have seen in such a dull movie.

4. *The Martyr Complex*

An individual with this complex makes exaggerated complaints about the obstacles he faces. He habitually blames his associates, wife, children, co-workers, and friends for his troubles. He's the fellow who complains about the way the *other* fellow drives, the poor service *he* gets, and a host of other things. Picture the respect-lowering effect on a husband when his wife makes martyred comparisons such as, "I'm always willing to listen to your problems. Why don't you listen to mine?" Unaware that her blame of him is responsible for his inconsiderate attitudes toward her, she resents him all the more.

These reactions are not unrelated; they comprise a unified, coordinated behavior response. If a person possesses any one of these reactions to inferiority, he must also possess the others. Thus, if you observe someone who bores you by his obsession with his own opinions, physical symptoms, or travels, then you can be sure that he also has a superiority complex. If a girl is in a state of anxiety about her job or social relations, then you can be sure she also has feelings of superiority and hostility, even though she may be afraid to express them openly. You'll observe her making snide comparisons in which she is the do-gooder, implying that others are to blame.

A simple formula to sum up these reactions of the emotional system to deficiency in respect is:

I → A + Ob + H + S + Mar.
I = the feeling of Inferiority or loss of self-respect
→ = generates
A = Anxiety
Ob = Obsession with oneself
H = mirage of Hostility
S = mirage of Superiority
Mar. = Martyring (blaming other persons and situations for our failures)

"Overdo nothing" is an ancient Greek maxim that many of us follow quite well when it is a question of balancing the budget or the front end of the car. Why is it so difficult to practice emotional balance? Because—as we'll see in the next chapter—of a lack of understanding of how to use our biological tools.

2.
Anti-Hostility Methods That Don't Work

Proverbs, maxims, and aphorisms are supposed to bring the wisdom of the ages to us. However, simply accepting the words of even the highest authority without putting them through your own thinking machine is an excellent way to come to grief.

For thirteen hundred years, doctors accepted Galen's version of anatomy as the ultimate truth without bothering to investigate its source: the human body. For all those years, the professors of anatomy continued to teach this subject in the medical schools by reading passages from Galen. Nobody disagreed with Galen, even though Galen frequently disagreed with himself! Not until the sixteenth century did Vesalius, a medical student in Brussels, check the facts by dissecting human cadavers and find that Galen was indeed frequently mistaken.

Enormous numbers of people still accept anything printed in a newspaper, pamphlet, magazine, or book as proven fact. Any number of articles advise us that we can overcome nervous troubles by controlling our temper, looking on the bright side of things, taking it easy, keeping busy, putting on a happy face, using our sense of humor, taking tranquilizers, or, venting our emotions. Many physicians dispense just this kind of advice, which is wholly ineffective in combatting hostility. To see why, let's examine these misconceptions one by one.

"CONTROL YOUR TEMPER"

Many persons are taught to do this from early childhood, sometimes to the tune of a burst of temper from the teaching parent. When

16

emotion does break through, the child is made to feel that something shameful has occurred. Some people are brought up to believe that only the uncouth and uneducated display anger. They say, with a touch of snobbery, that it's a pity some people have never learned to control their emotions.

Even persons who were permitted to express their emotions in childhood may become victims of "emotional control" later; others become so disgusted with their parents' constant bickering that they resolve to shun it in their own adult lives.

Because they make it a practice never to argue, many people claim they have learned to control their temper. Far from being controlled, their hostility becomes suppressed. When we attempt to avoid argument and maintain a calm exterior, the hostility remains inside, disrupting mental and even physical processes. For instance, when a person is repeatedly provoked, but is unable to express his anger, he becomes vulnerable to a host of serious diseases.

Regularly synchronized nerve impulses open the mouth of the stomach for oncoming food, stimulate the glands of the stomach to discharge digestive juice (including hydrochloric acid) into the cavity of the stomach, and then cause the muscles of the stomach wall to churn.

The stomach does its job with remarkable smoothness and efficiency—with one hitch: When hostility is suppressed, it disrupts the correct sequence of electrical discharges from the brain to the stomach, resulting in extreme contraction (spasm) of the stomach muscles and excessive secretion of hydrochloric acid. The sustained tension of the muscle tissue and the excess of acid make it more liable to erosion and ulceration. This all-too-prevalent condition not only causes gnawing stomach pains, but in some cases life-threatening hemorrhage as well. Advising a patient suffering from ulcers to avoid argument only results in his keeping *more* hostility inside, thus aggravating his symptoms.

If you are the docile, gentle, smiling, pleasant, compliant type who makes it a practice to avoid argument, then you are also more likely to come down with high blood pressure and coronary heart disease. After years of bitter arguments in a marriage, one of the partners may become so fed up that he or she resolves to avoid arguments at all cost. As a result of the advice of some self-styled authority, such a person may switch to the "peace at any price" philosophy. Time and again I've encountered these people in the hospital; within a few years after giving up quarreling, they have developed a physical disease. When asked if there was any friction in their marriage, a smug look would appear, then the inevitable reply: "We never argue."

"LOOK ON THE BRIGHT SIDE OF IT"

Back in 1910, a French pharmacist, Emile Coué, treated nervous disorders by instructing his patients to "think positively." According to this form of therapy, all you have to do to overcome fear, lack of confidence, negativism, pessimism, and nervous symptoms is to *tell* yourself that you can. He had his patients repeat the phrase, "Day by day, in every way, I'm getting better and better." Physical pain was treated by stroking the painful area while murmuring, "Going, going, gone."

Although Couéism failed to live up to its claims, it is now practiced more widely than ever. Today it is referred to as "positive thinking." Its advocates tell us that we can rid ourselves of feelings of inferiority, defeatism, and depression simply by filling our minds with thoughts of confidence, faith, and success. This is guaranteed to expel all feelings of inferiority and doubt. When you awake in the morning, the first thing to do is to say, "I believe this is going to be a wonderful day." If things don't clear up by noon, you simply add, "I don't believe in defeat."

Not only does such advice fail to overcome inferiority, worry, depression, illness, and personal problems, it actually makes them worse, since the practice of positive thinking leads to suppression of hostility and anxiety, and consequently increases the likelihood of personal failure and emotional and physical illness.

"TAKE IT EASY . . . RELAX . . .
LET BYGONES BE BYGONES"

Most physicians advise their patients to avoid worry, tension, aggravation, and depression. Well-meaning friends tell us to relax. However, you can't achieve relaxation by "trying" to relax.

There are those who tell you to just sit still, let your muscles go limp two or three times a day to achieve relaxation, and whenever you think of any of your worries, simply repeat a particular word a guru has given you. However, this does nothing about the anxiety and hostility producing the tension. The commonest advice of all is "Don't worry." This makes no more sense than advising a patient with a little patch of cancer not to worry about it.

We are frequently told by government, business, and religious authorities that we should not "wallow" in past trouble, but should "forgive and forget," as if our troubles would vanish if we only followed this advice. Now, if you think about it logically, you'll see why this isn't so. The reason is that the brain stores our learning and emotional experience. Thus, after a year of repeated scares by the life-threatening blasts of artillery shells and rockets, a soldier returning to his hometown is apt to be startled at the sharp report emanating from the exhaust of an auto, while the friend who accompanies him isn't startled in the least.

We can't get rid of thoughts and emotions that are troubling us by forgetting them. And hostility doesn't disappear when we try *not* to worry about what is bothering us. The word "worry" is the popular term for anxiety or fear. To worry occasionally about one thing or another is a normal part of living. When a person worries a good bit of the time about matters that seem trivial, most of his family, friends, and fellow workers treat him as if he is some sort of inadequate weakling. They say in a disparaging tone, "He shouldn't worry so much" or "He doesn't have anything to worry about." Yet the worrier really has good reason to worry, for no one worries without adequate cause.

Worry is the mind's way of alerting us that there's real trouble going on and that we're not remedying the trouble that's causing the worry. Any problem that's troubling enough to produce anxiety can't be forgotten. If we try to ignore it, it is merely more deeply suppressed, becoming a source of much more harm than if we tried to think it out. The fact is that the emotional system is doing its best to keep us in a state of worry for the very sensible purpose of prodding us into ascertaining the *cause* of our worry.

"KEEP BUSY . . . GET OUT OF THE HOUSE AND DO SOMETHING"

Sometimes, when a husband brings his wife to the psychiatrist for the first time, he favors the doctor with a knowing look and delivers this blockbuster: "She needs to keep busy, doesn't she, Doc?"

Winston Churchill, when asked if he worried about his immense responsibilities in the midst of World War II, replied, "I'm too busy, I have no time for worry."

Some have interpreted this statement as evidence that keeping busy is actually a successful cure for worry. But in reality, the reason Churchill didn't worry was that he was emotionally fortified by a high level of self-respect. Such persons characteristically embrace activities which give them the opportunity to serve because they are fulfilling, not because they need to keep themselves from worrying.

Even a person with a fairly healthy level of self-respect is likely to go through a period of excessive worry as the result of a sudden crushing blow, but soon regains his or her composure because of an underlying strong respect level.

A case in point is that of Osa Johnson, who achieved worldwide fame as an explorer. After twenty-six years of marriage, her husband, Martin Johnson, the famous explorer, was killed in an air crash. Yet, within a few months, Osa Johnson resumed her fascinating lectures on their explorations. When she was asked why she did it, she replied, "I did it so I would have no time for sorrow and worry."

However, it wasn't her busy schedule that relieved her worry. When she married Martin Johnson at the age of sixteen, she already had a high level of self-respect from the emotional nourishment received from her parents and the grandmother who lived with them. This was followed by twenty-six years of marriage to a devoted husband who also had received excellent emotional nourishment from his parents. Their sturdy respect levels were further strengthened by twenty-five years of brilliant achievement as explorers. Fortified by this background, her worries cleared up rapidly not because she kept busy, but because she strengthened her self-respect still further by carrying on the work for which she and her husband had been acclaimed.

Dr. N. was a general practitioner whose workday began early in the morning and often extended to the late hours of night. Each of his patients received his undivided time and attention. Beloved by the patients he administered to, and admired by his fellow doctors, he seemed every inch the ideal doctor. But Dr. N.'s career came to an abrupt halt when he fell dead from a heart attack at the age of forty-one. Does this mean that a person shouldn't work hard at his career?

Not at all. Dr. N.'s career brought him great pleasure and fulfillment; the long hours he devoted to his practice did not harm his health. It was through his wife that I learned what had really done the damage.

Three years before his death, she told me that she was proud to be the wife of a doctor who was so devoted to his patients. "But I don't see him in the morning because he leaves the house at six; he's rarely home before ten P.M. I save him supper, but no sooner does he sit down to eat than the phone rings. He's on the phone with patients until midnight because he instructs them to call after ten. Our three children, eight, six, and four, are as frustrated as I am. What can I tell them when they cry, 'I want my daddy.' Of late, they insist on staying up and waiting for him. All they get is a hug and a word and then he's on the phone again."

At the beginning of the marriage, Mrs. N. had reconciled herself to the long hours he worked as an intern. She didn't complain after he completed the four years of internship because she knew he had to work hard to build a practice. As his practice grew, she was partially appeased by her pride in her children, her lavish home, and her participation in the Women's Medical Auxiliary. "Then I realized that my husband and I were becoming strangers. Talking to him about it didn't change anything. He'd promise that he would cut down on his work, but his schedule remained as busy as ever. Occasionally, we went off for a week to a medical convention, but he seemed more interested in discussing medical topics with the doctors than in talking to me. I began pleading with him, complaining, and for the first time we quarreled bitterly. He said that he had given me everything a woman could ask for and that he was fed up with my nagging. That was about six years ago. I've continued to nag, but he won't argue anymore. I've become nervous and depressed. I scream at the children. I know I should have done something about this years ago. What can I do?"

Hard work is not always based exclusively on dedication to one's career. Many busy, hurried people don't realize that their frenzied overactivity is frequently due to an urge to escape from frustrating and hostile relationships. In order to avoid quarrels with close associates they retreat into hard work, hobbies, sporting events, and other activities which remove them from the line of fire.

Mrs. N. was advised to take a course of therapy to learn how to deal with her husband. After her first visit, she asked him to participate in the therapy, but when he refused she failed to return. His heart attack occurred one year later. There was no doubt in my mind that a long-standing circle of hostility had existed between the doctor and his wife. As usual, the survivor was the one who openly vented hostility. Even the eminent medical scientist John Hunter, whose pupil Edward Jenner discovered the immunization against smallpox, lacked the knowledge of how to immunize himself against such attitudes. He declared, "My life is in the hands of any rascal who chooses to annoy and tease me."

Cutting down on working hours and taking vacations won't solve our problems. Many people believe they can become relaxed by engaging in exercise; but this doesn't relieve the conflicts at the root of the tension. Exercise is great for the appetite and the muscles, but has no effect on hostility and anxiety. You can't rid yourself of hostility toward your mother-in-law by hitting a golf ball and imagining that it's her cranium. This is no more effective than hitting a baseball in an effort to convince yourself that you're a leading home-run hitter in the big leagues. Abandoning tension-producing projects only makes for more tension arising from the failure to complete the projects. A mechanic wouldn't advise repairing a motor by keeping it running. Yet he may advise his wife that she can overcome worry by keeping busy. How can that reduce the anxiety resulting from her faulty way of relating to other people?

"PUT ON A HAPPY FACE"

"Keep a cheerful disposition" is the precise phrase that appeared recently in a newspaper article given national distribution. Let me quote the author, a researcher from one of our leading medical centers: "It would seem that the best way to increase longevity is to maintain a useful role in society and keep a cheerful disposition." Would he tell a patient that the best way to a long life is to keep in good health?

One of the human face's most attractive manifestations is the genuine smile. But when we smile in the futile belief that it will cause our troubles to vanish, we're only deceiving ourselves. "Smile Though Your Heart Is Breaking" is a beautiful song, but following this advice may lead to a heart attack.

If you try to act friendly and agreeable and keep smiling, what happens to the anger, despair, hurt, and discontent that you so frequently feel? Why, you try to hide it, of course, in an effort to impress yourself and everyone around you that you're a person of good cheer. Most people believe that if they're diplomatic enough they can conceal their dislike or disapproval of another person. But in a way, this is the cruelest trap of all, because human beings are rarely fooled. We can readily tell from a person's eyes, the expression of his mouth, his tone of voice, and his entire demeanor how he *really* feels toward us.

The sureness of feeling transmission was brought home to me when I first began treating patients. Little Bobby, age five, complained that he couldn't stand his father's yelling at him about sucking his thumb. I spoke to the father privately, explained that the antagonizing effect of his yelling was only causing Bobby to suck his thumb *more*, and suggested that he not mention the thumb sucking any more.

When they returned for their next visit I anticipated a brilliant cure and confidently inquired of Bobby whether his father had said anything about his habit. "No," Bobby replied ruefully. He didn't *say* anything, but oh, those looks!"

Put on a glad face, and no one, including your dog, is fooled. Hostility is impossible to conceal. All it takes is contact—in person, via the phone, or the written word. Even if you praise, smile, agree with, or give in to him, the other person can tell that you resent him. In Shakespeare's play, Cassius feigned great devotion to Julius Caesar, but that Caesar felt Cassius' resentment is clear when he said, "Yond Cassius has a lean and hungry look; such men are dangerous."

Even Sir Isaac Newton, one of the greatest minds of all time, was completely unaware of this transmission of hostility. Embittered by the criticism of his work by other scientists, he declared that he was giving up his scientific career and wrote to the Secretary of the Royal Society, "I see a man must either resolve to put out nothing new, or else become a slave to defend it." Only because his devoted friend, the eminent astronomer Sir Edmund Halley, prevailed upon him "not to let your resentments run so high as to deprive us of your third book" was Newton persuaded to return to his studies. His keen scientific insight into the nature of matter gave us his Third Law of Motion, which states, "To every action, there is an equal and opposite reaction." But despite his superior intelligence, it apparently never occurred to Newton that his own resentful feeling was activating an equal and opposite resentment in a number of his fellow scientists.

I want to emphasize that many people who are loaded with suppressed hostility really believe they're free of it. Simply ask someone, "Why are you such a resentful person?" or "Why are you always griping?" Not only will this usually evoke an emphatic denial, but a hostile reaction as well. Many people feel that it's not "nice" to be hostile. Consequently, they strive to convince us and themselves that they're not hostile by an assortment of alibis: "I'm not angry, I'm just hurt," or "I'm not mad at you, I'm just disappointed."

A young woman patient complained about the selfishness and indifference of her fellow workers. I told her that this was a hostile reaction to her resentful feelings toward them. "But I never show any resentment," she countered in a resentful tone. "In fact, I go out of my way to be nice. I'm always doing favors for them. Yet they haven't even got the decency to thank me," she declared in martyred tones.

"How do you *really* feel toward them?" I asked.

Without a moment's hesitation she blurted out, "I detest the whole lot of them!"

It seemed so unfair: In return for being so kind, she received only hostility. However, there was nothing unfair about the exchange of feelings. She was getting back no less than she was dishing out.

Those who deny their hostility are unaware of their part in transmitting it to their loved ones, friends and co-workers. Far from being hidden, it is as obvious to others as a barrage of obscenities would be. And since those around us recognize that we are trying to hide our hostility, they look on us as hypocritical. The suppressor of hostility *can* sometimes fool people because he may not hide his anger on all issues. Nevertheless, he cannot face arguments on the crucial personal issues in his life—for example, his wife's or boss's complaints about him. Because of the critical lowering of his self-respect in these issues, the hostility is too intense to face.

"USE YOUR SENSE OF HUMOR"

"Laugh it off" we are told, "it's all in a day's work." If your boss berates you at a staff meeting, can a sense of humor rid you of your hostile reaction? And if someone belittles you, and then tells you to use your sense of humor by saying, "Aw, come on, can't you take a joke?" will that lessen your hostility? The kidder may have to pay dearly for his antics. Even when we kid without any intention of ridicule, some have feelings so sensitive that they react with exquisite pain. Feeling ashamed, they often try to conceal their hurt, but it makes them disgruntled and uncooperative.

"A PILL FOR SIMPLE NERVOUS TENSION"

In his medical training, the doctor learns that too high a level of any of the normal constituents of the body, such as calcium, blood pressure, sugar, or temperature, is a forerunner of disease. The same thing is true in the manifestations of the personality. The person who is forever smiling, come hell or high water, is almost invariably a suppressor of hostility and, therefore, unhappy and predisposed to premature physical illness.

Denial is one of the chief obstacles to correct analysis of interpersonal problems. Since the person with suppressed hostility almost always *denies* that he's hostile, it's more accurate to go by your feelings than by what he tells you. But when the doctor unearths the hostility factor, how does he treat it? The most common treatment is the admonition to "avoid controversy," and a prescription for a tranquilizer.

The recent biochemical revolution in brain physiology has resulted in a wealth of information that holds out great promise for advances in psychiatric treatment. This revolution has been accelerating ever since pharmacologist Dr. Oleh Hornykiewicz's discovery of the chemical L-Dopa, whose action on the brain has brought dramatic relief to thousands of patients with Parkinson's disease. At Johns Hopkins Hospital, the brilliant researches of Dr. Solomon Snyder and Dr. Joel Elkes are uncovering exciting revelations of the role that chemical changes in the brain may play in mental illness.

The wealth of new psychoactive drugs have proven of immense value in relieving symptoms of schizophrenia, depression and the manic phase of manic-depression.

But anxiety—the average case of nerves—is the condition for which these drugs are most commonly prescribed. Valium, only one of a host of tranquilizing drugs, is far and away the most prevalent treatment for nervous conditions.

"VALIUM SENDS MORE ADDICTS TO
HOSPITALS THAN HEROIN"

This was the headline of an article on the first page of the *Baltimore Sunday Sun*, January 26, 1975. Investigation by the Mayor's Office on Drug Abuse in Baltimore revealed that Valium was landing more abusers in hospital emergency rooms than any other drug in the United States, including heroin. According to Charles Cox, Director of the Baltimore Drug Abuse Program, "There are an awful lot of housewives walking around like zombies. I'm talking about the housewife who has nervous tension and calls her friendly doctor, and it's the first thing that pops into his mind: Valium."

This has the distinct advantage of saving the doctor a lot of time, but he must reckon with the accidents and blunders of the patient, unpleasant and occasionally toxic side effects of tranquilizers, antidepressants, and antipsychotic drugs. You have only to consult the *Physicians' Desk Reference*, the doctor's drug bible, to learn that Valium can produce withdrawal symptoms similar to those produced by barbiturates and alcohol: convulsions, tremor, abdominal and muscular cramps, vomiting, and sweating. Despite its dangers Valium is the most prescribed drug in the United States.

The widespread use of tranquilizers has led the public to believe that they actually reduce anxiety and hostility. But despite the vastly exaggerated claims made for these drugs in medical journal advertisements, they unfortunately fail to reduce these disturbing emotions. In fact, as in the case of alcohol, they may precipitate an eruption of rage and violence. A tranquilizer's only effect is to reduce the patient's *perception* of his anxiety and hostility; but since these emotions remain in the brain in full force, they continue to exert their harmful effects. Consequently, not only does the "tranquilized" patient continue to transmit hostility, but he becomes increasingly susceptible to physical disease.

The worst danger comes about when the drug actually "works." When it does, it is as harmful psychologically as alcohol. Relieved of the perception of anxiety, the patient is only more encouraged to continue avoiding his underlying problems. Since the drug soon wears off, the perception of the anxiety returns and another dose, often stronger, of the drug is taken—just as in the case of alcohol.

"VENT YOUR EMOTIONS . . . CLEAR THE AIR"

A study conducted in the late forties compared the incidence of coronary heart disease in Italy and in the United States. It was found that the American percentage was five times as great. The reason may very well be the difference in the way Italians and Americans deal with their hostility. The Italian is far more prone to vent his hostility vociferously, while the American is more likely to "control" this emotion.

Many psychotherapists and physicians in other branches of medicine recommend "blowing your top"—and the statistics on individuals who follow this practice seem to support them. John L. Lewis, the labor leader who spilled out his anger for F. D. Roosevelt in no uncertain terms, lived vigorously to the age of eighty-nine. But Roosevelt, who more often smiled than expressed anger, died at sixty-three of cardiovascular disease. Harry "Give 'em hell" Truman lived to the ripe old age of eighty-eight. And the way George Meany, the eighty-three-year-old head of the AFL-CIO, habitually speaks his beliefs out in anger, he should be around for many more years. Dr. Frank A. Finnerty, Jr., a leading researcher in high blood pressure, emphasized this point in an article in *U.S. News and World Report*, October 21, 1974: "The psychiatrist tells us never to keep things inside—that you should ventilate your feelings. The worst thing to do is keep your mouth shut. It's better to blow off steam, and that is certainly true for anyone with high blood pressure."

This distinguished professor of medicine is right when he tells us that the worst thing we can do is keep our mouth shut. No doubt it's possible to avoid much of the anxiety and tension of suppressed hostility by openly venting our feelings. But what about his advice to "blow off steam"? What is a person to do—blast his boss, wife, or child whenever he feels like it? Admittedly, some of the "give 'em hell" types live to a ripe old age, but how about the effect on their associates? Wives may be driven to insanity or serious physical disease; children often grow up emotionally maimed and eternally bitter; and the motivation, cooperation, and health of one's co-workers are significantly impaired.

If you are the type that yells, fights, and argues whenever you feel irritated, it is unlikely that you'll be the victim of a premature heart attack. But most people vent their anger only with those they don't fear. For example, a man who does not hesitate to express anger toward his wife and children may suppress his anger toward his boss. If he fears arguments only with women, he suppresses his hostility to his wife, but may speak up to his boss. These types are *still* liable to heart attacks and other diseases since they are suppressing intensely hostile feelings.

Venting your anger can cause you to lose your mate, child, job, and sometimes your life. At the very least, you're going to have to suffer unpleasant consequences, since your expression of anger will antagonize its recipient, and you'll soon be angry again because of the hostility you receive in retaliation. The more contacts you have—with the foreman, wife, husband, or child—the more the circle of hostility widens. The net result resembles the pie throwers in the old Mack Sennett comedies. While the person who started it may have initially felt better for having vented his hostility, it wasn't long before he himself got creamed as a result of the battle he began. The habitually hostile person becomes trapped in a vicious circle since the hostility he uses to protect himself only incites ever-increasing incidences of the behavior it was meant to protect him from.

3.
The Method of Overcoming Hostility

You don't have to be a biologist to observe that animals are less inhibited than man in expressing their desires and emotions. But Konrad Lorenz theorizes that the evolution of aggression in the animal kingdom offers valuable lessons in how to save humanity from annihilation by hostility. Lorenz believes that the animal species flourishing today managed to escape being wiped out by their aggressive instincts only because they developed aggression-inhibiting mechanisms.

Lorenz's description of such ceremonies as the triumph dance in greylag geese and the ritualized ceremonies of Siamese fighting fish reminds us of the greeting ceremonies and ritualized customs of man, as in the European and American custom of shaking hands, and the Japanese custom of bowing—both of which are meant to express friendliness and, in their earliest origins, to assure each of the participants that the other was not carrying a weapon. The purpose of these rituals in animals is to inhibit aggression between them. He demonstrates how animals, like man, employ humility as a useful measure to protect themselves against physical aggression.

Lorenz observed these mechanisms in a variety of animal species. He described how young night herons escape annihilation by the older birds in narrow confines where every tree branch is the subject of disputes between neighbors. As soon as the older bird approaches, the young bird importunes it with begging calls and wing flapping, and tries to milk the beak of the older bird. This humble attitude, conferring respect on the older bird, inhibits its aggressive instinct.

A similar inhibition of aggression appears in wolves. When an enormous timber wolf encounters a weaker, younger one, bared fangs flash in a rapid exchange of snaps. The growls of the stronger wolf are angry, but there is a note of fear in those of the younger wolf. Incredibly, the younger turns his head so as to offer unprotected to his enemy the bend of his neck, the most vulnerable part of his whole body, since directly under the skin lies his jugular vein! Whereas during the thick of the fight both wolves were intent on keeping their teeth in opposition to each other, the weaker fighter now proffers intentionally that part of his body where a bite would surely be fatal. Dr. Lorenz tells us that an inhibitory instinct prevents the stronger wolf from executing the fatal bite, though he continues to growl ominously and snap with his teeth, and even carries out the movement of shaking something to death in the empty air. However, this biting inhibition persists only so long as the defeated wolf maintains his attitude of humility. Should the "under-wolf" abandon his rigid attitude of submission, the other will fall on him again.

What a striking similarity to the critical role of submission and humility in inhibiting aggression in man! The on again-off again switch between aggressive fury and its inhibition in response to humble submission is illustrated by an incident involving a man whose truthfulness none of us had any reason to doubt.

Jack had the reputation at our gym of being the man one would least wish to tangle with in karate, jujitsu, or any other type of violent activity. Nevertheless, Jack was always the soul of gentleness and modesty. It took us several years to get him to admit that he had once broken his vow never to use his murderous art except in defense. After years of successfully resisting opportunities of teaching a lesson to some insulting bully, Jack finally weakened. While driving down a highway, he was roundly cursed by a vicious-looking pair who had tried to take his right of way. A wave of sudden hope enveloped Jack. Wasn't he entitled, just this once? Before he could restrain himself, he fired back an obscenity. This was all the two thugs needed to rekindle their urge to violence. They turned toward Jack's car and he obligingly pulled over as he gleefully contemplated the golden opportunity Fate had bestowed upon him. However, as they approached him, Jack's need to honor his long-standing creed prevailed, and he said, "I'm sorry, fellows, I didn't mean it."

Just as in the case of the wolf, this humble submissiveness on Jack's part inhibited the aggressive instinct of the two bullies. "All right," they yelled as they turned back to their car, "but watch your mouth, punk."

As they walked off, Jack's urge to use the fighting art got the better of his vow, and out came an "expletive deleted." Enraged, the two bullies came charging again. As Jack drove off, honor did prevail: He notified the police the location of the two battered bodies.

Like animals, man possesses a brain which is ancient from an evolutionary standpoint. The pioneering studies of neurophysiologists Paul D. MacLean and J. W. Papez point to an area of the brain, the limbic system, as the anatomical site of emotion. This structure was named "limbic" because it winds around the brain stem at the base of the brain.

According to Dr. MacLean, Chief of The Section on Limbic Integration and Behavior of The National Institute of Mental Health, the limbic system is an evolutionary inheritance from the reptilian and paleomammalian brain. The primitive cortex of this brain region and its connections with the midbrain and brain stem comprise the limbic system, which is found as a common denominator in all mammals. Two of the subdivisions of the limbic system are closely related to the olfactory cortex (smell apparatus) and are involved in oral, alimentary, and sexual functions that ensure preservation of the individual and the species.

Recent research has focused on the amygdala, two little almond-shaped structures in the limbic system located side by side on the inner surfaces of the two cerebral hemispheres. They appear to be a critical center for hostile emotion, as was demonstrated by Dr. James Woods in an experiment with sewer rats. Normally these rats are so fierce that they kill mice at the slightest provocation. But after surgical removal of the amygdala, these savage creatures became tame.

Removal of the amygdala in monkeys was also followed by a decrease in hostility. In man, when the midportion of the amygdala is electrically stimulated, an angry or fearful mood is induced, indicating a connection between hostility and fear. On the other hand, stimulation of the outer portion of the amygdala has a calming effect. Dr. José M. R. Delgado, a recognized authority in brain physiology, experimented with a brave bull, bred to respond with a raging charge at the sight of a human being. When the bull charged, did the good doctor's own amygdala register fear? No indeed! He merely pressed a button on a transmitter, sending a signal to a battery receiver attached to the bull's horns and, lo and behold, the beast ceased his ferocious charge and became as placid as Ferdinand.

You might conclude from this that all that's necessary to calm down an angry world is to implant such electrodes in the brains of the populace. Such a possibility, however, is regarded with the greatest skepticism by most brain physiologists, neurologists, and psychiatrists. In their view, human brain stimulation does not produce a specific and predictable response from the same anatomical structure in different individuals, but varies greatly with the patient's recent and past emotional state. Moreover, the modern concept is that no one area is the anatomical seat of hostility; instead, these emotions are produced by the interaction of a number of structures in the limbic system and neighboring areas.

The science of biology has amply demonstrated an ongoing process of evolution aimed at progressive correction of earlier models of the brain. Evolution has not only brought about the remarkable advances in thinking, symbolism, and language possessed by the New Brain (later evolutionary development), the neocortex; it has simultaneously changed the Old Brain (evolutionarily older).

Hostility, fear, and affection are products of the Old Brain. When threatened with a deficiency, this area reacts first—the greater the deficiency, the stronger the reaction.

Dr. MacLean expressed his belief that man is an evolutionary blunder because the neocortex (New Brain) is not properly integrated with the ancient brain (limbic system). He referred to this inability to coordinate reason and feelings as "schizophysiology." Despite the New Brain's capacity for logic, it often leaves untouched the primitive, illogical, and destructive emotion of the Old Brain.

One of the few animals that attacks its own species is the brown rat, but even these rats seldom kill members of their *own* clan, as man does. Since the inhibition against killing members of the same species is so much weaker in man than in lower animals, it would appear that evolution is taking us in the wrong direction: toward the annihilation of humanity. Does this separation of brain function doom us to continue our imbecilic conduct of human affairs? Are we destined to become extinct along with other species which were the victims of evolutionary mistakes?

Surely it wasn't the purpose of the Designer to manufacture a creature lacking the capacity to improve. I believe there is a way out, a way based on the very structure of the brain that Dr. MacLean calls schizophysiologic.

Take another look at the difference between animals and man. Two eleven-year-old boys are playing on the lawn. One trips. His left shoe flails out and strikes the family dog. The dog automatically turns and sinks his teeth into the boy's ankle. It's obvious that the dog's hostility is due to the automatic response of his balancing mechanism. He can't help his mistake because this mechanism always goes into action when his equilibrium is disrupted. Thus, it *compels* him to act *as if the offender was to blame.*

Animals are limited to this automatic hostile response because they lack the thinking equipment required to understand that the bumping was an accident. Most people are aware of the limitations of the animal brain and, therefore, are more tolerant of misbehavior of their dog than of their husband or child. But while most of us like to think we're smarter than dogs, the fact is that when our emotional equilibrium is disrupted, as when we're blamed, our balancing mechanism, too, causes us to believe that the other guy is at fault. Nevertheless, since man alone is equipped with the neocortex, this fantastic advance in evolution makes it possible to understand *why* another individual is *not* to blame.

Consider this incident: having become annoyed with myself for being late for an appointment, I wanted to phone the party who was waiting for me. I was standing in front of a newsstand on the first floor of an office building, so I laid a quarter down right under the eyes of the newsstand vendor and asked for some nickels.

"How many nickels?" the vendor asked.

I became angry. Just as I was about to ask how many nickels he thought there were in a quarter I looked up and saw that he was blind. My anger vanished and was replaced by sympathy. What caused the hostility to dissolve so rapidly?

I had been feeling inferior because of my tardiness for a most important appointment. As you know, the Old Brain's first response to inferiority is a feeling of hostility and superiority to others. That's why I became angry. However, when I saw that the vendor was blind, my New Brain had all the information it needed to see that the "offender" wasn't to blame—whereupon my New Brain fired off a message to the Old Brain that dissolved the hostility.

Of course this blind vendor wasn't to blame. But what about the guy who's downright rude? A wife who greets you with a string of complaints? A child who giggles at your reprimand, and then repeats his misbehavior? Aren't *these* people to blame for their actions?

Not really. On rounds, during my first year of internship, a professor mildly reprimanded a patient for the way he had been behaving on the ward. The patient looked the professor right in the eye and replied, "Well, Doctor, I'm only doing the best I can!"

The more I thought about this, the more I realized why the professor didn't reprimand him further: He had recognized the truth in what the patient had said. All the doctor had to do was consider the mistreatment that this patient's family had subjected him to and he understood why his emotions functioned as poorly as they did. After all, wasn't that the reason he was in the hospital for psychiatric treatment? A person can become hostile only as a result of inferiority—which means that someone has *done* something to him to make him act that way. (That's why when Joey complains that Petey hit him, Mother asks, "Did you hit him first?")

I find that it's easier to explain this in terms of a three-car accident. If you are suddenly slammed in the rear by a fellow motorist, of course you react with anger. But what happens when you learn that a third car had slammed into *him*, causing him to crash into you? Of course your hostility disappears. What you must understand is that whatever grief someone gives you is a result of someone who "hit" him. *He's not to blame for the way he's behaving since his behavior is determined by what he's been through.*

Admittedly, we get mad and act moronically before we can get a message from the New Brain to the effect, "Don't be a chump; if you yell at him, you'll turn him against you." By nature we are so short-sighted that we seldom see any farther than the person who blasts us, blissfully ignorant of the forces that propelled him. But the New Brain has connecting nerves to the Old Brain enabling these two areas to influence each other. When you realize that $I \rightarrow A + Ob + H + S + Mar.$ (Inferiority results in Anxiety plus Obsession plus Hostility plus Superiority plus Martyring) you also see that anyone displaying those traits does so because he's feeling inferior. You realize that you're not being pushed into the inferior position after all—he's merely reacting, as all of us must, to the balancing mechanism's action aimed at extricating him from his concept of inferiority.

Whenever anyone belittles, acts superior, or is hostile to you, think of who or what's been bugging *him*. No matter how great the provocation or how obnoxious a person seems, your awareness of the forces responsible for any person's behavior will help you feel less inferior—and thus, less hostile.

Anyone who applies this method will find that it actually does lessen his feelings of inferiority. It is this knowledge which enables us to cooperate with the other fellow's brain and with our own.

Where there is only a small deficiency of the respect requirement, your New Brain comes into play, enabling you to act with common sense. Thus, if your boss provokes only slight inferiority and hostility in you, your New Brain goes into action. You figure out that you'll serve your own interests best by not telling the boss off. A message is delivered by a connecting neuron to your emotional area, inhibiting any hostile action. True enough, your hostility would still be there, but at least it would be held in check.

This understanding of the basis of $I \rightarrow A + Ob + H + S + Mar.$—as we'll abbreviate these terms from now on—helps clear away your feelings of blame toward persons with repugnant traits. Remember that H was *designed* to be offensive and repugnant in order to turn away the enemy, as in the case of a skunk's odor.

But in order to overcome H to such irritating traits it is not enough to understand that the person who manifests them is the innocent victim of his I feelings. You must recognize one more factor to which most of us are quite blind. *You, too,* manifest unattractive, repugnant traits for the same reason that the rude person does: as a reaction to your own I. But you're not to blame for this. We do this as naturally, unconsciously, automatically, and innocently as does the person who offends us. Since every human being regularly produces H, you should no more be ashamed of it than of the sugar your liver manufactures or of the hydrochloric acid your stomach produces.

When Albert Einstein was asked by a fellow scientist why man had solved so many problems of physics, but not of human relations, Einstein replied, "Physics is simple; human relations, complex." Yet the laws governing human relations are just as simple and orderly. *You can only reduce H in proportion to overcoming its true source: I.*

Many persons will insist that it's not I feelings, but offensive behavior of others that makes them hostile. This is like blaming pneumonia on a virus. Your doctor will tell you that the principal reason for viral pneumonia is the lowered resistance of the patient. This is the case with H. We can no more insulate ourselves from irritating remarks, attitudes, and actions than we can hide from germs. But we can protect ourselves by maintaining a healthy resistance: a healthy level of Self-Respect. Since we become hostile only because of our I feelings, the logical method of removing H is by elevating our level of Self-Respect.

Let's see how this knowledge is applied in a case of marital unhappiness.

Rita, a thirty-four-year-old housewife, had been under the care of her family physician for abdominal pain, anxiety, tension, depression, fatigue, and sleeplessness. Her doctor informed me that physical examination and laboratory tests failed to reveal any organic disease. When Rita was asked if she had any complaints about her work, she said no. And when asked about her husband, Mike, she said that she considered herself lucky to have such a wonderful man. "He's a devoted father, a good provider, and he doesn't drink, gamble, or run around."

The way she lavished praise on her husband gave the impression that she was protesting too much. Excessive praise is often because of underlying hostility which causes feelings of guilt. Only after I gained her confidence did her complaints come to the surface.

She said that Mike ignored her. "All he seems to care about is that I cook his meals, go to bed with him, take care of the kids, laundry, and cleaning. Instead of conversing with me, he buries himself in the newspaper or TV. I don't even think he hears me half the time. Finally, in order to shock him into listening, I told him I had become a prostitute."

For a moment, I thought that she was serious. "You must have really become desperate," I said.

"Oh, I just made up that story to shock him," she replied rather testily.

"What did your husband do when you made that statement?"

"Nothing," she replied bitterly. "He didn't even hear me."

I asked her whether she usually poured out her complaints to Mike.

"I used to in the early years of the marriage. But he'd only become sullen and ignore me even more. He'd walk off into another room or out of the house. Then he wouldn't say a word to me for days on end. I couldn't take it, so I quit fussing at him."

Since nagging had made matters worse, Rita believed that her new policy of keeping her complaints to herself was a sign of maturity. But something was wrong, since Mike continued his indifference and selfish ways. It's hard to be affectionate to someone who has repeatedly hurt your feelings. In recent years, therefore, Rita had lost her physical desire for Mike.

When someone says, "Oh, I'm not angry, it's just that you've hurt my feelings," you know you're being reproached because you can feel their hostility. Think of any situation where your own feelings have been hurt and you'll recognize that the essential ingredient of hurt feelings is hostility. This first step of recognition is essential, since there's little likelihood of getting rid of our hostility when we don't even know if there's any present.

Rita was entirely unaware that her hostility was contagious but it showed in her eyes, mouth, tone of voice, and her gestures.

It makes no difference which partner starts the hostility: it forms a vicious circle with increasing hostility on each side.

Mike's own H was manifested by his disdainful and indifferent attitude toward Rita, which made her feel that sports, the newspaper, and TV were more interesting to him than she was. Misinterpreting the true meaning of his actions, Rita had feared she wasn't personable or intelligent enough to share conversation with Mike. Now, however, she realized that this interpretation was based on her self-concept of I, which caused her to see herself in a poor light.

Well, if she weren't inferior, why did he ignore her?

Because of pronounced I feelings, each frequently became hostile to the other. When Rita's H had lowered Mike's Respect Level further, she forced him into an involuntary action to extricate himself from this position, causing Mike to visualize himself as superior and Rita as inferior—unworthy of any serious conversation with him.

Both Rita and Mike feared they were incapable of being sufficiently appreciated—a consequence of their low Respect Levels. Because of low levels of self-respect, they were especially offended by attitudes of S. The result was a vicious circle in which each's Respect Level progressively dropped. Since H causes increasing contrariness to each other's opinions and desires, there was scarcely a subject on which Rita and Mike did not disagree. But each was completely oblivious to the vying for S that was at the root of their disagreements.

Many unhappy wives complain that their husbands refuse to go visiting with them. "He just wants to stay home all the time. When I put my foot down and literally drag him to a party, he embarrasses me by getting drunk." Here, again, vying for S is at the root of the trouble. By insisting on having her way, the wife lowers her husband's self-respect. The inevitable reaction of H causes him to retaliate by humiliating her at the party.

All of us react to hostile, superior, belittling, and martyred attitudes with progressive feelings of I. Since we are not to blame for this I, then we shouldn't be blamed for the H it invariably generates.

When Rita understood that she had become hostile through no fault of her own, she poured out her bitter feelings to Mike in a torrent. But Mike was no more to blame for his H to her than she for her H to him. For the first time in Rita's life, she recognized that she became hostile for the same reason that Mike and every other person does—because of a low Respect Level.

We earn the other fellow's receptivity in direct proportion to our elevation of his respect. "Well, then," said Rita, "what I really need to do is to build up his Respect Level. Should I give him a lot of praise?"

Praise doesn't do the job. Since Mike was quite aware of Rita's resentment, he would not be fooled by a sudden outpouring of compliments. But by giving Mike sincere credit for his suggestions, she would raise his Respect Level a notch.

Unless we cleanse ourselves of H, though, nothing we say or do will alter an unhappy relationship. Rita's H was now considerably reduced, but further reduction of H required that she learn how to overcome her own I, which was causing her to blame Mike for their unhappy domestic life. For example, on one occasion when he was absorbed in the newspaper, she blurted out reproachfully, "You never talk to me." Whereupon Mike put the paper down, walked over to her and said with what he thought was the ultimate in consideration, "Okay, go ahead and talk." Naturally, Rita was so taken aback by this retort that it left her tongue-tied.

It isn't necessary, nor is it possible, to rid ourselves of every bit of I. A small amount will always remain and, in fact, is a factor in stimulating achievement. Rita understood this. "How can I reduce my I down to a healthy level?" she asked.

I told Rita that she could remove much of the deeply embedded I by an understanding of the factors in childhood that produce an undernourished level of respect. As far back as she could remember, she had been picked on, scolded, and punished by her mother. No matter what the issue, the mother had repeatedly insisted that she was right and Rita wrong. Her know-it-all attitude relegated Rita to the know-nothing, or inferior, position. Mother had to run the show, have her way, couldn't be crossed. She blamed Rita for piling burdens on her back, forcing her to slave so that Rita could have the things she wanted. By portraying herself as a martyr, she made Rita feel guilty, ashamed, inferior.

"But I could do no wrong in my father's eyes, and he'd give me anything I wanted." His warmth, affection and approval provided the nourishment she required to feel respected, cared for, and appreciated. However, by giving in to so many of her wants, doing much of her homework, and solving lots of other problems for her, Rita's father unwittingly prevented her from working them through on her own.

While appreciation from her father raised her Respect Level, his overindulgence lowered it. This lack of working-through experience contributed to the I she experienced later as an adult. After being spoiled by her father, Mike's indifference had come as a rude shock.

Rita could see that she was mistaken in believing that *she* was the cause of her I. Now she realized that she was the victim of the attitudes and feelings of her parents. She had always been perfectly worthwhile. In Victor Hugo's *Les Misérables*, little Cosette had been repeatedly scolded and punished by her foster parents. She was bound to react to such abuse with pronounced feelings of I, fear, and distrust of adults, which was why she feared Jean Valjean, who liberated her from her guardians' clutches. Since Valjean understood the reasons for Cosette's fear and H, he felt neither blame nor S toward her, only sympathy and affection. This nourishment of her self-respect gradually lessened Cosette's fear and H to him and replaced them by trust and affection.

"Why don't you apply the I → H Reaction to your mother? After all, it applies equally to everyone."

"Yes, I can see where she got her I feelings. Her mother lived with us and would pick on her for every little thing."

Just as the belittling by Rita's mother had caused Rita's I feelings, so her grandmother's belittling must have had the same effect on Rita's mother. It was the three-car-accident analogy all over again. Rita had not been aware that her mother had been propelled by the impact she had received from her own mother. The transmission of H from one generation to the next explains why her mother was as innocent of blame as Rita, since she was actually in the middle.

Rita could see how her I was causing her to pick on her little girl, just as her mother had picked on her. Her mother and grandmother probably couldn't have done otherwise, since they hadn't received the Anti-H instruction that Rita was getting. "But," Rita said, "my mother is still resentful, belittling, and domineering."

"As your H to your mother disappears, so will hers toward you. You've always wanted each other's love. Now you can bring this about. Remember what you told me about her bringing soup over for Mike? Not only didn't you give her any credit, but you were actually resentful. You've complained about her attitudes, but all the while you've been manifesting the very same kinds of attitudes toward her. Your mother needs credit, appreciation, and recognition like all the rest of us."

Rita could now see why her mother so often took the opposite view from her on all things. The problem wasn't at all because of any inherent inability to see eye to eye. The intensity of such vying for S between two or more persons is proportional to the degree of I in the communicators. In any discussion of national policy in Congress, for example, it *seems* that the anger generated pertains to the matter under consideration. This is not the case. The hostility is specifically caused by a contest for superiority.

Observe any conversation, even over trivial topics, and you'll soon recognize this underlying contest. Note how frequently marital partners unceremoniously interrupt each other. No matter what one is trying to get across to the other, the response often commences with "But." This is equivalent to stating, "You're wrong in this matter; just listen to me and you'll get the right answer." The actual source of their differences is not the particular subject being argued, but the universally overlooked vying for superiority between them. To prove that the inferiority, not the topic, is generating the heat, simply remark to one of the discussants, "You're wrong." You'll see an immediate reddening around his collar.

The more inferior we feel, the more the balancing

mechanism pressures us to use any issue, no matter how trivial, to show that we are right and the other fellow wrong.

The more Rita had been relegated to the inferior position by her mother, the stronger her impetus to the superior position. No matter what subject they were discussing, a contest would inevitably take place. Each was constantly making the other feel more inferior and therefore more hostile.

Rita realized that she had been trying to get her mother to admit her errors about many of the issues they discussed. This only made her mother feel more I. The increase in S resulting from this increased I intensified the domineering traits that were so repugnant to Rita.

"Your mother is like you; if she gets what her emotional system requires, she'll be sweet and lovable. Now that your resentment to her is diminishing, you're in an excellent position to improve her attitudes."

Because of vying for superiority, even the most trivial issues can give rise to the most pernicious H. But suppose the subject really is of great importance. How can you go along with someone sincerely when you really believe that he is wrong?

Well, don't blurt out, "You're wrong," while looking as if you're so much smarter. Here, too, your best tack is to use the subject only to raise the other fellow's self-esteem. He will appreciate and like you for your validation of his opinion.

Suppose your spouse expresses the opinion, absolutely contrary to your own, that you should sell the house and move into an apartment. Instead of trying to point out why he is wrong, just ask him for his reasons. When he recites them, don't look at your fingernails or turn your eyes inward. Even a four-year-old could tell immediately that you aren't listening, just champing at the bit until you can espouse your own views.

Make sure that you're giving him your sincere attention and ask an occasional question. Don't interrupt with some opinion of your own. As he goes on he may mention a point that has some merit. Then you could say something like, "Well, that makes sense," or, "I hadn't thought of that." While this won't result in changing his opinion that very day, repeated norishment of this kind will gradually make him more receptive to your opinion. Without receptivity, our opinions are wasted anyway.

A simple reminder of this principle is the formula:

$$R = \frac{1}{H}$$

This formula shows that R (Receptivity) increases as H (Hostility) decreases, and that R decreases as H increases.

Why fire a competent employee because he offends you?

Why put up with an aggravating husband, wife, or child? Isn't it better to use this technique to help rid such persons of their offensive traits? Offensive traits gradually diminish in proportion to our respect-elevating measures and are replaced by affection, respect, receptivity, and unselfishness toward us.

I know you're anxious to find out how Rita and Mike's marriage turned out. When one has been the victim of repeated blows to his self-respect, the deposit of H is very concentrated. Because of strong force of habit, Rita could easily have slipped back into her former resentful self. Therefore, I warned her that the gains she had made would vanish unless she continued to practice what she had learned.

Rita's feelings of appreciation, sympathy, and affection, no longer contaminated by resentment, progressively reduced Mike's H. At the same time, she reduced the vying for S between them by means of the feelings she transmitted and by the measures for nourishing Mike's Respect Level. Mike's increasing Receptivity to her opinions helped raise her own esteem. Since her sexual coldness was caused primarily by her H, she regained her natural capacity for enjoying sex with Mike.

The very same measures applied to her relationship with her mother brought about an affectionate relationship between them. By providing her mother with the respect she needed, she evoked respect and approval in turn. For the first time, mother and daughter attained what they had always yearned for: each other's love, untainted by H.

Because of the excellent record of the Designer, there is every reason to believe that He will eventually produce a New Brain which will automatically compute understanding and transmit it to the Old Brain. Meanwhile, since the present model isn't equipped with such an automatic transmission, we must go to the trouble of shifting our own gears. The method I am discussing here is designed to provide a smooth transmission from the low gear of H to the high gear of respect and affection: the basic ingredients of health and success.

Despite greatly reduced H, problems may still remain, of course. For example, years of a husband's H may turn his wife toward another man. The best treatments fail when applied too late. However, one thing is certain: Although such a man loses his wife, he saves himself; instead of being poisoned by H, he is able to preserve his mental and physical health and use his new learning to find happiness with someone else.

Admittedly, maintaining an existence of minimal H can't rid you of all of life's pitfalls and miseries. You'll still be more liable to sickness if you don't exercise and eat properly. You can be divorced, lose a loved one, get fired, injured, or become sick despite adherence to anti-H. However, as we have touched on, and will go into later in more detail, H sets up cravings which lead to carelessness about diet and overeating; it consumes so much energy that we don't feel up to exercise; it is the principal cause of divorce and loss of friends, and often brings about disease in ourselves and our loved ones.

But for those of us who have learned how to keep ourselves cleansed of hostile feelings, living becomes an increasingly more joyful experience. Anxiety and depression are replaced by relaxation and optimism; fatigue gives way to a plentitude of energy. And somewhat surprisingly, we can even *think* more clearly and logically.

4.
"Whatever Made Him Do a Thing Like That?"

A retired schoolteacher came to the hospital to find out why she felt so hot and smothered while her husband felt comfortably cool in the same room. A simple test revealed that their opposite reaction to temperature was based on the H between them. No sooner had she sat down in the examining room than she complained that it was too hot. As the interview progressed, I felt increasingly sympathetic toward this troubled lady. After about fifteen minutes had elapsed, I asked her if she would like to change to a cooler room. She replied, "No, thank you, Doctor, it's quite cool in here now."

The room temperature hadn't changed, of course; it was because of the relaxation of her feelings that she felt more comfortable. I soon learned that she and her husband had been thrown together a great deal more at home since their retirement as teachers. The increased number of contacts provided more opportunities for points of dissension, one of which was the question of the most comfortable temperature.

It is inscribed in the Hebrew Talmud that "as a man gets angry, he falls into error." Cardano, one of the greatest physicians of the sixteenth century, stated, "When a man is hostile, he is insane." When emotion comes into play, memory, concentration, and judgment are impaired. An otherwise intelligent, competent executive will make idiotic blunders; a sensible, loving mother loses her reason and will say and do things to her husband or child which she later sorely regrets.

How often we declare in disgust, "How could I have behaved so stupidly?" The answer is most often found in the past accumulation of $I \rightarrow H + S$. It insures the continuation of stupid mistakes and, therefore, fouls up our future.

Many a capable political leader comes to grief because crushing blows to his self-respect make him more vulnerable to gross errors in judgment. The case of ex-President Nixon is an unfortunately good example. Most political analysts predicted that he would win the 1972 election by a large margin. What impelled a man who had risen so high to resort to underhanded methods of getting the vote, and to use dirty tricks against potential election opponents? What was the source of Nixon's doubts?

The degree of anxiety, H, S, doubt, and lack of self-confidence is proportional to the degree of I. Nixon's self-concept of inferiority was the result of devastating blows to his self-respect —being implicated in the scandal that led to the "Checkers Speech," having to serve as second fiddle under Eisenhower, his narrow defeat for the Presidency by John F. Kennedy, and his failure to be elected Governor of California.

For those with an excess of I, it isn't enough to merely win. The craving for S is so intense that the win must be huge, as in the case of a gambler in a losing streak. This explains Nixon's urge for a landslide win in the 1972 election. At the same time, the craving for S leads to a Mirage of infallibility and exaltation, sometimes referred to as the King Richard complex.

Since H generates an equivalent amount of fear, the greater the H the more fearful one becomes. It is this extreme fear which is at the root of the paranoid's desperate need to eradicate those to whom he is hostile—as exemplified by the dirty campaign tricks and the Watergate break-in. The lower the Respect Level, the greater the urge to vengeance and S. Not content merely to defeat their opponents, such persons are driven, because of their own previous humiliations, by an uncontrollable urge to exact revenge by humiliating others. When his H reaches extreme proportions, this type of individual isn't satisfied to stick the knife in, but is impelled to twist it. This gives rise to the urge to let the object of one's H "twist slowly in the wind."

What about the wild risks taken by the other men involved in the Watergate scandal? Professional commentators, high-ranking government officials, and professors of law and political science stated that they couldn't understand why men of such high intelligence behaved so "stupidly." However, some members of Nixon's staff followed him blindly in these illegal acts, while others did not. Why was this?

Gullibility is a product of inferiority. The staff members who were ridden with I followed, while those with high levels of self-respect (such as Richardson and Ruckelshaus) were not vulnerable. This is borne out by the fact that the "followers" had little if any record of competence in government. Nixon selected comparative unknowns for his Vice President and most of his staff because his I unconsciously motivated him into seeking greater S by surrounding himself with aides of comparatively inferior status.

Baseball fans may recall the losing streak of an L.A. outfielder in the 1966 World Series. How could he, an outstanding fielder, possibly have dropped three fly balls in rapid succession? The balancing mechanism does an efficient job of maintaining equilibrium in the healthy individual in the face of moderate stress. Subject such an individual to moderate stress (a dropped ball or belittling remark) and he doesn't become unduly upset. Nor does the expert with his high Respect Level go to pieces after an error. However, when the stress is severe, as in dropping an easy fly, the anxiety becomes so great that coordination is impaired.

A normal level of I provides enough stimulation to make us competitive. However, as you have learned, with increasing I we become overanxious and overcompetitive, as manifested by H to our associates and the urge for S. The Mirage of S eggs him on to excess in trying to outdo others. This will cause a man to run with the ball or attempt a goal shot when he should have passed it to a teammate. A player with an excess of I often lunges for a ball which is impossible to get. In spite of his knowing better from experience, the Mirage of S creates the belief that he can do it.

The same process occurs in any sport or endeavor. For example, if one of your fellow workers or employees who had previously always performed well is in a streak of blunders, it's most likely caused by S and suppressed H. The same is true when a child who has previously done well at school or college is in an extended period of poor schoolwork.

Professional athletes generally manifest less H than amateurs. Experience has taught them that H to opponents or teammates results in costly errors. However, injuries traced to H are all too prevalent. The H may follow angry reprimands by a manager or coach who can't manage his own H. Although the Mirage is fleeting, by the time the player has realized his mistake, the damage is done. Recently, a leading jockey became so enraged after being blocked in a race that he rammed his fist through a door in the jockey quarters. The result was that he broke his hand and had to be sidelined.

Now, it's only natural to want to look good, but the need to lord it over the other fellow and humiliate him by superiority and contempt prods us into dangerous extremes. A chess champion may lose his title because of inability to manage the H his opponent provokes in him.

Have you read about Ilie Nastase's hostility on the court? Recently a referee insisted that Nastase quit stalling between games.

Where the Respect Level is low, as a result of long-standing under-nourishment, the response to even mild criticism is one of overreaction. Instead of being brought back to the healthy level of feeling equal, the individual conceives of himself as superior to others and becomes angry; more than ever he is convinced that *he* is right and therefore refuses to heed the criticism. Nastase cursed out the referee, and that gentleman promptly disqualified him.

This bad-tempered fellow claims that discharging his anger during a match helps him play better. It's true that one's performance is impaired by suppressing H. But Nastase doesn't realize that the gain from venting anger is far outweighed by the liabilities. His anger turns the referees, linesmen, and spectators against him. The feedback from them multiplies his H. His concentration and judgment must be impaired by this escalation of H. He doesn't realize that H turns his mind away from his real goal—applying the mind's reasoning faculty to strategy—to the unconscious goal of hostility: humiliating and hurting the enemy.

Nor do I believe his assertion that he *deliberately* becomes angry; H can only arise unconsciously and involuntarily. If Nastase learned Anti-H as well as he has learned tennis, he would not only win more matches, but also more respect and affection.

Ex-heavyweight champion Bob Fitzsimmons used to tell his boxing trainees, "Try to put your fist right through your opponent's body. But don't get mad at him." This ex-champion knew that anger interferes with concentration and judgment and often goads one into hasty, impulsive action.

One of the consequences of success in any sport may be the S Mirage. Even champions are sometimes the victims of such a Mirage: "I beat this guy four straight times, so of course I'll beat him again." Because of the Mirage, the champion may overlook such significant factors as:

1. The change in style of his opponent;
2. A change in the surface of the court or ballpark;
3. Failure to make an exhaustive investigation of the many factors that could spell the difference between winning and losing.

Another problem is that professional athletes seldom understand the basis of ridicule and H from the fans. Most fans are drawn to a game through identification with the local team. Much of their satisfaction when their team is ahead is based on the normal level of I feelings. The more inferior a fan feels, however, the less able he is to tolerate the loss of the game, and so he seeks a scapegoat. Given an understanding of this, the taunted player won't be antagonized and, therefore, will avoid fights or errors resulting from H.

Ridding yourself of H *doesn't* mean giving up firmness, fight, resolution, and the drive to win. Eliminating your H only strengthens those forces. Therefore, we shouldn't be deceived into believing that an athlete who is angry at the opposition has any kind of advantage.

H is also a large factor in errors and accidents in "individual" sports such as jogging, golf, and fishing. The medical profession recommends jogging as one means of contributing to the health of the heart and blood vessels. Nevertheless, your doctor will insist that you not overdo it. Here again, the jogger most likely to overdo it is the one with the most I and, therefore, H and craving for S. It is from the small group with pronounced feelings of I that most injuries occur in sports and exercises. Most of the sportsman's H and anxiety is initially directed at himself, in the form of self-condemnation.

You can see how this works with the golfer. When charged up with H and anxiety he is apt to begin with a stroke below his usual form. Failing to realize that his lack of coordination is due to his disturbed mood, he becomes angry with himself and can usually be heard muttering something like: "Idiot, how could you be so stupid?"

This increase in H makes the next stroke worse, and the ensuing vicious circle is likely to cause a succession of poor shots. At the end of such a day the golfer doesn't like himself at all, and is apt to go home talking to himself. Of course, the next time he plays he's the victim of the increase in I $\rightarrow$ H due to the previous poor performances. This is often the basis of an extended losing streak.

Positive thinking doesn't change anything, because if you tell yourself to forget the bad stroke, that you're going to make good strokes from now on, you're not doing a blessed thing about the real cause of the trouble. This is the time to apply immediately a dose of anti-H therapy. While most folks look at a game as a chance for relaxation, away from the problems of work and family, it's a mistake to believe that you can forget unresolved problems that are heavily laden with H and anxiety. Don't be afraid to ask yourself if you're carrying such a load. If you are, then you can recognize that the poor stroke was due not to lack of ability, but to an honest-to-goodness emotional burden that would have interfered with the strokes of a champion.

Of course, if you had been making it a practice to keep your home and work problems cleansed of H, you would have been much less likely to muff the stroke. Now, having recognized that you've overlooked your H, give it some attention. Even if there's not enough time to think it out right then and there, you can at least acknowledge its presence. This keeps it from being suppressed, in which state it creates the greatest havoc with concentration and coordination. Mistakes are seldom due to stupidity. Recognizing that the bad stroke was caused by self-blame will enable you to make the next stroke with more self-confidence. Remind yourself that you only did the best you could *at the moment*, that your mistake was the result of $I \rightarrow H + S$.

Make it a rule never to blame *anyone*. If you're well along in a losing streak, apply this technique and it should help pull you out. Now that you're reversing the vicious circle—from self-blame to self-confidence, you can expect to improve with each stroke.

H is easily provoked in any activity where self-respect is involved. Thus, when a driver with a low respect level is passed by another driver, he feels as if he's even more on the inferior end. This may goad him into speeding up in order to assert his superiority. This places the other driver in the inferior position and therefore, he's apt to speed up. Although both started out for the purpose of going to work, they're now going in for drag racing. Or, you may be driving along, quite free of H and suddenly find someone trying to bulldoze you. The temporary state of H provoked when someone takes your right of way may incite you to cut him off despite the risk of a collision.

Even a good-natured person is quite unmindful that his recently acquired H makes him an unsafe driver inasmuch as H incites us to attack by any means at our disposal.

Like the animals, we often attack anyone who crosses our path when we're unable to attack the person that angered us. The reason for H to perfectly innocent strangers is easy to comprehend when you consider H's purpose: to relieve us of the intolerable concept of believing ourselves inferior to others. The $I \rightarrow H$ not only increases the chance of an accident, but also the likelihood of a ticket for speeding or outright mayhem.

Not infrequently, a couple of pugnacious bruisers actually attempt to lure a solo driver into honking his horn by refusing to move when the light turns green. Then while they've got him blocked, they come over and indulge their need to bully by making a remark such as, "Wutzuh matter, you wanna get your face mashed in?"

But even an "impromptu" provocation can lead to violence. Take the case of Jim; at the age of seventeen he was considered to have an excellent chance to fulfill his ambition of becoming a professional baseball player. One day, as he pulled up to an intersection, a pedestrian, fearing that Jim was going to take his right of way, became angry and snarled at him. Jim was willing to overlook the matter, but then the pedestrian made an obscene reference to his mother. Angered by this remark, Jim stepped out of his car, and a fight ensued.

Since Jim was a powerful athlete, he easily battered his adversary to a pulp. Although he won the fight, the fractured bones of his hand didn't heal properly, thus ending his prospects for a baseball career.

Some will say that Jim would have despised himself as a coward if he hadn't fought to defend his mother's virtue. Let's see why this isn't true.

Derogatory remarks have only one meaning: an uncontrollable reaction of the belittler to his own feelings of inferiority. I explained to Jim that the pedestrian had become hostile only as a result of what others had done to him, just as Jim himself had. This is the only way any of us can become hostile. The pedestrian's remark was merely a hostile reaction to his mistaken belief that Jim was crowding him at the intersection as a gesture of disrespect.

In the course of our discussion, Jim raised a point that indicated that he had brought his own share of I to the altercation: "Yeah, but if our positions had been reversed, I wouldn't have made any nasty remarks to the driver."

Such statements, indicative of a need to think of oneself as superior, arise from a deficient level of self-respect. I reminded Jim that if he had been subjected to the same conditioning emotional experiences as the pedestrian, he would have reacted in the same irate manner. Hadn't Jim also become hostile when he believed he was being disrespected? Jim understood that the pedestrian was as blameless as himself, so why fight him?

You often hear the indignant remark, "Why, I would never have done anything like he did." But you must reckon with the fact that the other person's mental responses may differ from yours because:

1. He may be unable to reason as well as you can.
2. He may lack the information necessary to come to the correct conclusion.
3. H, S and anxiety cause gross errors in even the most intelligent person's judgment. You have already learned why we are not at fault or otherwise responsible for any H, S, or anxiety.
4. Your own H or S to a person may be the instigating cause of his misdeed or mistaken thinking.

You must reckon with the sharp increase in H that occurs to a driver after some experience which has lowered his self-respect. For example, when walking across the track parking lot on your way to the racetrack you'll find the drivers reasonably friendly and courteous. However, it's a different story on your way out. Since most of them have wound up losers, their self-respect has taken a sharp drop. Accordingly, their H levels have risen. So if you're too close, beware: they're a lot more apt to snarl and bear down on you.

The urge to belittle others is less inhibited when driving since it appears easier to get away with it—for instance, mashing down on the horn to prod someone into speeding up. It may be that the car in front of you can't move because of motor trouble. Sometimes we've honked only to find out that the driver was one of those old ladies who seldom uses her car, except when she has to visit her sixty-four-year-old sick brother. All in all, you're better off not to blow the horn except as a safety measure. The average person is apt to feel humiliated by this pointed reminder that he's goofing and, therefore, usually responds with H. Since H causes automatic contrariness, he's likely to slow down even more. His hostile response may increase yours to a point where you'll either blow the horn louder and longer, or try to speed up and get around him despite the danger.

Check your H when you get into your car and check it frequently during your trip. Also, you must learn to protect yourself against the H aroused by your wife, husband, child, or other passengers. An irritating remark from a passenger can ignite your H just as you are entering a freeway, approaching a fork, or signal. Since H dominates the mind to a point where the individual may lose sight of his own safety, watch out lest it goad you into a speed contest when you're passed or berated by an irate motorist.

It's because of $I \rightarrow H + S$ that so many drivers go through red lights. Since you have no way of knowing how hostile other motorists are, you can avoid danger by always assuming it may be present. Whenever a driver manifests hostility toward you, use your training to diffuse your H immediately. At the same time, you can diminish the other driver's H by some type of respectful gesture; for example, by simply saying, "I'm sorry, I was in the wrong."

Maybe you weren't. But in giving him the benefit of the doubt, you'll quiet him down and prevent a potentially dangerous altercation. Furthermore, by helping him feel he's respected, you help him become a safer driver. Your own self-respect will arise for having contributed to road safety, and your passengers will admire your coolness under fire. You'll arrive at your destination relaxed, instead of being charged up with tension.

Just as you must be able to turn on the windshield wiper or

apply your brakes instantly, so you must learn to be equally alert in applying the method of dissolving H. You'll find that it is your best protection against altercations, accidents, and traffic tickets—and you'll acquire the love of your insurance company to boot.

GETTING BETTER SERVICE

Suppose you arrive at the gas pump, and when you ask for premium gas the exasperated attendant growls, "How in hell do you expect me to reach your tank from there?"

Since it's obvious that he *can* reach your tank from there, your first impulse is to indignantly inform him of this fact. With Anti-H training you'd know that it wouldn't be to your advantage to assert yourself in this indignant way. Now, why did he become hostile in the first place?

For the same reason that you did: in reaction to someone else's disrespect. The fact is that he, like yourself, was the innocent victim of a chain reaction he didn't originate.

Communication between employees and customers is a source of H that inflicts a much greater toll on the employees, since they deal with a succession of customers. The H provoked by one customer is apt to cause irritability with the next, so that H, anxiety, tension, and fatigue grow as the day progresses.

Let this bank teller tell you about her day at work: "All day long we have to take abuse from customers. Just ask for identification, and they act as if you were accusing them of forgery. Don't they realize we service so many customers that we can't recognize all of them? And the glare you get if the line's been moving slowly! Why can't they see that it's not the teller's fault? So many customers haven't made up their minds what to do with their money when they arrive at the window. Many of them haven't endorsed their checks or filled out their deposit slips. Some come in with a bag of change and bills rolled up in a ball that's hard to count. Then we have to listen to the same old complaints—'What took so long?' or, 'If I can't get better service, I'm going to transfer my account.' "

Have you ever noticed how frequently waiters and other public service employees sneak off for a smoke? The principal reason is the tension arising from a succession of hostile encounters. One veteran waitress remarked, "Many of the customers are so demanding and grumpy that I make it a practice to go back to the kitchen and cuss them out there. The waitresses who keep it in don't last. They get ulcers or some other sickness."

An irritated employee indeed deserves our sympathy. "But," you say, "he hasn't any right to take it out on me."

But H is an automatic involuntary reaction. Unless we're trained in Anti-H therapy, it envelops us and we transmit it immediately. Remember that the other person hasn't been trained in managing H—as you have been. Human beings complain, blame, and adamantly insist they're right only because they too have been subjected to similar attitudes, not because they're out to give you a hard time.

"Look," you might say, "why bother with all this? Why not just express my anger and tell the gas station man that my car's already within reach of the pump?"

The reason is that your anger would aggravate his, leading to an argument or some form of retaliation, then or in the future. Many of the multitudes of people charged up with H are so disturbed that they badly need psychiatric treatment. Some are under the influence of illegal drugs, tranquilizers, or alcohol, or embittered by the conviction that they are being ill-used by their families, employers, or government.

A hostile attendant might tell you that your oil, battery water, or radiator checked out okay when they were actually low. Besides, his hostile response will aggravate your H. This could very well be the basis of some carelessness, such as racing out of the station. Even if you exited without mishap, your H might get you into an altercation with another motorist or provoke an accident.

Your understanding that the attendant and yourself are the innocent victims of a chain of reactions which neither initiated will help you manage this provocation without any loss to yourself—of pride, time, or anything else. As you move your car closer to the premium pump, your new-found understanding will show in your voice when you say, "Sure, I'll move it up."

Whenever you are the customer, it will pay you to be alert to $I \rightarrow H$ in yourself and other public service employees. Remember that they have been in contact with irate customers and their supervisors throughout the day. Since they can't retain their jobs if they vent their anger, suppression of H is the rule.

Occasionally a waitress mistakenly adds $1.85 on your check for an item whose price is included on the dinner. Such mistakes are generally due to the H that you or other patrons may have provoked. Even though she wouldn't deliberately cheat anyone, the H exerts its unconscious vengeful effect, feeding the extra $1.85 into her brain's computer and causing her to believe that it's a legitimate part of the bill.

If your waiter walks away when you're in the middle of asking for something, remember how many times he's encountered $H + S$ from previous customers and check your own $I \rightarrow H + S$. Not only will your considerate feelings melt his H, but also your own, to say nothing of saving yourself from an unpleasant meal and a case of indigestion.

If, instead of the hostile response his arrogant manner provokes in other customers, he receives a respectful response from you, he'll be agreeably surprised and react appreciatively, not only then, but on your future visits. You'll be pleased with your adept management of the situation and go on your way without the serious liability of a system charged with H.

5.
H on the Job

Consider the managers of firms that sell and service equipment. I got to meet many of these fellows as patients hospitalized with such illnesses as high blood pressure, heart attack, headache, pain in various parts of the body, and alcoholism. These men had become ill as a result of their daily contacts with complaining, demanding, and irate customers.

Since the salesmen hadn't done anything wrong, why are the customers angry? The reason is that they are reacting to $I \rightarrow H$, just as we all must do. Make it an invariable rule to use the $I \rightarrow H$ formula to assign your H to its real source.

Your understanding that anger is a chain reaction, in which each person is the victim of attitudes and circumstances which cause him to feel disrespected and to treat others disrespectfully in turn, will quickly free you of any H. Your self-respect will be restored since you'll be aware that other people's H has nothing to do with any misdeed on your part. This will not only safeguard you against the accumulation of H throughout your day, but will also fortify your self-confidence.

When H develops between members of a team, cooperation deteriorates and losses really multiply. Take the case of Herb, the manager of a firm that sold and serviced tractors and bulldozers. He attended a lecture I gave on "Hostility In Business"; after the lecture, he told me that it had seemed to be all about him. "The first thing in the morning the salesmen are after me about equipment they've sold which isn't ready for delivery. But I've told them time and again not to make commitments they can't fulfill. Then I have to listen to their complaints and catch it from the customers as well."

Herb felt as if he were being attacked from all sides. He complained bitterly about his mechanics. They were angry at the men in the parts department for not supplying parts more quickly. The parts men complained that they couldn't get it through the mechanics' heads that they were not responsible for delays in shipment from the factory. His sales manager was angry with him for not allowing him to fire several of the salesmen. There were frequent phone calls from the head office taking him to task for not selling more equipment.

Herb had been coming home from work in a state of tension, depression, and exhaustion. His wife had urged him to quit his job, lest he have a breakdown. "How can we sell more equipment when the factory isn't even delivering what we've already sold?" he demanded. "Do you think I should chuck it and look for another job?"

I told him that this made no more sense than to discontinue selling some of their fine tractors because some customers mishandled them. His men knew their business, but, like everyone else, workers need to feel that their contribution on the job is appreciated by management. When, instead, they are treated with indifference, ridicule, and hostility they become disgruntled, uncooperative, and inefficient. Herb was angry with his boss, sales manager, salesmen, mechanics, men in the parts department, and the complaining customers, and he had no idea whatsoever that he was infecting them all with H and thus causing them to work against him and each other.

WHY WASN'T I PROMOTED?

Promotions aren't handed out for technical competence alone. They're also based on how well a man is liked. Many an employee becomes bitter because he is passed over for promotion in favor of someone who does not measure up to him in job performance. In most cases that old nemesis, H, is responsible. Since this emotion is contagious, an employee antagonizes his foreman, manager, supervisor, and anyone else to whom he feels hostile.

A recent article in *The New York Times* cited the fact that large numbers of executives are fired not because of lack of technical competence, but because their personalities are offensive to higher-echelon officers. Even when a man knows that he may not be promoted—and may even be fired—because of the boss's resentment, there is nothing he can do about it if he doesn't know how to deal with the H.

Besides H, the worker often overlooks his involvement with his immediate boss in a contest for S. As if this were not enough, the gradual accumulation of suppressed H makes him especially prone to serious illness. For example, a foreman was referred to me because of his increasing depression. Al complained bitterly that although he sincerely tried to help his crew, his efforts were often unappreciated. He cited a typical instance: Although his men were supposed to repair the machines they operated, one of them, Sam, asked him for help. Al readily obliged. However, Al complained, "This joker didn't bother to watch how the repair job was done. To add insult to injury, he didn't even thank me, but simply turned his back on me." Al went on to say that the frequency of this kind of incident had made him disgusted with some of his men. "What's wrong?"

A knowledge of the source of H makes it easy to analyze such problems. First, the presence in Al of H meant he must be feeling inferior. In his therapy, Al's I was traced to his frustrations with his wife and children. The I generated by this domestic strife had caused him to be unduly harsh and dictatorial with his crew. Because of his obsession with his own troubles, he hadn't realized the antagonizing effect of his harsh attitude. This hostile force was behind his crewman's lack of attention and his failure to thank Al. Attempts at friendliness, working extra hours, and doing favors failed to change the situation for Al, because his own H, which had caused it, was still present.

You already know why the worker who blasts his boss may be fired. Yet, as we have seen, the individual who *suppresses* his H is *also* disliked, fails to get cooperation, loses out on promotions, and gets fired as often as the fellow who blurts out his anger. He soon comes to feel that others are working against him. The resulting H causes tension, carelessness, forgetfulness, indecisiveness, poor concentration, and fatigue; it is also the chief cause of costly blunders and absenteeism in industry.

That certain individuals are accident-prone is indicated by a study in which it was found that only 10 percent of the workers were responsible for 70 percent of the accidents. Other studies have shown that from 80 to 90 percent of all accidents are not due to defective machinery, physical or mental defect, or lack of skill, but to an X factor in the worker's personality. The result is loss of skilled manpower, huge medical compensation costs to industry and, inevitably, higher prices for the consumer.

The prominence of the H factor in industrial accidents is seldom recognized; the foreman or injured worker usually blames the accident on carelessness. The fact is that most carelessness is due to a mental state of H and anxiety that makes even a skilled worker operate without his usual caution.

The result of suppressed H in an employee is unconscious

sabotage of anything you may want him to do—even though he may consciously feel that he is trying to do it. For example, a foreman who could not leave the plant had to make a bank deposit in order to keep a check from bouncing. He gave one of his men the money, stressing that it was imperative to make the deposit before the bank closed. Unfortunately, although there was plenty of time, the man stopped for a leisurely lunch and did not arrive at the bank until after closing time. The foreman was thus caused the embarrassment of having his check bounce.

What went wrong? The foreman had overlooked some cutting remarks he had made to this man on several occasions. Since the employee hadn't talked back, the foreman failed to reckon with the H those remarks had aroused. But the H had remained and had become the source of vengeful behavior. The moral? *You cannot rely on a person to whom you have been hostile.*

Don't overlook the critical influence of home life on job efficiency. Motivation, creativity, and cooperation at work may be seriously impaired as a result of domestic unhappiness. Many men proudly maintain that they don't bring their domestic problems to work with them, and can "forget about" the day's aggravation at work once they get home. The trouble is that anxiety and H aren't reduced in the slightest by "forgetting"; in fact, they exert an even greater force when we try to ignore their presence.

Richard, the president of a large firm, was referred to me after suffering persistent stomach pain. A specialist had examined him thoroughly and could find no evidence of any disease process such as ulcer or cancer. The commonest cause of pain anywhere in the body that is not the result of organic disease is suppressed H. Accordingly, I interrogated Richard carefully to find out if such a pattern existed.

The story soon unfolded. While dressing for work one morning he suddenly realized that he might be late for an important appointment with his sales manager. He called to his wife, "Sweetheart, would you fix me some breakfast?"

At that moment she was propped up in bed puffing on a cigarette and looking over the paper. She called back to him in an annoyed tone, "Oh, for goodness sake, you can fix it yourself."

Richard was already feeling a sense of self-blame because of running late, and therefore her remark only increased his I feelings, generating immediate anger. However, he had long since learned that voicing his anger to her only provoked a bitter argument. So for the past five years, he had walked away from arguments and tried to overlook and forget his disagreements with his wife. This bottling up of H had caused a disturbance in the function of his stomach and small intestine, resulting in the physical distress he was now suffering.

As usual, he now "forgot" his irritation and made the breakfast himself. On his way to work, suppressed rage led him into verbal clashes with passing motorists. Indeed, ensuing events at his office had all the characteristics of a chain reaction of turnpike collisions:

1. Richard's increased H paved the way for biting criticism of his sales manager at their conference.
2. The provoked sales manager then proceeded to a monthly meeting with his three hundred salesmen where his irritation led to caustic remarks which, in turn, antagonized them.
3. Three hundred hostilized salesmen then left to call on their clients. In their state of irritability they were primed more to provoke than to persuade their clients.

In failing to realize that he is functioning poorly because of his own H feelings, a man is likely to blame others for his poor performance. Richard's suppressed H had, of course, been transmitted to his employees. Being human, they had to respond accordingly; and by the time he arrived home, he was so irascible that he was apt to provoke even more dissension.

Through therapy Richard became able to understand that his wife couldn't have resisted the forces that had made her hostile. He was eager to have her come in with him and learn how to manage H, too. I explained that I preferred to have him first see for himself that he could make her more receptive by applying what he had learned.

There were many ways, unbeknown to himself, in which Richard's suppressed H had manifested itself:

1. When his wife spoke to him, he frequently did not listen. She knew this by the expression of his eyes and mouth.
2. If he was supposed to accompany her to some place she wanted to go, his H would unconsciously slow him down. For example, he would dally in the bathroom when she asked him to hurry because they were late for dinner at her mother's. Had he vocalized his feelings, they would have been something like, "To hell with the old battle-ax and you, too." Even if his wife appeared on the verge of convulsions, he couldn't get himself ready in less than an hour and a half. Yet she couldn't fail to note that on his night out with the boys he was able to shave, shine, and shampoo in twenty minutes!
3. While he put in so much time at work, he found little time

for her. As he had told me in his first visit, "She has nothing to complain about, I give her everything." Unfortunately, "everything" included his hostility—akin to giving someone a strawberry shortcake "accidentally" laced with pepper.

4. In his discussions with his wife, he failed to realize the effect on her of his insistence on having his opinion and his way at the expense of hers. If she disagreed, he would become annoyed and abruptly terminate the conversation.

Richard's H diminished when he realized that, like himself, his wife felt inferior and became hostile and depressed when deprived of appreciation and affection. He realized that he had never applied himself to thinking about her emotions with the same concentration and thoroughness he bestowed on his business. Telling her he loved her and how well he provided for her could never replace her need to feel that he understood and respected her.

I asked if he thought that she counted as much as the business. He replied that she counted for much more, and that he was going to do a lot more thinking about his attitudes and feelings toward her. His new appreciation and interest in her soon led to stimulating discussions—and sure enough, she began making his breakfast.

It might seem that Richard's increased attention to his wife's emotional needs would result in neglect of his business. However, in ridding himself of H he also got rid of his stomach pain and fatigue. Whereas he had often come to work in a state of pain and irritability, he now came in feeling energetic and cheerful. By applying his knowledge of emotional dynamics to his dealings with his staff, he reduced their H to him. They, in turn, became less irritable and more helpful to other employees and to the firm's customers.

A person with a low Respect Level is victimized by the Mirage effect into an even stronger conviction that he is right. The result is the continuation of erroneous policies by intelligent, well-informed persons whom you would have expected would know better—a practice known in business as "throwing good money after bad." That's why you shouldn't make a decision when angry; instead, first apply Anti-H. Then you'll be able to make a decision based on your accumulated knowledge and good sense.

Let's consider a case involving Hawks, the president of a steel firm, and his assistant, Byrd. The latter, a very capable executive, had developed a superb plan of reorganization which he submitted to his boss. However, there had been an undercurrent of resentment between the two for more than a year. After taking into consideration all the pros and cons of Byrd's plan, Hawks truly believed that it would not be useful and rejected it. He was quite unaware of the real basis for this rejection: his hostility to Byrd. H neutralizes any data that might give credit to someone who arouses that feeling in you. No matter how well such a person does his job, your H will lessen your appreciation of him.

I first met Hawks at a seminar on Emotional Dynamics conducted for a group of business executives. Following the discussion, Hawks asked rather indignantly, "How can you help but feel resentful toward an assistant who doesn't cooperate and who is so unreasonable?"

I replied that his own H was a potent factor in making his assistant uncooperative and unreasonable.

"Why, I act very friendly to him," Hawks rejoined. "I never let him know that I feel resentful."

After I pointed out that concealed H is *always* perceived by the other fellow, he became sufficiently interested to call for a consultation the next day. During our discussion he learned how hard it is to see anything favorable that emanates from a person to whom we are hostile. This was why he hadn't thought much of Byrd's plan. Since Byrd had perceived Hawks's hostility, he could only believe that Hawks had rejected his plan out of prejudice. For the first time, Hawks realized that he had been blaming Byrd for uncooperativeness that he himself had been instigating.

A boss who harbors resentment toward someone on his staff soon infects the entire firm. H spreads between the chairman of the board and the president, between sales manager and the head of the parts department, faction against faction. In this atmosphere, motivation and productivity are impaired, tardiness, absenteeism and illness mount, and competent men quit. Even though Byrd had tried to cooperate, his boss's H turned Byrd against whatever Hawks might propose. To make matters worse, Byrd's resultant bitterness and frustration stifled his motivation and creativity. Not only was Hawks the loser, but the company lost the benefit of an excellent reorganization plan.

The consultation ended at this point. Hawks was depressed because of the fear that he had botched things up. (He became even more depressed when I presented him with the fee for the consultation.) However, during his next visit he brightened up some when he saw that the entire mess could be straightened out by ridding himself of H. He felt more sympathy when he recognized that Byrd, like himself, also reacted with hostility to anything that lowered his self-esteem, and acknowledged that he had been doing Byrd an injustice by blaming him. Now he was eager to try his changed feelings on Byrd and the rest of his staff.

Hawks had always been able to walk into the plant each morning and quickly detect anything that was not functioning properly. However, when he returned for his next visit, he reported that in addition to checking the factory, he was now checking his feelings regularly. Whenever he detected any H, he would utilize the I → H + S Reaction to remind himself of its source. Then, by thinking through what he had learned, he was able to get rid of his H.

He also noticed that Byrd responded to his changed feelings with decreasing H. However, he had been hostile to Byrd for over a year, and this had badly dented Byrd's Respect Level. How could Hawks restore it more rapidly?

Now that he felt much less H, he was capable of giving credit when it was due. A practical way of accomplishing this would be to validate Byrd's opinions as often as possible. Byrd's Respect Level would improve in response to this approval since it would now be sincere. Hawks could manipulate many situations so that Byrd, rather than himself, would get the credit. If Hawks made a mistake, he should readily acknowledge it. On the other hand, if Byrd made a mistake, instead of blaming him, Hawks could lead him into a discussion of the issue, minus any evidence of know-it-all or any suggestions of blame.

When a person feels blamed, he unconsciously resists seeing his mistakes. The reason for this is that blame causes a drop in the Respect Level to a point of intolerable anxiety. The mind attempts to protect us from this anxiety by blinding us to anything, such as our mistakes, that we interpret as belittling. But, in this blame-free atmosphere, Byrd could more easily see his mistakes and acknowledge them.

By dissolving his own H and by raising Byrd's Respect Level, Hawks gradually earned the other man's respect and affection. Freed of H, he was able to see the merit of Byrd's reorganization plan. He admitted that his previous reaction had been unwise, the plan was adopted, and Hawks saw to it that Byrd got the credit for it.

Hawks's relations with Byrd were improved on the basis of knowledge he acquired in twelve hours of instruction. The more he applied it, the more confident he became of his ability to bring about better motivation, creativity, cooperation, and efficiency in his staff.

If you are a boss, how can you rid yourself of hostility and yet remain firm, forceful, and resolute in dealing with your staff? Examine yourself carefully for $I \rightarrow A + Ob + H + S + Mar$. If you find them present, first be sure that you have a thorough knowledge of the basic principles governing the operation of your emotional system, as set forth in Chapter 4. Read that chapter again and discuss it with your wife, family, friends, and associates at work.

DO YOU RESENT YOUR BOSS?

Suppose you find yourself resenting *your* boss, honestly believing that he has been unfair to you. Sue felt just that way. She had just typed a letter for her boss. "Sue, there's no need for that last sentence, so just delete it," he said.

Sue reacted with immediate I to the boss's criticism. When she was a youngster, most of the criticisms from her parents had been accompanied by a belittling attitude. Accordingly, she construed the boss's criticism as belittling and therefore had to react with $I \rightarrow H + S$. Her S Mirage was manifested by her reply: "Oh, that sentence will help get your message across." However, this necessarily made out the boss's suggestion to be wrong, and he became annoyed at her because of this contradiction. Her only gain was the transitory satisfaction of believing that she was right—and therefore not inferior. However, her remark consigned the boss to the inferior position and thus made him hostile. With a knowledge of $I \rightarrow H + S$ she could have quickly overcome her H and turned this incident to her advantage, simply replying, "Of course, that sentence isn't necessary."

REDUCING H IN THE UNCOOPERATIVE

Can we reduce another person's H whether he cooperates or not?

When I told the editor-in-chief of a publishing house that most emotional problems could be remedied by my method of getting rid of H feelings, he replied rather indignantly, "I don't believe you're aware of the kind of dog-eat-dog society we live in. There's no way anyone could reduce my boss's hostility."

Most people believe that you cannot change another individual's negative personal traits—his temper, resentment, nervousness, contrariness, selfishness, opinionatedness, uncooperativeness, disloyalty, dishonesty, or poor motivation. The fact is, however, that the knowledge of Anti-H equips you with a workable method of changing these traits—not only in yourself, but in your associates. This method most emphatically *doesn't* include "turning the other cheek." In fact, the knowledge you acquire will safeguard you from any hurt or upset from another person's hostility.

One member of my Anti-Hostility course was Peg, a real estate agent. She had recently completed the sale of a luxurious townhouse. When she returned to her office, her boss asked her about the sale. No sooner had she begun to discuss it when he interrupted and began telling the other agents that it was through the techniques *he* had shown her that the sale had been consummated.

Peg felt a surge of resentment toward him for robbing her of the credit, and became even more resentful when he repeated this performance at lunch in front of his partner and several other agents.

"Wouldn't anyone resent such behavior?" Peg demanded. In the next few weeks, communication with her boss rapidly worsened and she was on the verge of quitting her job.

The knowledge of I → H guided her to a consideration of her own I feelings. Peg had gone into real estate sales not out of a need for additional income, but because of fourteen years of "putting up with my husband's belittling." It was because of this failure to get respect from her husband that she sought it all the more outside the home.

Why had her boss hogged the credit for her sale? His appropriation of credit pointed to his own craving for Superiority. Peg had been so obsessed with her own S cravings that she had been oblivious to the fact that her boss had the same craving. But his bragging about what he had taught her didn't mean that he wasn't fully aware of her outstanding sales ability. The only force that could keep him from readily acknowledging her ability was H from her.

Peg learned that the resentment she believed she had been concealing was the source of her boss's H to her. A member of the class suggested that she let her boss know how frequently she used the knowledge he had taught her. This helped Peg earn his respect, which he showed by his greater ease in communicating with her —and by ceasing his attempts to usurp the credit for her sales.

HOW TO GET AHEAD BY YOUR MISTAKES

Having made a mistake, you can convert it into an asset rather than a loss to yourself and your organization.

Suppose Joan, a secretary, is told to type letters only after sending the bills out. However, on her own she decides to get the letters out first, thus provoking her boss into reprimanding her.

You can see the uncomfortable position in which Joan finds herself. When you are deprived of respect, whatever you say, do, and feel thereafter is dominated by the need to extricate yourself from this I status. The urge to relieve yourself of distressing I feelings pressures Joan into an alibi: "Oh, I didn't think it mattered, as long as I got the bills out today."

Joan would not have been ashamed of her I feelings if she had realized that they were a natural reaction to her need for respect. Her boss's hostile attitude was caused by the I *he* felt because of his fear that she didn't respect him enough to follow his suggestions. A knowledge that most mistakes are due to anxiety and H would have prompted Joan to ask herself if she had recently undergone any upsetting events. She would have realized that because of the dent in his self-respect, she had reacted with an urge to do things her way. With this relief from the burden of self-blame, it would have been easy for her straightforwardly to admit her mistake. She could have truthfully said, "It was pretty poor judgment to do the letters before the bills."

This validation of her boss's criticism would have served to elevate his Respect Level and therefore increase his respect for her. By making it a practice to honestly acknowledge her mistakes he would become increasingly receptive to her opinions. Inevitably he would compare her with others and recognize her superior ability to get along with people. Under these circumstances, her chances for promotion would be optimal.

WHY IT'S A MISTAKE TO BLAME ANYONE

Since your goal is to get the other fellow to see his mistake, you only make it *more* difficult for him to do so when you blame him. Even if you're not at fault, don't blame the boss for reprimanding you since his I, like yours, compels him to find fault.

When you're up against a boss who is loaded with H, you must cleanse *yourself* of H and apply the method repeatedly in every contact with him—face to face, and via phone or memos.

When he blasts you for being uncooperative, don't make the mistake of replying, "I feel that I've been very cooperative." *Never, never alibi.* Your alibis rob the other person of the credit for his criticism and therefore antagonize him. Your contradicting him will make him feel even more inferior. In order to reduce his H, your reply must elevate, not lower his Respect Level. "I'm sure you'll find me more cooperative from here on in." Since you're not hostile, such a reply would manifest respect for his opinion.

If you understand his legitimate need for respect, your feelings will transmit this message. Then the words you use will convey your honest humility. The knowledge of how a person's mistakes come about will exonerate anyone of blame.

What if he makes another derogatory remark, such as "What makes you so stupid?" You trump card is the knowledge that he doesn't *really* think you're stupid; you know he's responding to his own I → H. As always, you must dissolve any H that you have noted in yourself. Again, your answer is based on your goal of using your self-respect as a lever to elevate his:

"Gosh, if I had a brain, I'd be dangerous."

Don't be surprised if this tactic elicits a complimentary reply such as: "If you didn't have a brain you couldn't work for me."

With practice, anyone can acquire the habit of admitting obvious error. Abraham Lincoln's readiness to admit mistakes played a large role in earning for him the respect and goodwill of his associates. When he saw that he'd been wrong in believing that General Grant should have marched downstream when he crossed the Mississippi in the battle of Vicksburg, he wrote to him, saying, "I now wish to make the personal acknowledgement that you were right and I was wrong."

The esteem level is like a lever—by humbly lowering your own level you jack up that of the other fellow. This is illustrated by an event in the life of Will Rogers. At the height of his fame, Will was invited to a banquet given in his honor by a group of English lords. An elegant dinner was preceded by cocktails and accompanied by several fine vintage wines. After the dessert, the diners were served finger bowls.

When you are raised as a cowboy, finger bowls are not a part of the scene. Will believed that his generous hosts were serving an after-dinner drink. He squeezed the lemon into the finger bowl and raised it, preparatory to drinking the contents.

You can imagine the reaction of the English lords around the table. As their eyes met, consternation gave way to comprehension and they immediately squeezed their lemons into *their* finger bowls and, simultaneously with Will, drank the contents. In accordance with the background of English gentlemen, they were motivated by only one consideration: to avoid lowering the other fellow's Respect Level by any superiority attitude on their part. They accomplished this adroitly by using their own position to equalize Will's.

Even if you're not a member of the nobility, an understanding of the balancing mechanism enables you to earn respect by elevating the position of others. Many years ago when I was an intern, I was attempting my first major operation, under the supervision of an experienced surgeon. Nervousness caused my hand to slip, and I cut the hapless patient's bowel. Overcome with self-reproach, I began berating myself for my stupidity.

With the utmost gentility, the expert surgeon replied, "Son, when you've made as many stupid cuts as I have, then you can start complaining about yourself." Had he been harsh and condemning, he would only have put another crimp in my badly dented self-confidence. Instead, by frankly admitting his own fallibility, he alleviated my feeling of worthlessness and therefore reduced my anxiety.

Another way to raise the other fellow's Respect Level is to make yourself the butt of the joke. On TV recently, a lady from Hollywood was being interviewed by the Emcee. When he asked her what had brought her to Hollywood she replied, "I had my heart set on becoming a movie star, so I came out to Hollywood thirty years ago—and I've been a waitress ever since!" The audience howled, not because they were glad she hadn't made it in movies, but because she had so unhesitatingly and unequivocally admitted her failure. We appreciate this because most people blame their failures on someone or something else.

Why do we laugh so heartily at W. C. Fields, Don Rickles, Groucho Marx, and other comedians whose antics feature hostility, superiority, and selfishness? We laugh because their outlandish inferiority gives us a feeling of relative superiority. When W. C. Fields unmercifully blames his ridiculous golf stroke on his caddy, we roar because his outrageous alibi makes us feel so far above him. Our pleasure is enhanced at the opportunity of despising a form of behavior that we have resented in an inconsiderate boss or some other associate. That hostility is often a key factor in arousing laughter is shown by our disinclination to laugh when someone we like commits a *faux pas*, but are quick to erupt into laughter when it's committed by someone we dislike.

The Marx Brothers threw us into laughing spasms by humiliating haughty, disdainful, selfish types: the supercilious society matron, the hard-hearted hotel clerk, the villainous store manager. By humiliating the very types who usually flaunt their superiority and make us feel inferior, the Marx Brothers reverse our respective positions, and our pleasure is expressed in laughter.

Why does Don Rickles make us so gleeful when he portrays a celebrity as one with outrageous faults? The fact that we look up to notables accentuates our feelings of inferiority. Consequently, when a celebrity is made to look ridiculous, our pleasure is the greater because of the satisfaction of topping a member of a group to whom we had always felt inferior. And, of course, along with Don Rickles, we can get away with our ridicule because the celebrity understands that it's all in fun, no harm intended. Besides, he'll be admired all the more for good-naturedly going along with a joke that's on him.

The "joke's on me" technique not only earned Jack Benny

the lasting affection of the public, but a sizable income as well. Employing a little humor about your *own* mistakes indicates to a co-worker that you don't get mad about *his*. He will feel more relaxed with you, and, consequently, be less apt to make slips of his own.

WHAT IS BEING DONE ABOUT HOSTILITY ON THE JOB?

Very little. While some companies are beginning to promote therapy groups, we still find too many men working together who understand their equipment, but not each other.

Bill, the plant manager, is in a state of irritability because of problems at home. When he arrives at work, he finds that the order that he had asked his assistant, Joe, to send out the day before has not been shipped. Because of his peevish mood, he's all the more prone to an angry outburst. When he finds Joe, he snaps, "I just can't depend on you. Why didn't you get that order out yesterday?"

Joe, in no mood to be raked over the coals, replies heatedly, "Look, it wasn't my fault. I've had so much to do that I would've had to neglect more important things to get that order out."

An alibi only makes the accuser angrier because it implies that his criticism is not justified. Consequently, Bill becomes irate and says, "I'm sick and tired of your alibis. When I tell you to do something, I want the job done, not a lot of excuses instead."

This, of course, exacerbates Joe's anger. Had Bill, the manager, not walked away, a fistfight might have occurred. Even without such a fight, both men are left in a disturbed mental state which mars their concentration and judgment for the rest of the day. Each goes home from work in a foul mood likely to incite friction with wife and children. As a result of the aggravation at home, they return to work the next day in a state of heightened irritability which leads to increased dissension at work.

Calling the problem to Bill's attention isn't enough. Unaware that his H is creating a vicious circle, Bill's reply is "Yes, but he [the other fellow] started it." This is not so: a person becomes hostile only as the result of what others have done to him. No one ever *starts* it; the chain reaction is responsible. It doesn't matter where the dissension originates, since it will soon spread from one area to the other.

Now suppose companies provided a course in how to handle hostility. (Everyone in the organization should have this instruction, since the lowest-echelon worker can be hostilized by a chain of reaction moving downward from boss to manager to foreman to worker.) First off, Bill would be alerted to his own hostile state when he arrives at work. Instead of blasting Joe, he would work on his own H, knowing that unless he thoroughly rids himself of such feelings, he has little chance of effecting any improvement in employees' performance. Knowing that H can arise only from a feeling of I, Bill would ask himself, "All right, now what's making me feel inferior?"

This is the question you must *always* ask whenever you detect any H in yourself. In Bill's case, one recent source of I was his disappointment in his twenty-two-year-old son, who since his graduation from high school has been afflicted with an over-whelming aversion to work. Bill's I is the basis of not only his H, but also the tone of superiority in his voice. Joe, like the rest of us, has no difficulty in interpreting this tone; it is exactly as if Bill had said, "Too bad you're not trustworthy like me."

Recognizing his I, Bill would concentrate on figuring out why he himself isn't inferior. The next step is to apply the $I \rightarrow H + S$ Reaction to the other fellow. Joe, like Bill, becomes hostile when disrespected. But while Bill has always realized how much he wants respect and approval, he has not reckoned with the fact that Joe has the same needs. The result is that Joe has been blamed in one issue after another. Bill learns that the issues are not as important as Joe's Respect Level; by elevating Joe's self-respect, he can earn Joe's appreciation. Then no matter what issue comes up, Joe will then be motivated to cooperate with him. Bill would find that Joe would do the job for him, even when he wasn't supervising him. The person whose esteem you have consistently elevated becomes increasingly trustworthy and loyal.

Of course, such profound emotional alterations in co-workers can't be accomplished in one transaction. But, like any other worthwhile, high-priority project, it's well worth the steady applica-tion one puts into it. The cost of such a training program is negligible compared with the saving in lives, limbs, and efficiency.

The pity of it is that so few have access to this knowledge. What a shame that capable employees must be ravaged by anguish and disease as a result of suppressed hostility toward their bosses! How tragic when strikers and "scabs" inflict violence on one another, instead of defusing their H and standing shoulder to shoul-der in fighting for their rights!

No employer is favorably impressed by resentful, superior, derogatory, and martyred attitudes. Most employers attach the highest priority to your ability to get the job done without dissension with fellow workers and customers. Even if you're one of the large number of workers who have been laid off due to the recession, the practice of anti-H will enhance your chances of getting another job and making a success of it.

You may be living with the short-fused temper of a husband

who has lost his job or a son who has dropped out of college. Your knowledge of Anti-H will enable you to reduce their hostility, reinforce their self-confidence, and thus prevent a state of bitterness, lethargy, and despondency. In this way, you'll contribute significantly to a mental attitude which will improve their chances of reestablishing their careers—and, incidentally, will rebound back on you in positive ways.

And, note that whether between boss and employee, salesperson and customer, management negotiator and labor leader, doctor and patient, husband and wife, parent and child, teacher and pupil, or between negotiating statesmen, the method of getting rid of H is always the same.

6.
From Loneliness to Friendship and Romance

Many men and women pass their lives in depression and loneliness because they have never learned that H is sabotaging their chances of building solid friendships and achieving a durable love.

Bill was a bachelor who longed for friendly companionship. His real estate business had brought him into contact with a large number of well-to-do people and, for a time, he was the recipient of many social invitations. At first he made friends, but years passed, and at the age of fifty he was living alone and friendless.

His efforts to repair his social life became increasingly frantic. The replies to his invitations, however, were uniformly negative. Former friends turned down his invitations to dinner with lame excuses. He had to go on his vacations alone; no one seemed to be able to get away at the time he was going. He had numerous blind dates, but seldom a second date with the same woman. Now, Bill wasn't a bad person. He often helped people—at considerable personal sacrifice. Those he helped became grateful friends—for a while. How had he arrived at this miserable state of isolation?

A lonely existence in itself causes a lowering of one's self-respect, because one is cut off from the various means by which one's feeling of self-worth is nourished: being heard, noticed, having one's opinions validated, and receiving approval and feelings of affection. We don't require the constant presence of people for satisfaction of this need, any more than we need to eat constantly. However, we can't maintain emotional health without a steady supply of the feelings that can only be obtained from warm human relationships. Bill's need to be the center of attention was so irrepressible that he would monopolize any conversation. If anyone else tried to speak, he would raise his voice and make gestures with his hands for the purpose of silencing them. He permitted occasional comments, but the slightest disagreement would provoke an angry rebuke and a burst of self-righteous oratory. Along with this, the other person was denounced in such phrases as "You don't know what you're talking about" or "That's sheer stupidity" or "It's people like you who are responsible for the mess we're in." No matter what the topic of discussion, Bill took over in tones of imperious authority. Because of his Mirage he adopted pompous airs. It was as if he were a king, while his friends were relegated to the level of peasants who should feel honored to be in his royal presence.

Lonely persons suffer from anxiety, indecisiveness, restlessness, tension, depression, and obsession with themselves. We are offended by persons who are obsessed with themselves because they confiscate our share of the respect. We can't tell them about our activities because they interrupt and elaborate on their own martyred complaints, which offend us because they imply "better-than-thou." It's as if the complainer is saying, "The only reason I'm not doing better than you is because I've been up against greater obstacles."

An outing with Bill was sure to antagonize everyone present, whether they were co-workers, close friends or relatives. The hostility Bill aroused in his friends merely served to aggravate his own obnoxious behavior. Since Bill frequently accused friends and relatives of plotting to do him dirt, they finally labeled him a paranoid. Bill wasn't crazy—his accusations were often well founded. He had incited so much hostility in his friends and relatives that they actually *did* sometimes conspire to avoid him and in various ways to get revenge for his humiliating treatment. But after Bill had threatened suicide on several occasions, his older brother became alarmed and persuaded him to consult a psychiatrist.

In therapy, Bill's superior intelligence enabled him to make rapid progress in understanding the basis of his loneliness and depression. A great champion of equal rights and help for the downtrodden, Bill came to realize that, while he had been generous to the poor, he had been downright stingy in meting out respect to his friends. He learned that he could get all the respect in the world from people by the simple expedient of using his own good sense to help *them* feel respected. The result was that Bill won back many of his former friends and made many new ones.

HOW TO LOSE FRIENDS AND TURN OFF PEOPLE

Here are some surefire ways of bringing about a loss of interest in the potential friends you meet:

1. Monopolize the conversation. If the other person has little to say, make lots of talk yourself, instead of asking questions that would elicit answers from him.

2. Make a long-winded story out of what could have been said concisely.

3. Interrupt frequently.

4. Contradict the other person's opinions; if necessary, quote a newspaper or magazine article, or your father, as the authority for your contradiction.

5. If he manifests any H or S toward you, retaliate with H and S toward him.

6. If he appears to be depressed, tell him how wonderful you feel and how well things are going for you.

7. Agree instantly with anything he says, although you believe the opposite.

8. Tell him what he should do for colds, headaches, and other symptoms.

9. Cover up your ridicule of him by putting it in the guise of a joke.

10. Advise him on his personal problems.

11. When he makes a point, begin your reply with "Yes, but . . ."

12. Refrain from conversation because you're preoccupied with your own problems; if resentful toward him, give him the silent treatment.

There are many other ways. In one case, a woman was monopolizing the conversation at a party. Her fiancé, embarrassed by this, tried to slow her down by waving at her. She attributed this to his jealousy of her sparkling personality and went right on talking and throwing her hands around for emphasis. Shortly thereafter, he broke their engagement. Some 500 years ago Leonardo da Vinci reacted in much the same way. He said, "The eye, as lord of the senses, does its duty in giving a fall to those who are always disputing with noise and much moving of the hands."

You've learned that every one of these offensive traits —obsession with oneself, Mirage of superiority, hostility, and martyring—are specific reactions to feelings of inferiority. You'll find them in abundance in the lonely person. Because of their antagonizing and repelling effect, he is shunned the more. The hostile person finds himself being progressively shunned by his wife, children, friends, and fellow workers. The misery of loneliness may finally prod him into friendly overtures, but since his associates are still smarting from his former hostility, he receives a meager return for his friendliness. Unmindful that he was the chief instigator of their unfriendly reception, he becomes more hostile and the result is increasing isolation and loneliness.

Indeed, loneliness is not limited to the unmarried. Husbands and wives often develop loneliness for each other after a separation of only a day or two. But even when both remain at home, marriage partners can experience intense loneliness when H and S have broken down communication between them. Inferiority concepts generate martyred attitudes, so that ex-husbands and wives, relatives, friends, the government, weather, and even the towns they live in may be blamed for the lonely lives they are living. But most of all, they blame the lack of communication on the selfish behavior of their associates.

Typical of this response was the behavior of a forty-year-old single woman who obviously suffered a great deal more from her loneliness than she cared to admit. She rarely went anyplace other than to the office where she worked as a stenographer. When asked why she didn't make friends with fellow workers, she replied, "I've tried going places with them, but they don't pay their share of the expenses. Most of the time I have to call them about getting together. I resent their not calling me."

This lady's feelings were so easily hurt because of her pronounced I feelings. She was quite unaware that the resentment arising from her hurt feelings was perceived by her friends and thus only caused them to avoid her all the more.

There are few employees who don't feel resentful toward one or more co-workers. Frank, a fifty-two-year-old clerk, consulted me because of loneliness and depression. He resented another clerk, Janice, a forty-five-year-old unmarried woman, who worked adjacent to him. In a tone of annoyance, he related how unpleasant it was to have to put up with *her* resentment. "It isn't that I haven't bent over backwards to be nice to her. For example, when she came in yesterday morning, I greeted her with a pleasant 'Good morning.' Her reply was a disdainful 'Is it?' She's constantly griping, but when I ventured a gripe the other day, she looked down her nose and replied in a surly manner, 'Oh?' It was the kind of 'Oh' that makes you feel that your complaint was unjustified. How in blazes can anyone like a person like that?"

One of the traits most resented is resentment. The reason for this paradox is the universal ignorance of the inevitability of the transmission of hostile feeling. Even in the occasional instance where a person is aware that his resentment is perceived, he is powerless to do anything about it since so few persons know how to rid themselves of hostility.

Several months after Frank had completed his Anti-H training, I received a letter from him telling how much he liked Janice, enjoyed working with her, and how much she liked him. What had Frank learned that enabled him to effect such a drastic change? First of all, he had learned that his own resentment had been firing up Janice's H day by day. Therefore, he could hardly blame her for the H *he* provoked. Since it was he who had taken the Anti-H training, he realized that it was up to him to cleanse their relationship of that feeling.

Now aware of the I → H reaction, he looked to his own I feelings as the source of his H. At the time he had met Janice, he had just been divorced, and had lost out in several subsequent relationships. He had tried operating a business of his own, but had had to give it up as a failure. He realized that repeated defeats had resulted in a progressive growth of I. It wasn't fair to vent on Janice the hostility which arose from his own I feelings.

He then applied the I → H concept to Janice. He knew that at the age of forty-five she was living alone, and probably as desperately lonely as himself, increasing her I to a point where she, too, was caught in the I → H trap. He noted how often her H evoked antagonism from her associates, thus constantly adding to her inferior concept of herself.

Frank set out to supply the respect that she so urgently needed. He began taking his work to her from time to time and asking her if she would check it; then he would thank her for her suggestions. He noted how she would brighten up after such ego-nourishing measures. When she was sarcastic or belittling, he realized that this didn't reflect any discredit on him: It was, instead, a reaction to her own I. Occasionally she still replied to his cheerful "Good morning" with a curt "Is it?" But now he responded warmly, "It sure is, because you have just spoken to me."

In his letter, Frank related that Janice had recently acquired a boyfriend. Frank believes that she had become a warmer person in reaction to his changed behavior toward her, and that that made the difference in her new relationship, since this man had always ignored her in the past.

If you have a friend or relative who suffers from loneliness, you can't overcome it by simply inviting them out. Their essential need is nourishment of their self-respect; in furnishing this, you help remove the repellents responsible for their loneliness—H and S. When a lonely person *persistently* fails to respond to your sincere efforts to nourish his self-respect, he is undoubtedly suffering from such extreme feelings of I that he requires professional therapy. Nevertheless, most people who suffer from loneliness on this overpopulated planet can overcome their misery by the method described in this chapter.

Take the case of Sadie. She had left her impoverished family in the Ozarks to seek work in Chicago. On each working day she arose at 4:30 A.M. and, undaunted by the harsh Chicago cold, made her way to her job at the tea factory. There, she loaded tea bags for eight hours a day, conscientiously refraining from overloading the bags lest the company's customers become spoiled. Although she had found a job, she had not found friends. Poor Sadie led a lonely existence, devoid of boyfriends, family, or recreation. Her pleasures were limited to weight lifting at the YWCA and eating. After work she would prepare her supper, clean her room, and spend the evening in loneliness. Feeling so left out, she was quick to notice that the foreman was partial to the more comely tea-bag loaders. Her belief that she was too homely and insignificant to be liked goaded her into efforts to curry favor. When the foreman mentioned something about having to exchange an item in a department store, she let it be known that she was going downtown and would be glad to take care of it. Other workers learned of Sadie's department-store sorties, and soon she became an established courier between the factory and the stores.

Then the trouble started. After ten years on the job, Sadie became ill with nausea and vomiting, and was hospitalized. After a thorough physical examination, including consultation with an internist and stomach specialist, X-ray examination of the gastrointestinal tract and scrupulous chemical and bacteriological studies of her blood, urine, and bowel contents, no physical disease could be found. The doctors agreed that Sadie was healthy; in fact, she had an appetite that would shame a horse.

Nowadays, when exacting examinations fail to uncover any physical basis for an illness, a psychiatrist is usually brought into the case to search for emotional factors. When Sadie learned that I was a psychiatrist, she indignantly informed me that her trouble was in her stomach, not in her head. This was only partly true; as it turned out, her stomach was not functioning properly because of trouble in her head. I explained to her with the help of a simple diagram how suppressed hostility and anxiety cause excessive secretion of the digestive glands and spasm of the stomach wall, resulting in nausea and vomiting. I assured Sadie that her stomach actually was upset, and that her symptoms weren't indications that she was "crazy."

What made this woman so hostile? Remember that a low Respect Level activates a Mirage in which we see ourselves as the martyred victims of our unfair associates. Sadie believed that the foreman and her fellow tea packers lacked the decency to appreciate what she did for them. As long as she saw them all as being beneath her, it provided some relief from the misery of believing that *she* was inferior to *them*. However, fearing that if she complained to them they would like her even less, she kept her resentment to herself. Of course, she didn't know that suppressed H is easily perceivable. Inevitably her co-workers resented Sadie and felt little gratitude for the errands she ran for them. Not being aware that her H was showing, Sadie privately branded the whole lot of them as "no good."

The case of Sadie is a typical illustration of how I feelings may prod us into doing things for others in order to gain their approval, rather than because we sincerely want to help them. Instead of gaining approval, such an attitude begets only a thankless return.

When I first explained to Sadie that the ungratefulness of her fellow workers was due to the transmission to them of her own H feelings, she refused to believe it. However, her intense craving for relief from her nausea and vomiting was a potent stimulus to opening her mind to anything that promised help. After learning that all of us become resentful, it was less difficult for her to admit that such a thing could occur to her, too.

Sadie returned to work with greatly diminished resentment. Since it was her H that had caused her nausea and vomiting, her symptoms diminished as her resentment faded away. Her new ability to understand and therefore appreciate her fellow workers gradually earned their appreciation and affection—just what she had always wanted.

THE WEIGHT OF H

"I can't understand why Dr. T. sent me to a shrink; I'm not crazy, my problem is fat."

This was the opening remark made by Lynn, a thirty-year-old woman who had managed to put on 105 pounds of fat since her marriage nine years before.

For all her 222 pounds, Lynn's doctor found her in excellent health. Since she insisted on having the last word with her husband, mother, mother-in-law, and children, she was unlikely to develop any disease from suppressing H. The doctor had warned that her excess weight was an invitation to serious disease, but Lynn's chief incentive to lose weight was her vanity. Knowing that her general practitioner was down-to-earth and competent, I was sure that he must have had a very good reason to send Lynn to a psychiatrist to get rid of her excess baggage. When I consulted him, he informed me that for the past five years he had been unable to get her to stick to a reducing diet and was convinced that emotional factors were at the root of her fragile willpower.

Lynn felt that she was eating too much and too often out of

boredom. However, it soon became clear that a key factor in her too frequent invasion of the refrigerator, cookie jar, and candy plate was that old bugbear, H. But why did this woman who was so jolly and sweet with her friends display such hostility toward her family? Don't make the mistake of thinking that fat people are happy simply because they appear so lively and full of smiles and laughs. They often talk and laugh so much in public out of frustration, bitterness, and loneliness at home, and this was precisely the case in Lynn's home life as a child, and in her marriage.

Lynn's father was one of those hard-working men who came home tired and irritable, ate his dinner, read the newspaper, and went to bed. This left her little time to talk to him about her feelings and problems. "I think Mother felt that I shouldn't have any fun because she had such a miserable life herself. Dad seldom conversed with her and wouldn't take her anyplace. Even now, it's no use taking my troubles to her; she doesn't want to listen to them."

After living with a father who ignored her and a lonely, depressed mother, Lynn entered her own marriage with marked I feelings. She described her mother-in-law as a cold woman whom she resented for her frequent criticism of the way Lynn managed her home and children. "I don't blame my husband for avoiding her; she's always picking on him and never gives him credit for anything." In marrying a man also saddled with an excess of I, the formation of a vicious circle of H was inevitable.

Lynn said that she and her husband, Hal, had nothing in common except meals and sex. After dinner, Hal would ignore her in favor of TV or magazines. She complained that although he would promise to do some job of home repair, he would postpone it for months on end. While she longed for romance, the only time Hal said he loved her was during intercourse. It seemed that any conversation between them usually ended in a quarrel, which she blamed on his being set in his ways and on his insistence that he was always right. Since I feelings ensure H in any close relationship, poor Lynn was bound to resent her mother-in-law and children, too. Lynn's two little girls kept her in a constant state of upset over their contrariness, and she found herself yelling at them a good deal. You can see that Lynn lived in an atmosphere of almost constant dissension, with no sweetness in her life except for that which she could find in cake, candy, and ie cream. Following a quarrel she would have an uncontrollable urge to eat something sweet.

If you're having trouble taking off fat, check yourself carefully for the I → H + S factor. Many of my patients insisted that they didn't have I or H feelings, but ate out of frustration over one thing or another. However, if you analyze any kind of frustration that persists, you'll find it is based on inferiority. A frequent kind is sexual frustration, which often leads to overeating as an attempt to substitute another pleasure. Frequent relations don't necessarily mean that the sex is satisfying. When a vicious circle of H has been built up between a couple, sexual fulfillment is lacking. Deprived of the pleasurable fulfillment that comes from being liked and appreciated, hostile persons develop a craving for other sources of pleasure. For those who shun alcohol, drugs, gambling, or extramarital sex, the most accessible pleasure is eating. Unfortunately, this pleasure is short-lived, and because one's real need for respect has not been fulfilled, the craving for more quickly returns, just as with other addictions.

It's clear that Lynn's pleasure in eating had to be replaced by the pleasure derived from affection and respect. Lynn learned that she was cheating herself out of getting this essential nourishment from her family by failing to provide a like nourishment for them. She came to realize that they, like herself, were unaware that they were the instigators of the H they received.

Fortunately, it only takes one of the parties involved in a vicious circle to break the circuit. Lynn realized that since the others had had no access to the training that she was acquiring, it was up to her. The recognition that the other members of her family were as innocent as she herself in being caught up in the H trap stirred in Lynn the compassion that always arises when we recognize the similarity of others to ourselves. Lynn's new warmth and appreciation for those about her gradually evoked the same feelings in them toward her, providing the pleasurable fulfillment that she had formerly sought from food.

YOU CAN'T MAKE IT ON BEAUTY ALONE

I don't mean to imply that a new, slim figure is the answer to loneliness. All too often, men and women gifted with good looks fail to find lasting happiness.

One reason is that from early childhood, their beauty often causes them to be fussed over and spoiled by the opposite sex. Good-looking girls frequently get jobs for which better qualified but less attractive ones are turned down. The handsome boy often finds that women are eager to pamper him for nothing more than his winning smile in return.

Beauty, like wealth, can get you started on the road to emotional satisfaction, but it can't keep you there. When such knockouts get into a close relationship, their conditioned expectation of receiving more than they give evokes increasing antagonism. Since they encountered little opposition in previous relationships, they are ill-prepared to cope with partners who expect tit for tat. In a 50-50 arrangement, such persons feel shortchanged.

Just because the good-looking person has been spoiled since childhood doesn't mean that he or she has to lose out in the attainment of lasting love. But when such persons don't get the favoritism they've come to anticipate, they feel that they are being treated unfairly, which inevitably leads to an escalation of H in their relationships.

On the other hand, a man who is not well endowed with good looks soon learns the value of being considerate, appreciative, and respectful. His competition with a more handsome man is apt to follow the pattern of the race between the hare and the tortoise. While the good-looking man gets off to an early lead, he loses ground because of spoiled attitudes, obsession with himself, and hostility. Meanwhile, his plain-looking competitor gradually overcomes his poor start by qualities that earn women's respect. Since *durable* sex satisfaction is based on respect, her attraction to the handsome man fades and often turns to repulsion.

If you're frustrated, examine yourself for the personal traits that rob you of sex appeal: obsession with yourself, martyred complaints, arrogance, opinionatedness, know-it-all, better-than-thou, bragging, and belittling attitudes. Remember, no matter how good looking, you'll never attain enduring love unless you learn how to provide your partner's need for respect and appreciation.

MISTAKEN APPLICATION OF ANTI-H THERAPY

Rose T., a pretty twenty-two-year-old girl, was enrolled in our Anti-H therapy class because of crying spells and confusion. She felt that she should break her engagement, but was unable to get herself to do it. "Every time I see Ed," she told me, "we wind up in an argument that leaves me a nervous wreck. But I'm so attracted to him that within a few days I call him and we get together again. He blames me for the arguments; never once has he admitted to being wrong."

After attending six sessions of the class, Rose realized that neither Ed nor she could be blamed, since all human beings react with H to H and S. Ed's elevated H was the result of a home life in which he had been deprived of respect. Rose complained that although she had been using her anti-H training, Ed was as angry and arrogant as ever. Why hadn't the method worked?

Rose had overlooked an essential factor in reducing the other person's H and S: reducing her own. For six months Rose's self-respect had been beaten down by Ed's vicious denunciations. The lowering of her Respect Level generated increasing H and S. She manifested her H by remaining silent when Ed denounced her. Since such feelings are invariably transmitted, Ed perceived Rose's "better-than-thou" attitude. Of course, this necessarily increased his $I \rightarrow H + S$. The essential step she had failed to carry out was the cleansing of her own feelings.

Rose was taught to see her H feelings as warning signals, alerting her to the need for corrective action: the immediate application of anti-H. The more quickly she did this, the less H she would transmit to Ed. In this way, she would reduce instead of increase Ed's H, and would thus remove the principal impediment to their love. "But sometimes he gets so mad that he becomes violent," she objected. "Are you telling me that I should let him beat me up?"

Absolutely not! Rose couldn't protect herself against the violence of a powerful man like Ed by trading blows with him, but each occasion when Ed had become violent had occurred only after Rose had fanned the flames of his anger with her own H and S.

Since violence occurs only with an *increase* in H, it isn't likely to occur when we *reduce* the H of a potentially violent person.

In her succeeding dates with Ed, Rose applied her Anti-H training to her own H and S feelings. She no longer blamed Ed when he flared up, since she understood the real meaning of H: a natural biological response in all of us to the belief that we are disrespected. This resulted in a progressive diminution of Ed's H, and a progressively more loving relationship.

SOUR GRAPES LONELINESS

Lila T., eighteen years of age, was tall and slim, her features marred by her sullen expression. She came to my office only after repeated urgings by her parents. They had become worried because in the past two years she had become increasingly ill-tempered and despondent. When they asked her why she didn't go out with her friends, she would fly into a rage. "They're nasty and selfish," she screamed. "I never want to see them again." She had recently returned from college, where she had been unable to complete the year because of her depressed, withdrawn state.

When I in turn asked why she had stopped seeing her friends, she replied, "I got fed up with their snobbishness and meanness. Their favorite pastime is ridicule. I can't wait until I get back to college, where my real friends are."

However, her parents told me that she had not been able to

keep any friends at college either. Her roommate had moved out after bitter arguments.

When I asked her about her relations with men, Lila said that she could get all the dates she wanted, but she wouldn't accept any because the boys were only after one thing. This is a common alibi. Instead of acknowledging that something might be amiss in their own personalities, many girls attempt to save face by labeling the boys around them "sex maniacs." Most boys can enjoy dates who are not "pushovers"; they are much more likely to drop girls with unattractive personalities.

Lila's eight months at college hadn't done much for her speech. She repeated the phrase "You know" five or six times in each sentence. The overuse of this expression is due to a lack of confidence—the fear that one cannot adequately express oneself or attain the listener's agreement. The "you know" really means "I can't express myself properly and I'm afraid I'll be contradicted, so I'm depending on you to figure out what I mean and agree with me." This habit is a reaction to anxious, overprotective parents who nod their heads and say "yes, yes" to indicate that they know what the youngster is trying to say. If such parents made it a practice to refrain from coming to the rescue in this way, their child would learn to rely on himself to express what he meant.

Lila's parents had no idea that they were harming her by such apparently "encouraging" tactics. Both were in a constant struggle with their own I feelings, and their S urge was manifested by their need to win out in any issue with Lila, no matter how trivial. For example, if Lila wanted an egg for breakfast, her mother might provoke an argument by telling her she should have cereal. Even when her mother gave in, Lila could read her mother's unspoken feelings: "I'm only giving in because you're a spoiled brat, not because you're right." Lila reacted with her own overwhelming need to be right.

Lila's speech was only a minor part of her unattractive image. She repelled her friends with ridicule, meanness, and insistence on having her way—the very traits she complained of in them. She hadn't dropped boys; they had stopped calling her. When she returned from college, her parents continued their practice of moralizing, telling her what to do, and contradicting her. Her stubborn resistance to these attitudes aggravated the circle of H at home.

Given Lila's aversion to being corrected by her elders, any attempt on my part to correct her resentful attitudes would only have been blocked by H. I realized that when Lila complained bitterly that her father insisted on traveling via the old road rather than follow her suggestion to take the beltway, she would naturally anticipate that I would side with my fellow adult. You have seen that one effective way of earning Receptivity is by using whatever topic is being discussed as a vehicle to prop up the other person's self-respect. Therefore, I deliberately asked Lila why she preferred the beltway. When she told me, I commented that her reasoning made sense.

After seventeen years of living with "can't-be-wrong" parents, Lila had been conditioned to believe that authority figures never admitted to being wrong. So when Lila tried to show me I was wrong, she succeeded—time and again.

Nor did I ever contradict her. You might think that this tactic would have been impossible in some cases. For example, suppose Lila had declared that the Johns Hopkins football team (average weight: 150 lbs.) could beat the Baltimore Colts. Instead of snorting that the Hopkins boys do their best work in the laboratory, I could have asked her what she based her opinion on, and then listened to her reasons. This, in itself, would have conveyed respect; she'd have appreciated it, since she'd have had to go a long way to find someone else who would listen to such a story. Furthermore, I might have found that one of her observations made sense, and I could then have told her that I hadn't previously taken that point into account. You can provide steady respect-building nourishment for anyone by simply helping them up the respect ladder, no matter what the issue.

After I had earned Lila's Receptivity, she responded eagerly to the instruction; she learned the meaning of $I \rightarrow A + Ob + H + S + Mar$. Instead of instigating H, she found that in elevating the self-respect of others she had no further difficulties in making and keeping friends. And by overcoming her former H to her teachers, she was able to do well in her college studies.

TACTICS FOR THE LONELY WOMAN

In our society, it is easier for a man to escape temporarily from loneliness. He can go to a bar or restaurant without experiencing embarrassment. Most women fear that they will be looked upon contemptuously if they go to these places alone. They are afraid that the patrons will suspect them of being social rejects, engaged in a desperate hunt for sex or male companionship. Because of this fear they remain at home, suffering the pangs of loneliness. The growth of I feelings resulting from their loneliness further increases their fear of going out.

I advise the lonely woman who is afraid of going out to a bar or restaurant alone to go with a woman friend. Such a woman's usual response is that there is no such friend available. Because of her H this is often only too true. Even when her only objective is male companionship, her chances are enhanced if she has at least one woman friend whom she can count on to go with her.

When two women go out together, each can help the other assess the men they happen to meet. Gaining the knowledge that will enable her to make friendships with women will stand her in good stead in relating to men, since it was the lack of this knowledge that caused her to lose out in her previous relationships with men.

SHOULD I GIVE IN JUST SO I'LL BE ASKED OUT AGAIN?

Many women attribute their loneliness to their unwillingness to go to bed with a man after a date or so. The question is often asked, "Should I give in, just so I'll be asked out again?"

The mistake here is in assuming that a woman can earn a man's respect by sexual compliance. His respect for her can be earned only by her respect for him. Since sex alone doesn't earn his respect, she soon becomes hostile and this cools her sexual response.

Suppose there *is* mutual respect as well as sexual attraction; should the lady give in for fear of losing the man? This depends on the convictions and emotional maturity of the man as well as herself. If a woman believes that sex is demeaning, she will suffer guilt as the result of premarital relations. Before she engages in sex she should find out why she has this mistaken belief. Such an attitude inhibits sexual fulfillment and may confine her to lifelong loneliness.

A woman should use her judgment to assess a man's response to her refusal to have sex. Some men, because of their particular moral and religious background, lose their respect for a woman who seems to have no compunctions about joining them in bed. Thus, a woman would be better off to avoid premarital sex with such a man even if she herself has no feelings of guilt about engaging in it.

Some people believe that lack of sexual activity causes mental illness. This is true only when it is accompanied by suppressed H and anxiety. A person compelled to live without sex is still able to earn affection and respect by enlarging the self-respect of his fellows. For example, some clergymen and nuns reap so large a harvest of affection and respect that they can maintain physical and mental health despite sexual abstinence. However, in persons whose work is an escape from personal conflict, the suppressed H and anxiety are likely to cause depression and premature onset of disease. Except in the special circumstances of unselfish service to others, such people should ask themselves if this void in their life is the result of a "sour grapes" attitude.

Most men don't lose respect for a woman who goes to bed with them, provided that she respects them. But if a woman persistently refuses sex with a man who wouldn't disrespect her for engaging in it with him, she might lose the man she loves because of his anguish in being repeatedly rejected by the woman he cares for.

7.
Sexual Dysfunction and Marital "Incompatibility"

H AND THE ORIGIN OF HOMOSEXUALITY

It is estimated that there are five million practicing homosexuals in the United States, from those who are attracted exclusively to members of their own sex to others with varying degrees of desire toward both sexes. A recent survey of public opinion revealed that almost half the public believed that homosexuality was a crime that should be punished by law. Homosexuals, however, rarely resort to threats, force, or other violations of others' rights to gratify their desire; and they do not seduce youngsters with any more frequency than do heterosexuals. Why, then, are they usually regarded with so much contempt and ridicule?

The reason lies in our strong egotistical need to belittle those who differ from us. You may have observed that those men who repeatedly tell the same stale jokes about "queers" are the very ones who seem to feel most inferior about their own masculine status. I recall as a teen-ager watching the girls walking home from school hand in hand with some of the neighborhood boys. This would usually evoke from me some derisive snort regarding "those hand-holding sissies." What I couldn't admit was my own profound fear that I wasn't man enough to do the very thing I was ridiculing.

Most homosexuals prefer to remain so and, therefore, very few seek to change through psychiatric treatment. In any case, many psychiatrists and psychologists feel that only a small percentage of cases can be successfully "converted" because the causes of homosexuality are so little understood.

Because of having been belittled too often when using his hands, a boy may grow up to be clumsy and avoid even the simplest manual work, gravitating instead to an accommodation that does not

84

overwhelm him with the fear of inadequacy. Some cases of homosexuality may represent the same process sexually—avoiding that which is feared: inadequacy with the opposite sex, leading to an accommodation with those of the same sex to whom he feels far less inferior. The reason for this is that he was repeatedly deprecated throughout childhood in his relationship with his mother. Many male homosexuals were dominated, belittled, ridiculed, and resented by their mothers, along with the love they received from her.

A boy whose mother is preoccupied with her own troubles grows up with H not only toward her, but often toward the whole female sex. When a boy is subjected to the tyranny of a domineering mother, he grows up feeling so inferior to women that he may fear intimacy with them.

The more we avoid a hated and feared object, the greater becomes our fear of it—and the result is a vicious circle. The fear is so overpowering that it inhibits any emotional intimacy with the opposite sex—the basis of genuine sexual intimacy. This may be the reason that many homosexuals find that when they attempt intercourse with a member of the opposite sex, they fail to experience any sexual satisfaction. (This is very little different from the deterioration of sexual satisfaction by *heterosexual* partners after an extended period of H.) This leaves only those of the same sex for gratification of the unrequited sex desire.

When a father's self-respect has been beaten down, he is driven to lower the boom on his children because of his intense craving for superiority. For instance:

Father: *Wilbur, take your hand off your hip. Are you a boy or a girl? What will people think?*

In fact, when such remarks are repeated often enough, they may cause a youngster to question his masculinity. Why does a father humiliate his son in this manner?

The cause stems from the many doubts about his own masculine status. His wife may be wearing the pants in the family, taking over decisions that properly belong to him. The H between her husband and herself often causes her to become sexually indifferent to him, and she may become overattached to her son because of her unfulfilled need for affection.

The affection she lavishes on her son causes the husband to feel that he is inferior to the boy in his ability to win his wife's affection. The more inferior his concept of himself, the stronger the Mirage in which he visualizes others as condemnable. His lowered status prods him into humiliating and belittling the object of his wife's affection. Whatever subject comes up, he has a compulsion to make the boy seem to be wrong.

Deprived of the vital nourishment of respect that a boy needs from his father, the son grows up with the conviction that he is inferior as a man. Such a complex may produce overwhelming fear of inadequacy with females. At the same time, the frustration of his need for love from the parent of the same sex gives rise to an intense craving for it. Such a youngster is especially vulnerable to seduction by an older person who supplies the understanding and tenderness he didn't get from his father.

At the same time, by turning to another male for affection, he alleviates the anxiety he experienced as a result of being smothered by his mother's excessive possessiveness and dependence on him for her affection. The emotional and sexual satisfaction he achieves with a man leads him to the conclusion that he is a homosexual. Basically he is not a homosexual at all. He may only have become so as the result of a childhood fraught with humiliation by his father and the smothering possessiveness of his mother. Admittedly, whether or not such a person will confine himself thereafter only to emotional or physical relationships with males depends on many other factors.

Still, the damage to which homosexuals are subjected early in life does not appear significantly different from that which causes other types of emotional disturbance. Why, then, homosexuality?

I do not believe that science has as yet any specific answer to this question. But when a homosexual asks if psychotherapy can change his sexual preference, my policy is to encourage him to undergo treatment. Like heterosexuals, homosexuals make a far better adjustment to life when equipped with the knowledge of how to deal with $I \rightarrow A + Ob + H + S + Mar$. However, I feel that it is only fair to tell them that even when emotional factors appear to be corrected, there may be no change in their homosexual pattern. This is in sharp contrast to other sexual conditions such as frigidity, impotence, or transvestism (a compulsion to wear the garments of the opposite sex), which respond well to psychotherapy. When the patient really is opposed to giving up his homosexuality, it is easy to understand why he does not respond to treatment. Although it has been frustrating to me frequently to fail to get results in those patients who earnestly desire to overcome their homosexuality, the improvement in interpersonal relationships via anti-H therapy has been gratifying.

With these considerations in mind, I cannot see why a homosexual should be regarded differently from anyone else suffering from a pronounced fear: for example, a youngster who drops out of school because of his anxiety at being confined in a room. Such boys often find happiness and success in some outdoor career such as forestry or farming. Just as we should not condemn a man who abhors being confined indoors, so we should not condemn a person for his sexual fears. The homosexual deserves the same respect and equality of treatment as the heterosexual.

IS SEXUAL INCOMPATIBILITY THE CAUSE OF MARITAL FAILURE?

Some of the modern day sex clinics claim that by using the hands and mouth freely and practicing a variety of positions, sexual pleasure and fulfillment can be obtained where there was none before. The fallacy in this approach is that it gives insufficient priority to the emotional disturbance that underlies almost all sexual disturbance. Too often, doctors apply treatment directly to the patient's sexual apparatus instead of to his emotional state. For example, a patient who is unable to get an erection is still sometimes treated by prostate gland massage. Some therapists even provide instructors who engage in sex with the client in order to teach him the new techniques.

Couples who divorce because of sexual incompatibility are making a tragic mistake. If they remarry, they often find themselves incompatible with their new partners. The sexual incompatibility is merely one of the many ways in which they can't harmonize. My observation has been that anyone who makes a practice of using alcohol, drugs, vibrators, or pornography as aids to lovemaking does so because his sex life has not been satisfying. These devices are stimulating only for a very short period. Soon the novelty wears off, and the sex reverts to its previous unsatisfactory state. Lasting sexual satisfaction is based not on technique, but on mutual respect. Most sexual disorders, including frigidity and impotence, are due not to a lack of technical know-how, or to hormone deficiency in one of the partners, but to a lack of respect between them.

MARITAL "INCOMPATIBILITY"

By far the most intense H is that resulting from the violation of respect in a close relationship. This was illustrated in the case of the casual association between mobster Bugsy Siegel and actor George Raft. When Raft became fearful that Bugsy was going to rub him out, he told Bugsy of his fear. "You have nothing to worry about," Bugsy replied. "We only kill each other." Shortly thereafter, Bugsy's opinion was validated when he was killed by the mob—with whom he had been so intimately associated.

Dissension among the members of any closely knit organization or team arouses the most intense anxiety and H that human beings can experience. Among persons who spend a great deal of time together—such as members of a family—vying for S increasingly multiplies H. H is much more oppressive here because it is between those who have given so much trust, respect, and affection to each other. This is why the highest incidence of violence occurs between members of families, unless inhibitory factors—affection, respect, and the fear of losing meaningful relations—far outweigh the H.

The greatest source of violence is intense H among family members. In a February 24, 1976, meeting of the American Association for the Advancement of Science, Richard Gelles of the University of Rhode Island, speaking for himself and two associate social scientists, reported that three years of research had turned up a massive amount of indirect but convincing evidence of the spread of violence in the American family:

- A study of nonfatal assaults in Detroit found that 52 percent occurred between husbands and wives. Another study of divorce petitions found that 20 to 40 percent charged physical abuse.
- Gelles reported physical violence between husbands and wives or parents and children in 54 percent of the families investigated.
- In Atlanta, Georgia, in 1972, 31 percent of 255 murders were the result of domestic quarrels. Each year, as many people are murdered by their relatives in New York City as have been killed in the conflict in Northern Ireland.

Gelles said, "All the evidence suggests that physical aggression occurs between family members more often than between any others. It can be said to be almost universal."

People are often puzzled that the daughter who resented her mother weeps and wails hysterically at the mother's funeral, whereas the daughter who was so fond of her mother remains relatively calm. This is because most people who live closely together develop some H as well as love for each other. When someone we hate and for whom we had little or no affection dies—for example, a Hitler—there's precious little guilt. However, when affection and hostility have coexisted, the hostility makes the survivor feel guilty. The one with the most H is left with the most guilt and, therefore, feels a greater compulsion to atone. If there had been either little affection or little H, very little guilt would have resulted.

Couples who build up H during the day may find themselves

sexually incompatible later in the evening. Such H often eludes conscious recognition because of a veneer of overconsiderateness the partners may display toward each other. The selfishness in the advances of a male under the influence of suppressed H is not lost on his partner. Although she may go through the motions of responding to him she cannot experience any sexual satisfaction, because of her real feelings. A reading of these feelings would be, "Don't expect me to be giving when you are so selfish." Although she may go through with the sex act, her cold response is so mortifying to her partner that he can get little if any pleasure from their sex encounter.

Unless there are other extreme difficulties in the relationship—in which case the couple should seek professional help—the best route to sexual fulfillment on a permanent basis is by eliminating the circle of H that is almost always the basis of frigidity in the female, and loss of sex desire for his partner, impotency, and premature ejaculation in the male.

SUPPRESSED H AND SEXUAL DYSFUNCTION

Premature ejaculation is a condition in which the male orgasm occurs either just prior to the penis being inserted into the vagina, or within seconds afterward, long before the female partner has time to reach her own orgasm. It is often seen in the man who fears that he will fail and, therefore, is conditioned to act hastily. His obsession with this fear causes him to lose sight of his partner's needs.

His sex problem is usually only a symptom of a more basic problem: overanxiety. This can be observed in a consistent pattern of impulsive actions in his life—quitting school or job, moving from one town to another and from one woman to another. The origin of this anxiety is rooted in childhood relationships, as illustrated by the case of Peter.

Peter was still a bachelor at thirty-eight. Both he and his mother had been victims of his father's cruelty. The boy had often heard his father trying to force his mother to have sex, and he suffered intensely at the thought of her being sexually violated. The father's cruelty had caused the mother to turn to Pete, her only child, for affection. Because of his father's hatred, Pete went through childhood without ever receiving a single toy.

The intense sympathy aroused in Pete by the brutal treatment inflicted on his mother carried over in his attitude toward other women. Although he craved affection, he could not go on to intercourse because of the memory of his mother's sexual violation. To avoid this "violation" of a woman, he learned to reach orgasm without actually inserting his penis. When a woman would ask for intercourse, Pete would save her from "violation" by resorting to an alibi.

After four years of this pattern his desire for intercourse became so overwhelming that he yielded to the temptation. Much to his chagrin, ejaculation occurred within seconds. To keep from ejaculating prematurely, he tried all sorts of expedients: concentrating on something else during intercourse, employing drugs such as marijuana or alcohol prior to sex. None of these devices helped since the real problem was his deep-seated fear of violating a woman (as his mother had been). Although his symptom served to protect him from this violation, the repeated humiliations multiplied his anxiety. Whenever he was about to begin intercourse, his record of repeated failures aroused such overwhelming anxiety that he would fail again. The anticipatory anxiety alone was great enough to bring about premature ejaculation.

In therapy, Pete learned that his conviction that his mother was the martyred victim of an evil husband was only one side of the story. His poor mother had never been aware that her husband's H was in large measure a reaction to her own H toward him, which had been manifested by frequent contradictions of his opinions, reluctance to give him credit for ever being right, and refusal to engage in sex. Since she had been sullen and complaining toward his father, Pete could understand why the man had developed so much I and, therefore, so much H. He could also see why he himself felt so rejectable: not because he was inferior, but because of his father's demeaning attitude toward him. This understanding did much to elevate Pete's concept of his own worth, and for the first time in his life he felt some affection and sympathy for his father. In fact, a by-product of his therapy was a lasting reconciliation with the man he had most hated.

The I feelings produced by Pete's sexual inadequacy had caused him to avoid women on his own level of culture and intellect. As he learned from his therapy that the premature ejaculation was not due to any basic inability on his part, his self-respect grew, and he felt more comfortable with women of his own type. As his obsession with himself decreased, he began paying more attention to the woman's need for respect. He learned to appreciate and enjoy the many facets of a woman's companionship and found that he was not feverishly seeking new partners as he had before.

This resulted in an intimacy in his relationships that he had not previously been able to achieve. "My personality has improved since I've been going with this girl," he told me one day. "I've learned a lot from her and feel that she has from me. Formerly, the minute I had my orgasm I had no further interest in the woman and wanted to get away from her as quickly as possible. Now I like to remain with her. I feel relaxed, mellow, and enjoy lying close with my arm around her." The intimacy between two people that comes from understanding each other is a fulfilling feeling. Pete's analysis of his parents' relationship enabled him to understand that it is H and S, not sex, that violates a woman. When a couple fulfills each other's need for respect, there is little H and S and sex is a tender, fulfilling experience for both.

He could now approach sexual relations without his former feelings of guilt and fear of failure. Under these circumstances the anticipatory anxiety gradually waned, and with it, the premature ejaculation.

SEXUAL IMPOTENCE

An even more serious condition is sexual impotence, in which the male loses his erection immediately, or almost immediately, after attempting to insert his penis into the vagina. Less than 5 percent of all cases of impotency are due to any organic disease such as diabetes, cancer of the penis, or hormonal deficiency. The large majority are caused by suppressed H.

Lora, an attractive forty-five-year-old physician, made an appointment for her friend, John. As soon as she came into my office with him, she declared emphatically, "I've been in love with John for six years and we want to get married. But he's become impotent. He's been examined and treated by an internist and a urologist, but he's no better. I'm telling him right now that if you can't restore his potency, I'm severing relations with him. I can't take it anymore."

John looked understandably ashamed. "Doctor," he said mournfully, "I've tried everything except psychiatry, but I don't think there's any use. I get a strong erection just thinking about Lora, but as soon as I try to enter her, it goes soft."

John and Lora's romance had begun soon after John had been referred to her for a minor ailment. He was instantly attracted to her and, being unhappily married, he began seeing her socially. Although he was in love with Lora, the fear that he would be abandoning his children had made John feel so guilty that he felt compelled to postpone divorce until they were grown. His obsession with his own feeling of unworthiness as a father had blinded him to the humiliating effect on Lora of his procrastination in marrying her.

Lora became increasingly embittered and threatened to go back to her former boyfriend unless John sued for divorce in the near future. John thought she was bluffing. When he still insisted on postponing the divorce, she became so angry that she married her ex-boyfriend.

John was deeply hurt when he learned of Lora's marriage. Since she really did not love her new husband, the marriage soon ended in divorce. John and Lora renewed their relationship and John shortly afterward traveled to another state and obtained a divorce from his wife. When he returned they had a joyous reunion, except for one detail: He'd lose his erection as soon as he attempted to enter her. They tried liquor, hormone injections, a variety of positions, but nothing helped.

Lora said that it wasn't for lack of love that she would leave John, but only because his condition had made her a nervous wreck.

Lora's self-esteem had been badly hurt by John's refusal to marry until his children were grown. H, the essential component of hurt feelings, had been the basis of her vengeful action in marrying her ex-boyfirend. At that point it was John's turn to become hurt. His self-esteem had been shattered by Lora's marriage, and his system responded to this I feeling with the production of intense H. When they were both finally divorced, he was so happy that he forgot about his H toward Lora, and didn't realize that it hadn't disappeared. The unconscious mind doesn't forget. Lora's vengeance had been marriage to another man; John's was failure to produce an erection.

In therapy both John and Lora were quick to understand how they had been tricked by their deep-seated feelings of H. I reminded John that he had instigated their trouble in the first place by his procrastination in marrying Lora, whose vengeful response was the natural reaction to feelings of humiliation. Nor was John to blame since he hadn't had the slightest intention of humiliating her. With the eradication of his "forgotten" H, John's potency returned and they were married.

ANTICIPATORY ANXIETY IN IMPOTENCE

An essential function in the human makeup is Anticipation. Because of this faculty were are able to experience self-confidence, security, and pleasure in the present for what we believe is *about* to happen. But when we are about to face a situation that resembles previous anxiety-producing experiences, our anticipation is so anxiety-laden that we not only suffer from the oppressive emotion of anxiety, but from physical consequences as well.

My first observation of the physical effect of Anticipatory

Anxiety was at medical school in our Proctology course. The professor, of English origin, still retained a pronounced British accent. He addressed all the charity patients who patronized the Proctology Dispensary as Percy—with all the dignity conveyed by an elegant British accent.

The patient was an enormous man whose complaint was soreness and bleeding in the rectum. He was instructed to get on his hands and knees on the examining table. The professor approached him with a sigmoidoscope, a long tube which contains a light enabling the examiner to see what the lining of the rectum and colon looks like. Sad to relate, the patient turned his head and saw the instrument. It must have looked like a bazooka. His eyes fairly leaped out of their sockets. The professor, however, wasn't looking at his eyes. His concentration on the anatomical region in which he specialized was so intense that he seldom recognized returning patients the usual way: by their faces. What he was looking at was the anus, which had reacted to the extreme Anticipatory Anxiety by shutting down so tightly that it would have taken dynamite to open it. The frustrated professor exclaimed in a tone of the utmost disgust, "Percy, you're anticipating!"

After repeated blows to his self-esteem because of inability to sustain an erection, a male fears failure each time he attempts intercourse. The anxiety resulting from this anticipation is so great that it alone can cause impotence, even after the H has been dissolved. Such anxiety occurs whenever a person attempts to do anything in which he has a record of humiliating failure. Thus, if a student was ridiculed by a sarcastic teacher when reciting, he would anxiously anticipate humiliation in succeeding recitations. Each time the experience is repeated, the anticipatory anxiety and, therefore, the performance gets worse.

After twenty-four years of marriage, Hal, a forty-nine-year-old insurance agent, became so fed up with the bitter quarrels he was having with his wife that he resolved to avoid them. The result was that for days on end he would not speak to her. After several months of suppressing his H, Hal became impotent. Shortly thereafter, his wife told him she had a lover. In spite of his pleas for reconciliation, and their visits to a marriage counselor, his wife divorced him and married the other man.

When Hal sought psychiatric help, I found that although he was still in love with his wife, he stayed extremely bitter toward her. He had attempted intercourse with other women, but remained impotent. The impotence was the result of his high level of suppressed H toward females, whom he believed to be unfair and deceitful, as his wife had been toward him. Moreover, his ex-wife's repeated taunts that he wasn't man enough had aggravated his fear that he was sexually inadequate.

After ten hours of instruction in the Anti-H method, Hal was able to understand why his marriage had failed. He learned that the circle of H between his wife and himself was the result of their pronounced I feelings. This had caused progressive impairment of their ability to cooperate with each other, in sex as well as other activities. Since neither had had any training in the analysis and repair of emotional problems, the deterioration of their relationship was inevitable.

Hal learned why neither he nor his wife were to blame, but although this understanding freed him of hostility, his impotence persisted. The reason was that the repeated failures caused Hal to anticipate failure every time he attempted intercourse.

Therefore, in order for Hal to overcome his impotence, he would have to overcome his negative anticipation.

The first step in accomplishing this was for Hal to achieve an improved concept of his personal worth. From early childhood, his mother had found fault with him. Even in his twenties, it was, "Put those magazines back where you got them" or "You can't go out in that shirt." The repeated blows to his self-respect had made him so sensitive that he had reacted with extreme hurt when subjected to his wife's duplication of his mother's derogatory attitudes. Hal hadn't failed sexually because of any constitutional inadequacy; all he needed was positive rather than negative anticipation.

"You mean I must tell myself that I'll succeed?" Hal asked.

"That won't work because you'd still be falling into the same trap of avoiding the 'thinking through' of your problem," I told him. "Genuine positive anticipation can be attained only by examining the facts. A commander would be a fool if he launched an attack without examining the situation he faced.

Hal could now recognize that he had been the innocent victim of Anticipatory Anxiety—an emotional mechanism for which no one is to blame. With diminished self-blame his anxiety diminished. As Hal practiced this kind of thinking, his sexual failures became less frequent and he approached sex relations with increasingly positive anticipation. Within six months, he was entirely free of impotence.

It took six months because the long period of failures had multiplied Hal's anxiety. Anxiety does not disappear the minute we arrive at a rational understanding of why there is no longer anything to fear. The more we have been emotionally hurt, the more the emotional system (Old Brain) continues sending out its alarm signal: anxiety. The purpose of the anxiety signal is to inform us that we have a problem that needs resolution. Most emotional problems can't be resolved without the requisite knowledge of Anti-H therapy. If we make it a practice to apply this therapy in response to the anxiety signal, we can resolve most emotional disturbances and free our-selves of $I \rightarrow A + Ob + H + S + Mar.$ sufficiently to advance in our careers and lead healthy and happy lives.

Patients usually resent doctors for asking questions about their sex life, but a doctor does so because he so often finds depres-sion, addiction to alcohol, drugs, or gambling, and the beginnings of physical disease in couples who are sexually incompatible.

The organs of sex, like those of digestion, are controlled by centers in the brain. These centers, operating like an electronic switchboard, send out impulses that regulate the function of the sex organs directly and indirectly through the activation of endocrine glands. When little anxiety and H is present, this control is not interfered with and the sex organs function normally. As the con-centration of these emotions increases, the brain centers are stimu-lated into sending extra electrical discharges. These can cause spasm of a female's tubes, blocking the passage of the ovum (egg cell)—thus preventing pregnancy—and strong contractions of the uterus, pro-ducing painful cramps during menstruation. The hormone balance, too, may be upset and thus inhibit menstruation or cause excessive menstrual bleeding.

DOES MENSTRUATION CAUSE NERVOUSNESS?

If you have a menstrual disorder you should be under the care of a physician. If he rules out organic disease, the cause is almost surely some emotional factor.

I know that many women insist that their irritability, de-pression, tension, and other nervous symptoms are present only at the time of menstruation, but this is a form of self-deception. If menstruation was the real cause, then all or most menstruating women would get these same symptoms during their period. The fact is, however, that the majority of women do *not* experience an increase in nervous symptoms during menstruation. The *normal* menstrual cycle does not produce nervous symptoms. Moreover, the woman with nervous symptoms at this time of the month also has nervous symptoms at other times of the month.

Why do so many women (and some doctors) cling to this

dubious belief? Our balancing mechanism attempts to relieve us of oppressive I feelings by inducing feelings of blame. So, by blaming her nervousness on her menses (a condition which she can't help), a tense and anxious woman hopes to exonerate herself of self-blame.

The doctor who is trained in the diagnosis of nervous conditions will have no difficulty in finding the real cause of this woman's symptoms: low self-respect and its constant companions, H and anxiety. Her response to this usually is, "So, you're saying my trouble is that I'm a hostile person." But this resentful reaction gives even more weight to the diagnosis. Because of her anxiety, the patient is frantically seeking an instant cure. A shot or a pill offers an easy escape from her fear of a confrontation with her real problems. For this reason she is apt to shop around until she finds a doctor willing to blame her symptoms on the approach of menstruation and prescribe shots or pills to relieve them. Because of the complexity of menstrual disorders, however, if you are a woman suffering from symptoms such as those described above, you should continue to remain under the care of a general practitioner or gynecologist. But in addition to this, you should check yourself carefully for the presence of suppressed H and anxiety. When a doctor finds that a menstrual disorder is caused by emotional disturbance, he usually prescribes a tranquilizer and advises the patient to relax, avoid worry and arguments, and take up a hobby. Such treatment fails because it has no effect on the H and anxiety at the root of the emotional disturbance.

Women are also more likely to suffer from pain during intercourse than men. Most of these cases are caused by suppressed H too, but since a small percentage is caused by infections, growths or other organic disease, examination by a physician is essential.

SEXUAL FRIGIDITY

Sexual frigidity is defined as aversion to sex. A person may feel this way only in relation to his or her mate, or may have a total aversion to sex in general. But desire and pleasure may be only partially blunted: There may be sufficient desire to enjoy sex, but an inability to reach an orgasm.

Occasionally women develop an aversion to sex because their mothers taught them that it was filthy, disgusting, and sinful. Such mothers often advise their daughters to engage in sex only for the purpose of having children and keeping their husbands from philandering. But in analyzing women, I seldom find that such attitudes persist after a young woman gets away from the prejudiced propaganda of her home. With few exceptions, most cases of frigidity are caused by deep-seated H.

Temporary loss of desire often occurs immediately for anyone who antagonizes us. A man who makes his wife hostile is likely to encounter all sorts of coldness—such as a cold supper or a cold tone of voice—in addition to a cold shoulder. Perhaps the woman would be able to cooperate in something where she did not have to give much of herself, as for example, in pouring a cup of coffee. But even in this instance her hostility might just cause her to spill it "accidentally" on her husband. One well-meaning husband made the mistake of ridiculing his wife's choice for President just as they had been served steaming hot coffee; she responded by tossing the coffee in his face. The frigidity following a derogatory remark or any H-producing attitude is apt to be short-lived. However, when people are in frequent contact, as in marriage, the vicious circle of H frequently gives rise to long-lasting frigidity.

No matter how generous he is materially, or how fancy his bedroom acrobatics, a woman soon loses sexual desire for a man she doesn't respect. Many a man believes that because he lets his woman have her way, he is doing more than his share of giving in the relationship. However, traits such as martyring, H, opinionatedness, or obsession with himself will invariably poison the atmosphere between them.

We have already seen that most people dislike being labeled hostile because they consider it demeaning. This explains why the person who so readily condemns H in others remains blind to his own.

Because of their abhorrence of arguments, many marriage partners bend over backwards to be agreeable. However, if you study them closely you'll detect many differences between them. The husband may have a penchant for being punctual, whereas the wife is seldom ready until the last minute. Have you ever encountered the husband who makes a show of being considerate, only as bait to get his own way. For example, he asks his wife, "Where would you like to dine tonight, honey?" Then before she can open her mouth, he declares enthusiastically, "Let's go to Trader Vic's, you'll love it."

The wife may try to cover her disappointment at not being allowed to express her choice, and agree in order to avoid the feared argument. However, her facial expression and tone of voice betray her frustration and resentment. Despite well-intentioned aims to be agreeable, neither partner fools the other. Feeling transmission insures that each feels the other's H and the pretense in their agreeableness.

A husband wrapped up in himself fails to nourish his wife's

need for respect. If a man doesn't listen when his wife is trying to get his attention, he can't expect her to be a passionate bed partner even if he uses every technique in the latest X-rated movie.

Women seldom seek therapy for frigidity. Most of the cases I have encountered came to me for other problems, and volunteered nothing about their frigidity. For the most part it came out only when I specifically asked about it. The husband is the one who is more likely to consult a doctor; not that he believes there's any deficiency in himself, but to find out what's wrong with his wife.

Asking a frigid wife for sex is equivalent to asking an enemy army to discard its weapons. Therefore, the husband is instructed to cease all attempts to instigate sex with his wife. If she can be persuaded to join the treatment, both are taught how to eliminate H. If the wife refuses to participate, her frigidity can still be treated by the husband's ridding himself of his own H. Since this necessarily brings about a decrease in his wife's, her frigidity is replaced by normal sex desire. Since frigidity is a form of revenge, it may disappear when it no longer serves its purpose. (For example, when a woman senses that she is losing her husband to another woman, her desire may return.)

When her hostility has dissipated, a wife will give some definite indication of wanting her husband sexually; only when this point is reached should he make advances.

HOW TO DEFROST A FRIGID HUSBAND

Many women are frustrated and depressed because their husbands avoid them sexually. The loss of sexual desire for one's wife is most often the result of a marriage marred by H.

One of the sources of H is that which occurs when one person rejects a proposal that he or she could easily have complied with. Take the case of a realtor who had to inspect a piece of property and didn't relish the hour-and-a-half drive each way. He phoned his wife and asked her if she would accompany him. She said, "I'm sorry, but I planned to do house cleaning today, I wish you'd have let me know earlier"—and on, and on.

Feeling rejected, he turned to his secretary and asked her if she could go. She replied, in a word—"Yes."

Knowing how long it usually took his wife to get ready to go anywhere, he asked his secretary, "How long will it take you to get ready?"

She replied, "I'm ready now."

The contrast between the secretary's willingness and his wife's frequent reluctance had a strong impact on the man's feelings. He became increasingly resentful toward his wife and began to find the respect he needed in his secretary's readiness to share his tasks. Eventually he divorced his wife and married his secretary.

A happier outcome occurred in the case of Mae. After eight years of marriage, her husband, Cal, moved out of the bedroom and would have nothing further to do with her sexually.

When one party in a marriage is frigid, the other's desire is apt to be stimulated. This is due to the action of the balancing mechanism aimed at restoring the lowered self-respect. A reading of Mae's feelings in this instance would express something like "If we had sex, it would prove that I'm not rejectable." Accordingly, after several months of unrequited desire, she overcame her hurt pride and asked for sex. However, the more the rejected one cajoles and pleads for sex, the more satisfying the revenge of the partner, for the unconscious core of frigidity is the need to believe "I am not rejected inasmuch as I am doing the rejecting." When Cal failed to respond to her overtures, Mae tried a new hairstyle, doused herself with exotic perfumes, and paraded around the house in scanty attire. None of these devices bore fruit. "Why," she complained to her friends, "would my husband absent himself from my warm bed? He should go see a psychiatrist." Since he refused, she decided to go herself.

In therapy, Mae realized that it was her H that had deadened Cal's sex desire. In their first year of marriage, discussion of family problems had ended in bitter arguments. Since then Cal had dodged her attempts to discuss what was wrong between them. Mae admitted that she had been nagging him, but maintained that this was only because he wouldn't talk things over with her. Cal's habitual avoidance of argument led to suppression of H and, in turn, to a gradual loss of sexual desire for his wife. Again, in either sex, frigidity is a vengeful response to the mate's disrespect.

Formerly Mae had interpreted Cal's H to mean that she was not worth respecting; now she understood its true meaning: a reaction to his own dissatisfaction with himself. As her self-respect increased, her compulsion to martyred complaints decreased. Accordingly, she began turning her attention to her H rather than to perfumes and other material allures. Formerly, when Cal would discuss an accomplishment in business or set forth an opinion, her facial expression told him that she wasn't interested. Often she would cut him short with a contradicting opinion. Now that she recognized that his need for respect was as vital as her own, she listened with sincere attentiveness and found many opportunities to corroborate his opinions. Persistent application of these tactics gradually reduced Cal's H, and he began coming home promptly after work. Within two months he asked if he could again share their bed, and Mae found that he was indeed defrosted.

Sigmund Freud, on whose theories much of modern psychiatry is based, erroneously believed that sexual frustration was one of the most important causes of neurosis. Actually, it is neurosis that causes sexual frustration. The I feelings at the root of neurosis generate the H that causes sexual incompatibility and, consequently, frustration. Therefore, in most cases, sexual compatibility is restored when the H is appreciably reduced.

With H removed, each partner derives great pleasure from bringing about fulfillment in the other. No longer impatient and selfish, each partner enjoys taking the time to do the things that please the other. Since this unselfish giving actually adds to sexual pleasure, it's therefore not so unselfish after all. Achieving sexual happiness is similar to the attainment of any other kind of happiness. It is based primarily on the knowledge of how to fulfill the partner's need for respect.

8.
Parents Are Always Right— Or Are They?

A common mistake is the belief that a parent can manage his child's behavior simply because he's had so many more years of experience. One doesn't become an authority in the field of human behavior by virtue of being a parent. Nevertheless, most parents follow their own pet whims in child raising, without bothering to acquire the knowledge necessary to do the job. Typical is the father who lost his daughter to a religious cult, and his son to a hippie commune. He had achieved success as a chemist only because of years of schooling in this field. But he had failed as a father because he had ignored the importance of psychological knowledge about children and their emotional needs.

While it is difficult to determine the emotional state of the newborn, by the age of three months he is reacting emotionally to those who handle him. Even in the simplest tasks of caring for baby a circle of H easily develops. When diapering her baby, for example, a mother may be in a state of anxiety because of her own troubles. This can easily cause her mistakenly to stick the safety pin into the baby's gluteus maximus instead of the diaper.

A mother, like the rest of us, becomes impatient as the result of anything that increases her anxiety. This impatience can lead to attempts to feed the baby at a pace faster than he can handle. He responds sensibly by refusing to swallow the feeding. The mother, dominated by the need to be the victor in getting the baby to eat at *her* pace, may force one spoonful after another. When she finds that this doesn't work, she may try turning on the charm: "Come on now, eat for Mama." The baby, however, senses that she is continuing to force her way on him and continues his opposition.

When handling a baby, it is as important for the parents to check themselves for H as for cleanliness. Infants respond to a mother's irritable voice and handling as sensitively as to hot and cold. They react with anxiety to the hesitant, fumbling, and erratic handling of anxious parents and with H to the rough, jerky, and abrupt handling of an annoyed parent. A baby who feels unwanted, disliked, or forced soon begins to react with a hostile, contrary, and resistant attitude. The H arising in this way is one of the key factors in children's behavior problems and their subsequent failure as adults.

I rarely encounter parents who believe they have contributed to their youngster's disobedience, quarreling, refusal to go to school, lying, stealing, running away, cruelty, destructiveness, withdrawal and isolation from other children, sexual promiscuity, drug addiction, or delinquency. One parent may blame the other, but rarely himself. Each sincerely believes that the fault lies in the youngster's teachers or companions, in movies, TV, or any influence except their own. The conviction of such parents that they were only trying to do what was right is an unconscious reaction to relieve themselves of self-blame. The suppressed feeling of guilt serves as a barrier to the admission that they might have erred.

It is because of this guilt that most parents react to criticism of their management of their children—even when it is not accompanied by any blame—with a profusion of alibis: "He's been getting in trouble ever since he's been going with that Jones kid" or "I even promised I'd give him a new car if he'd get passing grades this year."

The truth is that parents aren't to blame at all, because they *have* striven to do what they thought was right for their children and themselves. No matter how decent, honest, and intelligent, parents are bound to err unless they learn to fulfill their children's need for respect. The knowledge of how to do this wasn't taught in school, and it's hard to get a working knowledge of it from newspaper columns, magazine articles, books, TV, or radio programs.

OVERCOMING H BY KICKING THE FURNITURE

If you come home and find your wife and child abusing the sofa and coffee table, don't conclude that your marital partner has gone the banana route. It could be her own original method of showing the child how to rid himself of H.

"Hostile feelings must be released" was the heading of an Ann Landers column in which a mother described her problem with her little boy's hostility. "Our son was two and a half when his little sister was born. I had to remain with them constantly to prevent him from pinching and hitting her." The mother tells us that her hostility became so great that "after months of policing the boy, I could stand it no longer. I became so angry I came within inches of spanking the daylights out of him." Then, God bless her, she had a flash of enlightment: "If I, an adult, could not contain my anger, how could I expect a two-and-a-half-year-old child to contain his?" In other words, she figured out that the boy *wasn't to blame for reacting like other human beings.*

 The mother went on to say: "When I get very angry I feel like striking out at something, too. I made a game of it. When we became angry we went together and kicked all the soft furniture in the room. You can't believe the change that came in this boy. Within days he was a wonderful boy again."

 There's no doubt in my mind that the boy's H rapidly cleared up—but not because he vented it by kicking furniture. His H could only have disappeared when his mother stopped transmitting hers to him. The boy was hostile to his baby sister because when she arrived, the attention to which he—as an only child—had become accustomed had been sharply curtailed. The deprivation of so much of his mother's participation and interest had relegated him to a position of Inferiority in relation to his sister—which automatically generated H. The mother reacted to her child's hostility with an equal amount. The result was a rapid growth of H between them. When, however, she finally figured out that his H was a natural reaction to a precipitous drop in her attention to him, her own H disappeared and was replaced by affection and respect. With the extinction of his mother's H, the child's diminished, and was further dissipated when she began paying attention to him as well as his baby sister.

BEHAVIOR PATTERNS THAT TURN YOUR CHILDREN AGAINST YOU

1. *Parental Self-obsession—Me-ism*

The more the parent is obsessed with his or her own problems, the more the parent neglects the needs of the child. Even infants display increasing H toward the self-obsessed, indifferent attitudes of their caretakers. A husband may spend as little time as possible at home, or a wife may go to work as a means of getting away from her husband. Such absences from home because of H between husband and wife make for neglect of their children.

This mother was so obsessed with having her own way that she was oblivious to the child's:

Mother: *Johnny, I've told you a hundred times to put your coat on when you go out. Do you want to catch your death of cold?*

Johnny doesn't want to die any more than the rest of us do. He is warm enough with his sweater on, and a coat will only impede his play.

Johnny: *Aw Mom, I don't need a coat.*

Mother: *Now don't be telling me what you need. If you don't put your coat on, you'll have to stay in the house.*

The disregard of the child's valid opinion results in a decrease in his self-confidence and an increase in H to his mother.

2. *Martyring*

A parent who portrays himself as a martyr causes the child to react with feelings of guilt. The martyr not only cites his burdens, but also often blames them on the child. For example: "I'm sick and tired of picking up after you. If you'd hang your things up I wouldn't have this aching back."

3. *Forcing the Child to Take Sides*

How often parents say, "Even if we disagree, we always present a united front and back each other up in any controversy with the child." Such a dishonest front, though well-intentioned, only harms the child, since he can perceive the true feelings of his parents. For example, if the mother actually believes that she is the martyred victim of a selfish, wrong-doing husband, then that picture is transmitted to the child, even though the mother says, "You have a good father, you must obey him." Unaware that her concealed feelings are apparent, the mother honestly denies that she is turning the child against her husband. Children require a harmonious atmosphere based on respect between their parents in order to feel secure and protected. Conflict between the parents fills the child with terror. But many parents wrongly believe that their children are protected as long as they avoid arguing in their presence. Children, however, are just as disturbed by the tense atmosphere produced by suppressed H as they are by angry fights.

4. *Overprotectiveness*

The human infant cannot survive without the help of someone who is capable of caring for his needs. Nevertheless, the development of self-confidence is retarded when parents habitually take over and do too much. Typical is this instance of a Ph.D. in engineering who saw a model of the Apollo spacecraft in the window of a toy store. A surge of affection for his seven-year-old boy prompted him to buy it. After dinner he spread the parts out on the floor and said to his son, "Let's put this Apollo together." The father's engineering background was, of course, of immense value in fitting the parts together, and so whenever the little boy picked up a part, his father would snatch it out of his hand and say, "I'll do it." These are the kinds of damaging blows to a child's self-respect that lead to lack of self-confidence and behavior problems in childhood as well as in adult life.

Many an adult has an abnormal fear of dampness and cold. Such fear often originates in childhood, when overanxious parents seeking to protect the child from fancied dangers, unwittingly frighten him or her by such remarks as "You can't go out; it looks like rain." So if your wife refuses to go out when it's raining, don't blame her; she is probably the innocent victim of a parent who believed that disease is caused by the body's contact with water.

Consider the plight of three-year-old Kitty. A summer shower had been followed by warm sunshine and puddles. The little girl was sensibly circumventing the afternoon heat by sitting in one of the puddles, when her mother yanked Kitty out of the puddle, pounded on the moistened portion of her anatomy, and screamed, "Do you want to get pneumonia?"

I doubt whether the little girl had any such desire. Pneumonia is a disease of the lungs which is not caused by wetting the behind.

The overprotected child is not given the chance to face problems. Consequently, he is as poorly equipped to face school, marriage, and a career as the undernourished physical specimen is to face exercise. The result is indecision, escapism, and panic when on his own. I know of no better illustration than that of a fifty-four-year-old man who had managed to make a trip on his own. However, when he was about to leave his hotel he was seized by anxiety as to whether he should wear his topcoat. Since his decisions had always been taken over by his mother, he called her long-distance, gave her the temperature, humidity, and wind velocity, and waited for her to make the decision for him.

5. Spoiling

If a parent habitually gives in to the child's demands, the child neither feels nor shows any appreciation. The parent, unaware that he or she is the instigator of these unsavory attitudes, becomes resentful, and a circle of H ensues. The son's room becomes a study in disorder and he is reluctant to eat meals with his parents. He seldom comes home at the time he is supposed to. As a result of his parents' belittling, he becomes sensitive to any form of criticism. He begins to make unreasonable demands and drives his poor parents to distraction. No sooner do they give in to one demand than it is replaced by another.

Since his desires are instantly fulfilled by the spoiling parent, the child enters adult life expecting the same from others. The instant gratification of his childhood desires prevents him from learning to face frustration as an adult. He grows up minus backbone and becomes panicky when called upon to face problems.

6. H and Other Forms of Belittling

A father may be extremely careful not to belittle his friends or business clients and yet have no compunctions about belittling his children. Father (to fourteen-year-old son): *Take your hand out of your plate. When are you going to learn manners?*

Mothers, too, may be quite unaware of the effect on their youngsters of belittling remarks, tones of voice, looks, and gestures. Mother (to fifteen-year-old daughter): *Your cousin Emma always keeps her room neat. Why can't you?*

Daughter: *Gee, Mom, I'll do it later.*

Mother: *That's what you always say, but you never do it.*

7. Superiority Attitudes

Moralizing is a form of criticism implying blame. Therefore, the child reacts to it with I → H. Of course, it is impossible for a child to understand that belittling or criticism does not mean that *he* is inferior—unless someone explains it to him. When the child is repeatedly made out to be bad, selfish, and ungrateful, it causes him to grow up with pronounced feelings of unworthiness.

Why are children humiliated by their parents? Why is it that so many parents don't permit children to do more for themselves? One reason is the Superiority Complex. When a mother insists that she knows best, it's because of the superiority complex that arises from her feelings of I. These feelings are intensified when wives fail to receive respect and recognition from their husbands. As a result of their resentful response to such treatment, their domestic chores become drab and tiresome. They are often too tied down to seek opportunities for achievement outside the home. As you have learned, the more unimportant you feel, and the emptier your life, the stronger becomes your craving for importance. A mother can't satisfy this need by giving orders to the mailman or the butcher; neither will hold still for it. The only readily available and defenseless victims of her urge for power and importance may be her children. This complex manifests itself in a "know it all," "can't be wrong," "better than thou," "do it my way" attitude. Here is a familiar example:

Mother to her son, who is enjoying his game with his chums: *Come in the house, you're tired.*

Son, who doesn't feel tired at all: *Aw, I'm not tired, Mom.*

Mother: *Yes you are. Now you get right in here.*

A mother's need to be important often causes her to draw up a set of rules for the children that resemble a manual of army regulations: meals right on the dot, this food forbidden, this food prescribed, bedtime at seven on the button, homework done immediately after supper.

Some parents demand nearly perfect performance. Few children can keep up with such demands. Consequently, they are unmercifully taken to task when, as they must, they fail. As adults, they feel inferior out of fear that achievements won't, once again, be good enough.

But this is nothing compared to the incalculable harm that can be wrought by authoritative opinions. The spongelike affinity of the child's mind for new information results in the retention of these opinions in adulthood. Thus, a mother's repeated insistence that sex is filthy may cause her daughters to feel guilty later about experiencing sexual desire. Racial and religious prejudice often takes root in childhood from sneering references made by parents about other races and religions.

A person who frequently refers to his father as if he were an oracle—"My dad always said"—is attempting to impress us with his "superior" breeding. This overdoing of hero worship of one's father is based on lack of confidence in oneself. Moreover, it is often used as a justification for questionable practices; as for example, when a man whose anger provokes him into beating his child states, "I believe in whipping because my dad whipped us."

8. *Physical Abuse*

National surveys estimate that between one and ten million children a year in the United States are physically abused to the point of requiring medical treatment. Statistics show that between 84 and 97 percent of U.S. parents spank or use other forms of physical punishment of their children.

Many parents maintain that whippings are necessary to teach a child right from wrong: "Spare the rod and spoil the child." Kids have been spanked since time immemorial, but axioms like that don't sanctify it. Nor does Boswell's recollection of Samuel Johnson's remark on whipping: "My master whipped me very well. Without that, I should have done nothing. He would ask a boy a question, and if he did not answer it, he would beat him, without considering whether he had an opportunity of knowing how to answer it." But Johnson omitted the fact that his great intellectual achievements were made possible only because of his endowment with a brilliant mind—one that produced the *Dictionary of the English Language* in three years, while it took forty members of the French Academy forty years to compile their dictionary.

An insidious error is to deal with one's family and co-workers as if they were enemy soldiers. While the objective in war is to defeat one's opponents, the goal in every other form of social life is to help our associates win; otherwise, we end up as losers along with them. As a parent, using force to make your point destroys your effectiveness as your child's teacher. Beating humiliates the child and leaves him with fear, guilt, and bitterness toward you and, therefore, makes him even more unreceptive and disrespectful. Because of fear of more punishment, he is conditioned to become a suppressor of H.

Physical punishment of a child is almost always the result of the parent's own H. You, the parent, may be feeling inferior because you haven't been able to earn your child's respect. On the other hand, when you work out the H in yourself, you can achieve a much better insight into his problem. This is illustrated in the case of one devoted father who, since his divorce, had been taking out his twelve-year-old son several times a week. While the two were dining out, the boy kept leaning against his father's arm. Feeling that the boy should have long since learned to behave in a more grown-up manner, the father became so angry with the boy that he slapped him.

When I suggested that he ask himself why the boy leaned on him so much, he soon unearthed the reason. He knew that his ex-wife had become distraught and despondent as the result of bitter arguments with her second husband. Because of her anxiety and distraction, her boy was being exposed to irascibility and neglect, instead of affection and understanding. It was because of this lack that the boy clung to his father. As the father thought about this, he realized that anyone deprived of intimacy, affection, and sympathy develops a craving for them. He recognized that he had reacted with so much anger not just because of the boy's behavior, but because of a pileup of recent setbacks in his own life that had deprived him in turn of some of those same human needs.

It is because of repeated subjections to these eight factors that so many children grow up with deep-seated feelings of I. The more inferior he feels the greater the activation of the balancing mechanism to extricate him from this biologically deficient state. It is this unconsciously acting force which prods him into a contest for superiority, manifested by H, contrariness, stubbornness, and disobedience.

Joey, age five, had been repeatedly scolded by his mother for playing with matches. The H her scolding generated in him caused a buildup of contrariness and defiance. This led him to play with a box of matches in the den while she was in the backyard. She returned on the double when she saw the flames leaping from the house. Little Joey managed to get off without being badly burned, and avoided a whipping only because the fire had singed his posterior.

At the very least, belittling, domineering, martyrdom, and "know it all" attitudes on the part of parents are sure to produce models of contrariness and selfishness in their children. No matter how diligently a child is taught, he'll do wrong in reaction to H and S, and right in reaction to genuine liking and appreciation. That's why a child will behave like an angel for a neighbor, uncle, or teacher, but badly toward know-it-all parents who ply him with sermons and threats.

SIGNS OF SERIOUS EMOTIONAL DISTURBANCES IN CHILDREN

If your child is the victim of nightmares, it's because his mind is overloaded with H and anxiety. As in adults, fatigue, stomach disorders, diarrhea, poor appetite, skin disease, allergies such as asthma, headaches, colds, sore throats, and virus infections in children often follow a protracted period of suppressed H and anxiety.

Sometimes the removal of a child from an emotionally injurious atmosphere results in a dramatic improvement of health and behavior. Just a few years ago, a large number of children with asthma were sent to a New York State sanitorium. One of the rules of this institution was that the parents were not allowed to visit. Within a month, although they had not been given any medicines or other treatment, most of the children showed amazing relief from their asthma. Sadly enough, when they were sent home, their asthma quickly returned. Since nothing was done to rid the parents of their H, the children were returned to the same emotional atmosphere that had brought on the asthma in the first place.

Sometimes a child's problems seem so severe that parents wonder whether they should take their son or daughter to a psychiatrist. Children have a marked disinclination for such treatment. They may hear from their parents or others that only nuts, kooks, and other objects of ridicule visit a "shrink." The youngster thinks he is being brought to a psychologist or psychiatrist because he has been bad; consequently, he expects to be scolded. Having already been subjected to his parents' domination at home, the child rebels at being taken to a therapist against his will. The H at the root of his disorder is only increased by such a show of force.

Rather than subject a child to more force, I advise the parents to come in by themselves for instruction in how to deal with the problem. One lady consulted me because of her fear of committing violence on her five-year-old daughter. She had become increasingly angry because of the little girl's refusal to bathe. The child's contrariness was due to the H she was getting from her mother. The mother was given instruction in the method of ridding herself of H. After three days of relief from her mother's H, the little tot asked, "Mommy, would you like me to take a bath?"

After the mother recovered from her shock, she managed to say, "That would be nice."

Sure enough, the child took off for the bathroom and returned minus a month's accumulation of dirt—whereupon the good mother had all she could do to keep from fainting.

With few exceptions, the most rapid and effective way to correct a child's behavior disorder is by correcting his parents' respect-lowering attitudes. When parents learn how to change attitudes of hostility, superiority, belittling, and martyrdom to approving, crediting, and humble ones, the child's behavior improves rapidly.

POSITIVE SUGGESTIONS TO IMPROVE PARENT-CHILD RELATIONSHIPS

You'll find that the very same knowledge that applies to emotional and personal relationships with adults also applies to such relationships with children.

In order to win any issue, we must first attain the other person's Receptivity—and a child is very much a person. Remember that in order to make him receptive to your views, you must raise his Respect Level. Thus, wherever possible, a child should be permitted to shift for himself, for in so doing he learns to have confidence in his own powers. Only when it appears that a child might come to harm should a parent come to his aid. An effective method of increasing your child's self-respect is simply by using whatever subject is being discussed. For example, when Johnny says that he doesn't need a coat, use this subject to prop up his Respect Level. A mother who recognizes this would reply along these lines:

Oh, you don't think it's cold enough for a coat?

Having his opinions respected and validated would nourish Johnny's self-confidence. In managing the situation so as to increase her son's self-respect, she would also increase his respect for her —and thus satisfy her own need for importance. *There is nothing wrong with your desire for importance as long as it is not attained at someone else's expense.* Parents who won't permit a youngster to have his way (when it won't cause any trouble) only increase I → H.

Consider the following incident: The mother has lamb chops on the table for the evening's dinner. Knowing that her seven-year-old boy does not like lamb, she has placed a dish of tuna before him. The father angrily moves the tuna aside and puts a lamb chop on the boy's plate.

The boy (in a whining tone): *I don't want lamb chops. I want tuna.*

Father: *Eat the lamb chop or I'll ram it down your goddam throat.* Needless to say, the boy is unable to swallow after this threat.

Although there are those who decry giving in, there is a time and place for it. If you have damaged someone's fender, it's only fair to submit to their claim for payment. In the same way, if you have inadvertently lowered your child's Respect Level, why not square the account?

For instance, if a boy is fiddling around with the food in his plate, his parents don't have to say sternly, "Come on now, eat your dinner or go to your room." Would you use that tone of voice on one of your clients or friends? His inevitable response to humiliation is revenge—easily obtained by fiddling around with his food more and thus escalating the contest for superiority between parent and child.

If he's not hungry, there's no reason why he should eat. Since his lack of appetite is mainly due to H, his parents could help him get rid of it by asking him about something that he takes pride in—his games, painting, or school projects. If he asks for some other food, they should let him have it (if it's no great bother) rather than making a superior or martyred remark like "You'll eat what the rest of us are eating," or "Mother worked hard to make you dinner, so eat it." His parents' understanding of their child's need for respect will prompt them to honor his request. In so doing, they are not only getting him to eat with relish, but supplying his essential need: respect.

Children who are deprived of appreciation and approval often develop a craving for worldly possessions as a kind of substitute. A case in point was that of Matilda, who had been picked on for most of her eight years. Under her mother's vigilant eye, Matilda was seldom able to go barefoot, as she liked. Her mother justified her demand that Matilda wear shoes at all times, except when she was in bed, by the unreasonable fear that the girl might cut herself and die of blood poisoning.

Her mother's insistence produced a hostile and therefore contrary reaction in Matilda. Despite her aversion to shoes, she prized one particular pair because she had bought them with her own savings and her father had commented on how nice they looked on her. The shoes gave her excellent service, but finally wore out and Matilda stopped wearing them. One day, while on a cleaning spree, her mother threw them out.

No doubt the closet became a tidier place without those shoes, but there was one small problem Mother hadn't reckoned with. When Matilda found out that her mother had thrown her shoes out, she hit the ceiling: "You had no right to throw my shoes away. I want my shoes."

Although they weren't retrievable, Matilda pestered her mother daily for them. Finally she demanded compensation —specifically, the $6.98 she had paid for them. "Forget it," her mother told her. "Those shoes were rubbish. They weren't worth a penny."

The belittling allusion to this valued possession only intensified Matilda's fanatic demand for adequate compensation. Day after day, she badgered her mother about the $6.98. Finally, when the father couldn't take it any more, he prevailed on his wife to give Matilda the money. But alas, when given the money, Matilda threw it back at her mother and screamed, "I don't want your old money, I want my shoes."

When the mother related this to me, her tone revealed how indignant she was. "After getting the money for shoes that weren't worth a penny, she had the gall to throw the money at me. There's no pleasing that child."

One moral of this story is: Don't try to overcome H with money. Even if the money is accepted, it won't lessen H one hairbreadth—because unearned money has little effect on anyone's self-esteem. This principle also explains why Christmas and other holiday gifts cannot reduce H. For instance, the father who fails to spend time with his children may be in for an unpleasant surprise if he expects to reduce their H by lavish gifts.

In Matilda's case, disregard for her valued possession made

her feel that she counted for little in her mother's eyes. What made the episode even more humiliating was that her mother had not thought her worth consulting before throwing out the shoes.

Why had the mother exerted her will without consulting Matilda? Her husband had diverted to Matilda a good bit of the appreciation and interest his wife needed. When mothers don't get their fair share of respect within the home and aren't free to attain it in the outside world via a job or other activity, they often become bossy and willful. The hunger for power becomes so overwhelming that they fail to realize that their children have exactly the same requirement. Had the mother known that Matilda's respect could be gained only by respecting her, she would have asked her about the shoes. Matilda might even have said it was okay to throw the shoes away, and that would have settled the matter without any trouble.

Even after the shoes had been thrown away, the issue could have been settled peacefully. With an understanding of what Matilda's possessions meant to her, the mother would have known that money could not repair the loss of self-esteem. Since she had made a mistake, she should have humbly acknowledged it and offered to buy Matilda another pair of shoes. As long as her mother's feelings matched her words, Matilda would have felt respected.

A typical case of vying for S between parent and child is the following:

David, age six, and Terry, age nine, were making such a racket that James, their father, couldn't concentrate on his newspaper. He knew that yelling at the boys wouldn't help. Therefore, he tried to hide his annoyance and, in a quiet voice, asked them to tone it down. After forty seconds of reduced noise, the boys started up as loudly as before. Now James really got mad. After all, hadn't he first asked them in a nice way? He angrily ordered them to their rooms with the threat of punishment if there was any more racket.

I doubt whether this particular father would have consulted a psychiatrist on his own initiative for such a trivial problem. However, he had attended a lecture I gave to a group of business executives, explaining how hostility diminishes cooperation between a boss and his staff. Shortly after this incident with his sons, he came to see me. He began, indignantly, "I can't go along with your statement 'Nobody's to blame.' My two boys are living proof that you're wrong."

I explained that much of the H was caused by the vying for S between the boys and himself. This contest goes on between parent and child just as it does between adults. Suppose you hold a baseball bat in front of a youngster and close your hand around it. The youngster will then place his hand above yours. When you top him again, he'll top you. As with all the rest of us, an automatic inner force prods him to get out of the inferior position. James was not terribly bothered by his inability to concentrate on the paper, what really hurt was that his sons didn't *respect* him enough to comply with his reasonable request.

James had always assumed that he was right in his disputes with the boys. He took pride in the fact that he always tried to reason with them. But under careful scrutiny, such reasoning usually turns out to be moralizing, simply another form of presumptuous superiority implying that the moralizer is the righteous one while the recipients of the sermon are the sinners.

James hadn't realized that when he thought he was asking them "nicely," the boys had nevertheless perceived the annoyance he was trying to conceal.

There had been many previous episodes in which this father told his sons something "nicely" and then followed up with an angry blast. "No one wants to cooperate with you when they feel you are trying to deceive them," I pointed out. "You can't conceal the H that you feel toward your children."

I added that the boys were hurt when he felt hostile to them, scolded them, or made them feel guilty with one of his sermons. You might say that they had become allergic to any H from their father, which is why they reacted with defiance to his hostile tone. James recalled that as a boy he would sulk when his father asked him to go to the store; yet he'd be glad to run errands for the man who lived next door. The difference was that this neighbor didn't moralize, scold, and belittle him as his father did.

How could James get his boys to behave? What should he do when the next incident of noisemaking came up? He assured me that this would occur within minutes after he arrived home.

What makes it so easy to get kids to behave is that they all have the same requirement: appreciation. How could James supply this need? Why not participate in their games? This would make them feel that they were getting some recognition from their father. His nonhostile participation would raise their Respect Levels —exactly the opposite of what had happened previously. Just one week of James minus H would melt away a good bit of accumulated resentment. Then he would find that when he made requests, they would respond willingly. I suggested that he return in a week and let me know what had happened.

In his next visit, James proudly reported progress. "I've learned to listen to myself. I can see that my tone betrayed my annoyance with them. Instead of getting after the boys, I took stock of myself and realized that I was hostile. I was able to put the l → H formula to work. I realized that I came home from work feeling put down by the boss."

"What did you do about those feelings?"

"I could see I'd been mistaken in taking out my H on my sons. Instead I realized the fact that my boss put me down didn't mean that I was inferior. The knowledge of I → H explained the source of his H. It was *his* personal problem, arising from his own I → H. Since understanding that I → H is as human a reaction in him as it is in me I've felt sympathetic rather than resentful toward the boss."

"Are your sons still making a racket?"

"Not much less," he replied, "but their noisemaking hasn't been grating on my nerves like it used to, because I realized that I was the original cause of it." James was astonished at his ability to tolerate the same intensity of noise that had been so irritating before, now that he no longer saw it as a defiance of his authority.

It is a fact that as H decreases, your sensitivity to noise decreases. Yet if someone you resent is disturbed by the noise, it becomes music to your ears. Have you ever noticed how people who resent you are so unconcerned about the racket their kids make when you're around?

"In fact," James went on to say, "I feel you helped me win fifty dollars at the race track Wednesday."

"How was that?" I asked.

"Well, I felt so much better Tuesday night that I was able to concentrate better on my horse handicapping. At the track Wednesday, instead of losing a hundred dollars as I usually do, I lost only fifty."

James learned that since it was he who had cast the boys in the inferior position, it was up to him to utilize the subjects or issues that arose during the week to raise their respect. Their noisiness was a prominent issue. Why not use that?

Sure enough, when James returned for his third visit, he told me how, in the midst of their noisemaking, he joined them and told them—truthfully—that when he was a boy, he had made even more noise than they did. "The racket would drive my poor father crazy." This humble admission demonstrated to the boys that he felt no blame toward them.

James had done his homework well: a humble admission to a child or adult does not cheapen you. By elevating another person's opinion of himself, you only cause him to appreciate you more. And you'll find that you can accomplish a lot more with humility than with punishment.

Omitting a whipping doesn't mean that you are sanctioning

whatever your child did "wrong." For example, if he's beating his sister, don't whip him; just remove him. Excessive H between brother and sister always traces back to the H fomented by their parents. You're not going to wean them from violence by a violent demonstration. With practice in employing this knowledge, you can consistently overcome your H and achieve the harmonious cooperation with your children essential for your own happiness as well as theirs.

9.
I→H in the Classroom

Twelve-year-old Guy was spotted chewing gum by his eagle-eyed teacher. She reminded him in icy tones that chewing gum was forbidden in class.

Guy's gum was removed, but not his hostile reaction to the teacher's scolding. Within a few days, this H had festered to a point where Guy again began chewing gum. This time, he was ordered to the principal's office. The principal asked Guy to sit down and wait until she returned to the office. As the time passed, the boy became increasingly anxious. The restlessness caused by his anxiety led him to pick up the phone and fiddle with it. Just at that moment, the principal returned. Guy was scolded again and sent home. When his parents came to the principal's office, they were told that their son was emotionally disturbed and must be examined by a school psychologist. That evening, Guy's father scolded him for his gum chewing and his fooling with "the goddam phone."

What had started out as a harmless bit of gum chewing had multiplied into three successive scoldings—from Guy's teacher, principal, and father. By the time the psychologist could give Guy an appointment, a week later, the series of humiliations had produced a fearful, confused youngster with greatly increased fear of and H toward adults. When the psychologist asked why he chewed the gum and picked up the principal's phone, Guy could only answer truthfully, "I don't know."

Because of Guy's adamant refusal to visit the school psychologist again, his parents consulted me. The father emphasized how much of his time he devoted to helping Guy with his problems—for example, with his reading. However, I learned that when

117

Guy made a mistake, his father would yell at him. The result, of course, was more mistakes.

You can't expect a child to react well to other forms of authority outside the home when his major sources of authority—his parents—have exposed him to constant berating. The bruising of his self-respect at home made Guy all the more sensitive to reprimands at school.

I explained to the boy as well as to his parents the chain of events and their emotional impact. Guy could see that if *he* became irritated from what other persons did to him, then his teacher could get irritated from what others did to her.

Children warm up to those with similar problems, just as adults do. I told Guy that I knew how bad it makes a fellow feel when he can't get any cooperation.

"It sure does," Guy agreed.

"Then you can understand how teachers feel when they can't get any cooperation." Guy had been so preoccupied with his own troubles that he had scarcely ever thought about anyone else's. For the first time, he saw the teacher as a person who was up against the same kind of oppression as himself. He felt a surge of sympathy for her and, when he returned to class, he no longer had the impulse to defy her, so there was no further misbehavior.

In many instances, parents learn only of their child's misbehavior, and not of the teacher's yelling, name-calling, sarcasm, ridicule, and belittling. Teachers, like other well-meaning persons, become hostile in proportion to the emptiness and frustrations in their own personal lives. The more I they're saddled with, the more intensely they react with H when a pupil doesn't comply with their wishes. When given a wrong answer, they may interpret it as a reflection on their teaching ability and scold or ridicule the child. If a child misbehaves, they're likely to interpret this as a sign of disrespect.

A teacher with a low Respect Level reacts to a child's misbehavior with H, unmindful that both the child and teacher are the victims of I → H. Even a teacher with a normal Respect Level is bound to react to misbehavior with H, since this is an invariable psychological reaction. Small wonder, then, at the prevalence of mental illness in teachers. A study made in 1959 revealed that approximately 10 percent of the nation's teachers were emotionally disturbed. The rapid growth in classroom disorder and violence since then has been accompanied by an alarming increase in mental and physical illness in teachers. Headaches and depressions alone account for much of teacher absenteeism.

The H aroused by roughneck behavior in the schools is

multiplied by the callous disregard of teachers' rights by parents, government authorities, and most of the public. Tragically, the children, already the victims of H at home, must face the H of their teachers. What good is it to teach Civics when the hostility that some teachers transmit breeds arrogant disdain for the rights of others?

It's easy to comprehend the emotional damage children suffer at the hands of disturbed teachers who hurl books and papers all over the classroom or who inflict cruel punishment. Such persons can be spotted and placed on sick leave. However, what about the large majority of teachers who are not mentally ill? Overwhelmed by the defiance and violence in the classroom, and abandoned by the public, their H has risen to a point which is emotionally damaging not only to themselves, but also to their pupils. It is this group that causes most of the emotional damage that children sustain at school.

Like most people, many teachers focus on the other fellow's H, while remaining blind to their own. This is especially the case in teachers who try to "control" their emotions. They fail to recognize that angry feelings don't disappear just because we try to keep them under cover, and since they are perfectly apparent to the child, he reacts with anxiety and H. He has no trouble understanding outright scolding, but veiled H has the menacing effect of an attacker whom he can't see. The child responds by disliking the teacher. Since the expression of anger by pupils is taboo, the child's H is usually contained. Subjected to a hostile teacher, such a student dreads going to school and returns home in a depressed, agitated state, often accompanied by a headache or stomachache.

There are other responses as well. Suppressed H makes youngsters as vengeful and contrary as it does adults. While the child can't have teacher write five hundred lines of "I must not demean my pupils," there are a few thousand other forms of revenge he can easily carry out—like doing whatever the teacher doesn't want him to do or simply doing nothing when the teacher has assigned a project. Clowning, picking on other children, throwing spitballs, truancy, and violation of rules are most often due to the pupil's H toward the teacher.

Learning difficulties are seldom the result of basic lack of intelligence. As the result of his H toward his teacher, a child's motivation to learn is stifled and he is often considered to be deficient in gray matter. Albert Einstein's schoolwork was so poor that his teachers and parents thought he was retarded. The headmaster at his school said, "He'll never make a success of anything." However, it wasn't lack of ability, but hostile defiance to his teachers that was stifling his natural gifts.

In many cases, when a supposedly stupid child is transferred to a class where he is not subjected to a teacher's H, his performance improves dramatically. Yet in the course of thirty years of interviewing teachers, I have seldom encountered one who is aware of the significance of his or her own H in causing behavior and learning problems in children. It's so much easier on the teacher's ego when a child's misbehavior and inability to learn can be attributed to stupidity, laziness, orneriness, daydreaming, or anything and everything from poor classroom lighting to faulty diet or an organic lesion of the brain. In spite of flimsy medical evidence for any such damage, a diagnosis known as "Minimal Brain Damage" is made in thousands of cases and followed by the prescription of tranquilizing drugs such as Ritalin. While the drugs may exert a quieting effect, they do not correct the real cause of the child's symptoms. Worst of all, the child is being influenced to use drugs rather than his own thinking powers when faced with anxiety—a practice which can pave the road to drug addiction.

Medical research has established that MBD is a misnomer, since the children who are so labeled rarely have been found to have any brain damage. This hasn't dampened the enthusiasm of the advocates of drug treatment for the nervous, hyperactive child. Instead of calling the problem brain damage, though, it is now more often referred to as Minimal Brain Dysfunction. What could that possibly signify? Isn't *every* known form of nervousness a form of brain dysfunction? Since a drug has no effect on the child's faulty attitudes, these can be expected to continue and serve as the basis of a mentally disturbed adult life. The most effective treatment of MBD (Hyperactive Child Syndrome) is to remedy the faulty attitudes of the child's parents and—not infrequently—his teachers.

Not many parents can afford the cost of a psychiatric consultation. The school psychologist is overloaded with examinations that require many hours of his time, and is seldom able to find time for therapy with youngsters. Wouldn't it be far more feasible to train teachers in the method of reducing H than to terrify a youngster by compelling him to undergo a psychiatric examination?

The only way teachers can reduce a child's H is by dissolving their own. Let's consider a typical example. Miss R. passes out drawing paper to each child in her first grade class. As she goes by Tim's desk, she notices that he has torn his sheet. She picks up the torn pieces of paper and says, "The slip is for you to copy, not tear." Tim feels her blame and is bound to react with hostility and anxiety. This makes him vengeful, contrary and unreceptive.

Teachers are trained to be aware of many items about themselves: their tone of voice, neatness, even their proximity to a child.

First priority, however, should be checking themselves for H—on their way to school and during the school day. In making this self-examination a habit, Miss R. would become aware of her H and recognize that its source was her own feelings of I—her interpretation that Tim's tearing the paper was a sign of disrespect. Had Miss R. recognized that Tim might have done it because of a child's natural playfulness or inexperience, she might simply have asked him to try it again with a new sheet of paper.

If he *did* do it out of disrespect, the three-car accident analogy can help her understand that a child's bad behavior is determined almost entirely by the emotional forces to which he has been subjected. Did she cause the disrespect in previous communications with him when she believed her H was hidden?

During his schooldays, Robert Watt, the eminent Scottish physicist, spent most of the day looking out the window rather than tending to his classroom lessons. His teacher did not punish him for this behavior; instead, she chatted with him about the beauties of the Scottish countryside. Had she scolded and threatened him, his hatred of authority would have intensified. But he reacted to her sympathetic feelings with an increased affection and respect for authority. Without this respect, he might not have been motivated to go on and get a doctorate in physics, and perfect radar for Britain in World War II.

An example of how this same wisdom can be applied in the modern classroom was related to me by Mrs. H., a young woman who served as a substitute teacher. One of her second-grade pupils told her that another little girl, Amy, was eating at her desk. But Mrs. H. was one of those teachers who took a child's home life into consideration. She walked over to the little girl and simply said, sympathetically, "You must be hungry."

The little girl answered with a nod of the head. After school, the teacher learned of the aftereffect of her remark from her own daughter, who was a member of the class.

"You know what Amy told me at recess, Mom? She said, 'Mrs. H. is sure swell; if it had been Miss K., she'd have scolded me.' " These incidents help shape the emotional content of the child's mind. You can't grow up with a dislike for people when you're raised with this kind of nourishment.

Can you recall how annoyed your teacher would become when one child giggled and how the annoyance would turn to rage when the other children were infected and the whole class got on a giggling kick? Angry threats might eventually restore order, but would leave the pupils with increased H. Instead of the usual angry command to cut out the giggling, a better solution would be for the teacher good-naturedly to let it continue for a minute. In this way the pupils feel that the teacher can understand their need for occasional fun. Now that he or she has won their Receptivity, they're far more likely to comply when the teacher says, "Okay, let's get back to work." Have you ever seen a middle-aged nun run the bases in a ball game with her parochial class? Sure, she may not be too speedy, but for her participation in their fun, she earns their obedience in class.

There are much better ways of improving a child's behavior than by reprimanding him. One teacher who understood this was Miss Q. During recess and lunch periods, quite a racket went on in the hall outside her classroom. One of the leading noisemakers was Jay, an eleven-year-old boy in her class. One day, at the height of the noisemaking, Miss Q. called him into the classroom. "Jay," she said, "those kids are making too much noise out there. I need someone who can control them. I've selected you because I think you have the ability to do it. Therefore, I'm appointing you as my monitor."

She took an armband from her desk with a large *M* on it and slipped it on Jay's arm. Jay, who had expected a reprimand instead of a promotion to leadership rank, was delighted: "Gee, Miss Q., I'll see that those kids behave themselves."

And that's exactly what Jay did, meanwhile behaving like an angel himself. Miss Q. had simply recognized that children are motivated to behave well for anyone who elevates their self-respect.

Mr. F. was another teacher who was able to convert a youngster's unruly behavior into respect for authority. In his eighth-grade class was a rambunctious youngster named Billy. One day, Billy was called on for oral recitation. Jumping at this opportunity to play the clown, he grabbed the dictionary off Mr. F.'s desk, held it high, and yelled, "What am I bid for this fine *Funk'n* Wagnall's dictionary?"

The way he pronounced the first part of the name provoked an uproar of laughter from the class. But Mr. F. was able to dissolve his own H. "Let's assume this is a real auction", he said, "and see how much Bill can get for the dictionary." Certainly Bill's behavior had been rowdy and defiant, but the teacher saw his job as helping Bill respect authority by demonstrating to Bill that he, a symbol of authority, respected Bill. After the auction was completed, Mr. F. complimented Bill in front of the class for doing a good job as a salesman. Interestingly enough, Mr. F.'s prophecy was borne out; when I encountered Bill forty years later, I found out that he had made a success selling real estate.

For teachers who know how to keep themselves free of H, teaching is a fulfilling experience. Like their pupils, they look forward to their day at school and return home without nervous tension, exhaustion, and headaches. They take pride in the scholastic attainments and good behavior they have inspired and, most rewarding of all, their lives are enriched and their health fortified by the affection they feel for the children and receive from them in return. However, it isn't the permissiveness *alone*, but the feeling that accompanies it that determines how children will respond. Permissiveness doesn't correct misbehavior when the permissive adult hasn't rid himself of hostility and arrogance. Therefore, it won't do any good for teachers to ignore a pupil's infractions. Their H and S will still antagonize the child into some other kind of contrary behavior. Nor does dissolving H mean that teachers should permit disorder and violence; they should employ every disciplinary measure available to maintain order and protect themselves and their pupils from harm. On the other hand, disorder and violence decrease as H on the part of the teacher decreases. Once H is reduced to a harmless level, permissiveness is helpful in gaining subsequent cooperation.

10.
Why Youngsters Rebel

Picture what happens when a father, the very embodiment of the Establishment, comes in from work. He is on his way to deafness because his twenty-three-year-old has the rock 'n' roll up to a pitch that would irritate an elephant's eardrum. He can't help worrying about his sixteen-year-old daughter's hot pants as an invitation to rape, pregnancy, and venereal disease. As he sits down at the dinner table, he finds in his path of vision a creature whose sideburns reach the inferior border of the jaw and whose hair approaches the collar bone. Unless this father has learned Anti-H, he'll either denounce his son as a sanitary menace or, at the very least, let him have his most scornful glare. His hostility isn't a sign that he doesn't care about his children, but it does contaminate the existing affection. It will only aggravate his son's hostile defiance toward authority, which is the real reason that he won't get his hair trimmed.

The divergence in views between the generations is a frequent source of bitterness and disharmony. Anger, hurt feelings, disappointment, worry, depression, and sickness are too often the lot of the parents. In the last two decades, young people's callous indifference, hostility toward authority, widespread use of drugs and alcohol, incidences of venereal disease and illegitimate pregnancy, crime and mental illness have been increasing at an alarming rate.

Here is a typical parent's viewpoint: "The trouble with today's youth is that their parents let them get away with too much. They've meekly given in to their every demand. That's why they've turned out so arrogant, contemptuous, vulgar, demanding, untidy, and violent. My generation was raised with iron discipline. If you

124

ever disobeyed, you'd be punished so severely that you'd never disobey again. That's why we grew up to be obedient and orderly instead of a bunch of uncouth, law-breaking, unpatriotic dope addicts."

A recent study of college students revealed that half of their parents had either used or threatened to use physical punishment during their senior year in high school. It would appear from this that a sizeable segment of the generation that underwent severe punishment at its parents' hands has been dishing out the same to its own children. Some fathers have the mistaken belief that laying down the law to a child in angry tones is effective because it results in obedience.

Certainly, the child obeys, but out of fear, not respect for his father. Having made his child hostile, the father will now have to reckon with his vengefulness. A boy can't get revenge on his father by ordering him to bed, spanking him, or forbidding him to use the car. However, if his father wants him to go on an errand, he may just happen to be too tired. If his father wants him to do his homework, he may lose interest in doing it. If his father asks him to carry a box up from the cellar, he may say that his back hurts. Yet when the father goes down to the cellar, he may find his son practicing his weight lifting. I'm sure parents can give dozens of other examples.

Too many prohibitions and restrictions at home creates an urge for uninhibited release outside the home. Out of father's sight, the child delights in going against whatever father stands for. This is one of the reasons for a well-nigh uncontrollable impulse to speed on the road, and is also one of the factors leading to alcoholic excess and drug addiction.

When parents lack self-confidence, their overanxiety prods them into taking over every little problem that comes their child's way. Since the child is deprived of the vital experience of working through his problems, he grows up lacking in self-confidence. By the time he reaches his teens, his hostile reaction to domineering parents has grown to a point where he can no longer tolerate their intervention in his problems. But, in dispensing with their help, he is beset with the overwhelming anxiety of facing problems with little previous experience.

The craving for relief from such anxiety makes him an easy prey to drugs and alcohol—expedients that bring quick but only temporary alleviation of the uncomfortable feelings. The trouble is that inasmuch as no progress has been made in working through the problem causing the anxiety, it soon reappears. No drugs, alcoholic beverages, or tranquilizers can give us the confidence to stay with our problems and work them out. Consequently, the lack of self-confidence and inferiority feelings increase, with the inevitable compulsion to seek relief by blaming others.

I agree that the way children turn out depends on how they were raised. However, just take a look at the attitudes of the parents of these children: arrogance, condemnation, know-it-all, better-than-thou—all of which are the result of having been subjected to the same kinds of attitudes by their parents. Since speaking up was not tolerated in their generation, they were forced to suppress their H and craving for S. When they became parents and there were no longer any restrictions on the expression of these hostile and superior attitudes, their children were bombarded with them.

However, the present generation have had much more exposure to liberal ideas from newspapers and TV. Their more affluent parents can afford to send them away to universities where they can live on their own. With so much more exposure to one another, they can openly express and reinforce defiant attitudes that had been suppressed at home. Students who feel inferior may follow the rules of their college until they read about student uprisings at other colleges. The consequent tipping of the balance may lead to arrogant, demanding attitudes in presenting their petitions for change. (The result, of course, is to lessen the receptivity of the administration to their petitions.)

Since adult authority consistently made them out to be wrong, their S Mirage is strongest in relation to teachers, police, bosses, and anyone else in a position of relative authority. This need to be superior to authority is coupled with the need to be contemptuous of it, and so the attitude becomes one of righteous indignation. Such students become obsessed with their own ideas and proposals and condemn the views and methods of constituted authority. Thus, when the Establishment supported the Vietnam war, these youngsters had a compulsion to wave the Viet Cong flag right under Authority's nose. Since the Establishment wants them to be discreet about sex, they often become consumed with the desire to be indiscreet.

This explains why most revolutionaries are products of homes in which the H became extreme as the result of repeated vying for S with opinionated, domineering parents. In these rebels violence is easily activated against persons and organizations that symbolize the parental authority they hated. Ironically enough, youngsters who have been subjected to the know-it-all, indignant, moralizing, and martyred attitudes of their parents respond by *duplicating* the very self-defeating attitudes they condemn. Since they haven't the slightest awareness of this duplication, you can see why they are sure to come to grief.

On the other hand, in my experience, youngsters raised with a judicious degree of humility, credit, and a minimum of S and H do not develop anti-Establishment attitudes. Since they feel respected by the older generation, they are eager to work cooperatively in achieving orderly progress.

When you read a newspaper account of some prominent person's child being involved in drugs or crime, or committing suicide, the parent's statement is almost always one of self-serving justification. In fact, the parent usually bends over backward to brag about how perfectly he raised his child: "I just can't understand why he [or she] ever did anything like that. We brought him up in a good Christian home. We taught him right from wrong. We gave him everything he wanted. When he misbehaved, we spanked him. When he was too big to be spanked, we meted out other punishments. I had no idea that he was despondent. He was liked by everybody. We insisted that he go to church." Etc., etc. They were the perfect parents; the crime, drug addiction, or suicide just had to be caused by influences outside the home. They'll blame it on the child, his teachers, the bad influence of his friends—on every conceivable influence except one: themselves. Occasionally they may go as far as to ask, "What did we do to make our child turn out like this?" Although one parent may blame the other, it's a rare parent who ever points the finger at himself for the way he raised his child, because low self-esteem inhibits the recognition of unfavorable facts that would arouse anxiety. Admittedly, it's most uncomfortable to admit that we've done wrong or acted foolishly. But if we at least permit ourselves to see our mistakes, then we know exactly *what* we fear. When self-blame is kept out of consciousness, we nevertheless sense that something's wrong and still retain the associated fear. This type of fear, in which one doesn't know what he's afraid of, is known as anxiety. Anxiety is frustrating precisely because it's impossible to deal with a problem we're not conscious of. But you are able to see your faults once you understand that you're not to blame for them. That's why, in most instances, all you have to do to get a person to admit a fault is to get him to understand why it doesn't reflect discredit on him.

Few of us manage to perform with equal competence in all the aspects of our lives. An example is that of a man who by dint of long hours of work, provides his family with a home, plenty of good food, and a college education for his son. Nevertheless, the son takes to gambling and drink and, at the age of thirty-eight, still can't keep a job. Now this father had set an example of hard work, honesty, and regular church attendance, and had striven conscientiously to bring his son up properly. What went wrong?

He had been so engrossed in his work that he had had little time, energy, or thought for his wife and boy. The neglected wife lavished her affection on her son. Since he was her sole source of companionship when her husband was still at work in the long evenings, she became increasingly possessive of him. As he grew up, her spoiling and overprotectiveness made the boy increasingly dependent and helpless. Feeling that his wife was paying more attention to his son than to himself, the father became increasingly hostile toward him. If he assigned him a chore, such as mowing the lawn, he'd become angry when he found that the job wasn't done. The mother constantly attempted to cover up for the boy to protect him from his father's wrath.

Of course, when the son finally went to work, his mother was no longer able to cover up for him. Nor could he tolerate the complaints of his succession of bosses; he resented them as he had his father. The inevitable outcome was that unless he quit first, he would invariably be fired.

HOW THE CHILD BECOMES INVOLVED IN A TRIANGLE

We usually think of a triangle in connection with the "other" man or woman. However, the most frequent triangles are those in which a couple is involved with their own child. A circle of H, involving the parents and gradually including their child, may begin as early as the infant's first months of life and continue throughout the child's growing-up years. The result is that the father may become overattached to his daughter, while the mother, becoming truly jealous of the daughter's ability to get more of her husband's affection and approval than she can, may become overattached to her son. In this case, the increase in resentful feelings lines family members up against each other: father and daughter versus mother and son. Each faction struggles to extricate itself from the inferior position by blaming the other.

In their frantic efforts to win a child over, the competing parents often resort to bribery, even submitting to a youngster's unreasonable demands to gain his allegiance. However, the child recognizes that he is being paid not as an expression of love, but to side with the bribing parent.

You can detect the presence of a triangle by asking yourself if you resent one child and favor the other. If you are a father, the resentment will usually be toward your son. Note the absence of resentment toward your daughter and your resentment of your wife's partiality to your son. Your wife and boy have the same need for appreciation that you do, and become resentful when they don't get it. When you repeatedly make them out to be wrong, you make it impossible for them to be receptive to your views.

Ask yourself if you have been contributing to your wife's I feelings by vying for S with her on a variety of issues. In fact, you may have picked up where her mother or father left off, duplicating their insistence on being right. Suppose she insists that the boy ought to have a bike for Christmas. You believe it is better for him to work and pay for the bike out of his own earnings. If you try to show her the merit of your opinion, you'll be implying that she is wrong. This will hit her where she's vulnerable, and she'll only oppose you more vehemently.

However, if you recognize how badly your wife needs your validation of her opinions, you'll take an entirely different approach. Admit to yourself that a strong force within you wants to assert that you know best. In being so obsessed with your own craving for respect, you've completely overlooked the same need in her. Your understanding of this will bring about a change in your feelings: from resentment and better-than-thou to a respectful consideration of her opinion. Ask your wife what kind of bike she has in mind. Does she think the boy will be able to use it safely? Above all, don't show her where she is mistaken. Maybe she will mention some aspects of the matter that hadn't occurred to you. If so, acknowledge them. Whenever she brings up the subject again, don't dodge it. Continue the policy of asking questions and acknowledging her answers. While S and derogatory contradiction will make for endless argument, building up your wife's self-respect will be rewarded by fruitful discussion.

WHAT A PARENT CAN DO

What can a father do to get his son away from bad company, defiance of the law, violent protests, disinclination to education and work, and aversion to grooming? "All right," an exasperated father challenged me, "how should I react to my children's long hair and sloppy attire?"

You have already learned what this father needs to do. His first step is to take a look at himself. By the simple procedure of examining his own feelings, he'll realize that he's angry at the person whose attitudes he wishes to change. In focusing his criticism on the boy's defects, the father has probably overlooked some of his own: the personal traits which are producing increasing emotional damage in his son. Almost invariably, when I remind such fathers that they should check themselves for self-obsession, superiority, hostility, and martyring, they respond with an angry recitation of all the affection, approval, and sacrificing they've shown their child. These generous attitudes *are* good for a child, and I don't wish to remove them. Nevertheless, we must still come to grips with the source of the child's problems.

The meaning of "Give and ye shall receive" seems clear: If one gives love, kindness, devotion, and unselfishness, one will receive the same in return. Yet this is not always so. It is an all too common observation that many parents give lovingly yet fail to receive love in return. The reason the love is not returned is that the parents have disregarded the hostile, superior, and martyred feelings they were presenting along with their love.

For example, a couple may sincerely believe that it was love alone that motivated them to give their daughter a $50,000 home as a wedding gift. What they may be overlooking is the attitude that accompanied the gift: "You don't appreciate what we do for you." Furthermore, the parents may feel that their gift entitles them to the right to run the daughter's home. When the mother visits, she may lecture her daughter on how to treat her husband and children. The result is that the daughter's hostility reaches a point where she doesn't want to see her parents. The father then complains, "The only time I hear from you is when you need something repaired"; and both parents feel bitter that they're not even invited to the house that they gave in love.

It's obvious that you don't have much chance to effect the changes you want unless you rid yourself of H and S. Consider this exchange between a mother and her eighteen-year-old daughter.

Daughter: *What should I wear to the party?*
Mother: *Why don't you wear your blue outfit?*
Daughter: *I think I'll wear my yellow dress.*

When her daughter stated that she would wear the yellow dress, her mother felt that her opinion was not valued.

Mother (with irritation): *Then why did you ask me?*

Because of her own need to dominate and control others, this mother was quite oblivious to her daughter's need for importance. And having been repeatedly relegated to the lower end of the respect pole by her mother, the daughter reacted with automatic contrariness.

The frustration of her mother's urge to dominate caused an immediate reaction of H. With a knowledge of the emotional forces involved, however, she would have recognized that her daughter was not really belittling her opinion, but merely reacting to the fear that her *own* opinion was not valued. I reminded the mother that for years she had insisted on making most of her daughter's decisions. This had resulted in the daughter's growing up with little confidence in her own opinions, depending instead on her mother's. However, victims of overdomination also gradually develop a rebellious resentment manifested by contrariness—based on the overwhelming urge to extricate themselves from the inferior position. With this understanding of her daughter's need for nourishment of her self-respect, the mother would simply have responded: "Oh, you *do* look nice in yellow."

Suppose your son is behaving badly. It's so easy to overlook how often you may have scolded him, belittled him and subjected him to know-it-all lectures. Think of the times you told him that you wanted to have a talk with him. He knew he was going to receive a sermon in which he would be labeled the wrongdoer. The only effect of those sermons was to place him in the inferior position and thus make him more hostile.

Bear in mind that he is constantly vying for S with you and with most of the others in his environment. Some of his hostility may certainly have been caused by his teachers, schoolmates, and the general society to which he has been exposed. However, his parents' influence is far greater in bringing about bad behavior.

When you understand that your boy's rash actions are the result of faulty emotional nourishment, you'll no longer think of him as bad or evil. Certainly his untidiness, laziness, and defiance are ugly. But he is behaving badly because his feelings have been injured. It isn't fair to blame him for what you and your wife have unintentionally brought about in him: instead, your understanding of this should arouse your sympathy. Just as you crave his respect and affection, so, too, does he crave yours.

Since his bad behavior is due to an excess of H, that's what has to go. No matter what the issue under discussion, Ob + H + S + Mar. will turn him against you. So, make it a habit to take a reading of your own feelings, to check for the presence of these self-defeating attitudes.

Learning to be aware of how you come across requires practice. Although you can't constantly study your expression in a mirror, you can learn to visualize how you look when you are talking to a youngster.

Listen to your own tone of voice, too. Although your words may be "Now, I'm not blaming you," if an attitude of H is present, it's perfectly conveyed by the tone of your voice. If you are feeling martyred, your tone will give this attitude away. The youngster can then only respond with feelings of guilt. He can tell by the look on your face and the gestures of your hands when you're discrediting the point he's trying to make. Are you monopolizing the conversation? Interrupting him? Drowning him out with a loud voice?

When he blames you for being a square, part of the military-industrial complex, even for having voted Republican, don't come back with denials, alibis or self-justifying arguments. Don't counter-accuse by trying to make a noble martyr out of yourself with such a remark as "Is it selfish for me to work long hours while you're out running around night after night?"

There's no reason to feel superior to him just because you don't behave as foolishly as he does. The fact remains that all of us have behaved foolishly, more times than we care to remember.

After ridding yourself of these feelings, use the issues *only* as a means of giving him credit. Remember that he can't behave well unless you provide nourishment for the growth of his self-esteem. You can do this by thinking of the subject under discussion as if it were a game the two of you were playing—a game not important in itself, but only in its potential for molding your son's character. Use the subject under discussion to show your child how right and well-meaning *he* is, while readily acknowledging any mistake or fault on *your* part. You can do this through a rejoinder such as:

"Well, son, what you say has made me do some hard thinking about myself, and I can see where I *have* been selfish."

A person acts unselfishly or selfishly because that's how he believes his interests will best be served. (I'm not advocating selfishness; I only want to point out that the selfish person is seeking the same goal as is the unselfish one, but is the victim of emotional forces of which he is entirely unaware.) All of us are selfish from time to time, so you've only admitted that you're one of us.

You can't turn your son around with one humble admission, however; after all, it took years to build up his H. Raising a boy's Respect Level is a job that requires steady application. Acknowledge any point on which he's enlightened you. This will prop up his self-esteem another notch. But be careful that you don't botch the job out of impatience. Even if it takes a year of using the new approach to make your child receptive to you, it is well worth the time and effort. Remember when he was three and you let him straddle your shoulders so that he could see the parade? He appreciated you for that. At twenty-three he'll appreciate you just as much for maintaining him in the same elevated position esteem-wise.

This kind of support must be supplied regularly in order to obtain progressive growth in emotional strength, as is illustrated by the case of Ruth and her sixteen-year-old son, Jim. All Jim wanted was four hundred dollars for hi-fi equipment. Ruth's Respect Level had already been considerably lowered by her husband's unwillingness to discuss their problems and by Jim's lack of interest in helping with family chores. So it was only natural that she responded with a flood of indignation and martyrdom rather than give the four hundred dollars. "All you think about is your own pleasure," she told Jim. "It doesn't matter to you that I don't have the money to buy the things that I need. When I ask you to take out the trash, you can't be bothered."

By applying Anti-H, Ruth learned how to manage any issue that arose. First of all, she made a practice of taking a reading of her own feelings before she spoke. Now when Jim asked for the use of the car for the weekend, her new understanding was perfectly reflected in her demeanor and tone of voice. She said that she couldn't give him the car because she needed it for marketing, but she omitted any reference to his lack of cooperation. Of course Jim was disappointed, but what mattered was that his mother hadn't blamed him, thus preserving his self-respect. Consequently he wasn't antagonized and would be more cooperative in the future. A child's Receptivity will grow when the goal of each discussion is to elevate his self-respect. Only when it becomes apparent that you finally have attained his Receptivity should you state your view on the matter. Your chances for success will be far greater because of his elevated Respect Level.

Perhaps I haven't sufficiently stressed that the humble, nonhostile approach does *not* mean being submissive in the face of demands that are obviously not justified. For example, if your boy failed to do a job you had promised to pay him for, giving in to his demand for payment would spoil him. Submissiveness does the greatest harm when it is accompanied by moralizing, martyred attitudes, or attempts to hide your H. Take the case of a high school dropout who refuses to work. After rising at 3:00 P.M., he demands money for his evening activities. His father lectures him in tones of righteous indignation: "If you won't work, you can't expect me to provide you with money to go out with those no-good bums. I have to break my back to provide for you. The least you could do is look for a job."

He then submits to his son's request. But since the demeaning, martyred lecture makes the boy more hostile, he has no qualms about demanding more money—or even stealing it. Since time immemorial, honorable men have had no compunctions about appropriating and enjoying the enemy's booty.

Many parents allow themselves to be bullied because of lack of self-confidence, and also to be able to have something to throw up to the bully afterwards, as a way of showing that they're better than he is. For example, take a seventeen-year-old who refused to continue at high school, ran up large bills with Dad's gas credit card, wouldn't look for work, or help out with household jobs. When the parents sought my help, they complained that despite their "giving in," their son continued to ride roughshod over them. The hitch was that they also blamed him, felt superior to him, and looked on themselves as martyrs; and these feelings made the boy feel inferior. He perceived perfectly well that their real message was "We're the good guys, you're the bad guy."

I explained to these parents that the answer to their son's demands should be No—without any hostility, martyring, or moralizing. Whenever the Anti-H technique is employed, the practitioner should not hesitate to be insistent and forceful when necessary. If a teen-ager has stolen money on several occasions, or taken the car without permission, the parents must make sure not to leave money around the house, and must keep the car keys where their son doesn't have access to them. These parents now had a clear understanding of how they had to change: no more giving in, but also no more H + S + Mar. Mindful of this essential principle, they firmly refused him use of the credit card and money on demand. Their son learned that he could get money in payment for mowing the lawn, painting the house, etc. The respectful attitudes from his parents, rather than the former demeaning ones, gave him the self-confidence to seek a career. He paid his way through barber school with earnings on a job. And the parents felt better because of getting rid of their H and for having earned their son's respect.

11.
The Drug Problem: What You Can Do About It

Since the early sixties increasing numbers of parents have been living in anxiety and despondency because of a youngster's involvement with drugs. If your child is using drugs, you can tell that his appearance and behavior are different: He's washed out, glassy-eyed, listless, slurred in speech, excited, and prone to lie. Since possession of drugs is illegal, you can't help worrying that he'll be jailed. The drug used most frequently is marijuana. A recent study placed the number of persons in this country using marijuana alone at more than twenty million. Although its possession is illegal, its users, most of whom are otherwise law-abiding, continue to multiply. They insist that their particular drug is harmless. However, while marijuana is not considered addictive, the fact remains that many users soon make a habit of it. Moreover, many more users than nonusers of marijuana become addicted to hard narcotics such as heroin. And many recent medical studies indicate that marijuana may be harmful to the human system, mentally and physically.

Pep pills (popularly known as speed), barbiturates, and cocaine are also frequently used, producing harmful mental and physical effects. LSD, commonly known as acid, is an exceedingly dangerous drug that often causes psychosis and various forms of self-destructive behavior sometimes eventuating in suicide. Other harmful drugs, including peyote, mescaline, psilocybin, PCP, and DMT are in less abundant use.

The most popular hard narcotic is heroin, a derivative of and considered even more addictive than morphine. It is estimated that there are approximately one-quarter million heroin addicts in this country. The consequences in physical, mental, and social deterioration of the heroin addict are catastrophic. Large numbers of them become criminals in order to support the drug's high cost. It is estimated that half of the crimes committed in the United States are for the purpose of obtaining money to support a drug addiction.

There is a great deal of information available to parents,* and there are increasing numbers of drug education programs in existence. But there is no reason to expect much help from either of these sources since they provide little understanding of the *cause* of drug addiction.

WHY A YOUNGSTER STARTS TAKING DRUGS

The principal reason a youngster starts taking drugs is his hostile feeling toward established authority. In a study involving hundreds of high school students, more of those who were exposed to drug information became users than those who were not given any information at all. When an authority-hating youngster is warned of the dire consequences of drug abuse, he may start taking the drug as a means of defiance.

Hostility toward authority is a natural reaction of a youngster to the anger, belittling, spoiling, know-it-all, moralizing, and martyring attitudes of his or her parents. When a child finds his efforts to counter a parent's opinion are futile, he develops a "what's the use?" attitude. Convinced that it is impossible to gain their approval, he believes his only chance to obtain what he wants from authority is through the tactics he used in childhood: He thus abandons discussion, suppresses his hostility, and resorts to subterfuge.

A large part of the thrill in taking a forbidden drug is the delight in defying authority. If such a youngster's feelings could be expressed in words, he or she would say "You're not going to have your way over me anymore." The feeling of exultation on taking a drug for the first time is in part based on the belief that, at long last, the individual is achieving liberation from hateful oppression.

Because H is always based on I, the drug user feels ill at ease when alone and lacks confidence in socializing. Fearing that without this drug his performance will be inhibited and impaired, he becomes increasingly dependent on it. When he tells you, "I get a lot

*"Drug Abuse: The Chemical Cop-Out" may be obtained free by writing to: National Association of Blue Shield Plans, 211 E. Chicago Avenue, Chicago, Illinois 60611. Another good booklet is: "Don't Guess About Drugs When You Can Have the Facts," National Institute of Mental Health, Publication No. 1006, November, 1969, National Institute of Mental Health, Chevy Chase, Maryland.

more out of sex with marijuana," he's entirely correct. Instead of perceiving his lack of sexual confidence, he acts on the Mirage that he's using marijuana because that's the only way *anyone* can get the most out of sex. Tricked by this Mirage, he never faces the emotional problems underlying his lack of confidence, and therefore never resolves them. You can now see why a heart-to-heart talk has no effect in getting a youngster to quit drugs. Telling your children what they should do, what's good for them, and how harmful drugs are is construed as a repetition of the same old "We're right, you're wrong, so do it our way" attitude. This only makes them more hostile to their parents, and therefore, more defiant.

"But," parents of a drug user declared adamantly, "we're not hostile to him, we love him; we'll do anything to help him."

Unfortunately, love doesn't dissolve H; it only makes it that much more unbearable. The drug user has an extremely high concentration of H resulting from the thousands of times his parents made him the loser in one issue after another. The following case exhibits some of these characteristics. Ron, a nineteen-year-old college student, had been smoking marijuana for nearly two years when his parents brought him to my office. Through hard work, Ron's father had advanced to a high-salaried position that enabled the family to live in comparative luxury. During Ron's first eight years his father's work had required a great deal of time away from home. The mother, an anxious, depressed woman, reacted to the father's absence with increased frustration. Her overanxiety manifested itself in an overprotective regulation of Ron's activities.

While the father had been concentrating on earning a living, the mother had applied herself to the care of her two boys. She had tried to find the intimacy with Ron that she lacked with her husband. Her fears had caused unnecessary protective practices that interfered with Ron's efforts to look after himself. For example, her fear that he would not eat enough resulted in coaxing, cajoling, and actual attempts to force food on him. As he countered her forcing, possessive tactics with increasing resistance, she became even more aggressive in her attempts to run his life.

Any child raised in this way develops a progressive lack of confidence in himself and an increasingly rebellious resistance. This causes the domineering parent to become even more agitated and insistent on having his or her way. As Ron responded to his mother with increasing contrariness, the affection she had formerly bestowed on him was lavished on his younger brother. Ron became jealous of any attention the brother received, and taunted, belittled, and bullied him unmercifully. When his parents found out that Ron was smoking marijuana, they pleaded with him to give it up. Their protestations that they only wanted to help him threw Ron into a hysterical rage, to which his parents responded with threats and punishments. After all their efforts had failed, they turned to psychiatry as a last resort.

HOW YOU CAN PERSUADE YOUR CHILD TO GIVE UP DRUGS

Ron regarded me as a member of the Establishment and manifested the same attitude toward me as he had toward his parents. He came to our sessions under protest and quickly informed me that neither his parents nor any shrink were going to stop him from using marijuana.

I told him that since his problems were primarily due to his *parents'* emotional trouble, I would treat *them*. He could help by telling me what he thought was wrong with them. He interpreted this to mean that his parents were mistaken in placing all the blame on him, and he was quite pleased.

The parents, as you might expect, were aghast at this turn of events. However, they quieted down when I explained that Ron wouldn't cooperate as long as he felt that he was being blamed. He would respond much better if they also came for therapy because it would signify that for the first time they were admitting that some of their attitudes could be wrong.

Although Ron was untruthful, selfish, and disdained any advice, suggestions, or preaching his parents offered, he was easily influenced by his friends. They shared his defiance toward parents and other authority figures since they, too, had been subjected to a similar brand of parental treatment. The gang's common meeting ground consisted of practices embodying defiance, such as the use of profanity and drugs. Because of their excessive I feelings, they also manifested excessive anxiety. For them, marijuana did tend to become habit-forming since it provided quick, albeit temporary, relief from these oppressive states of mind.

Ron's mother complained bitterly, "I wait on that boy hand and foot, but he won't listen to anything I say."

Her husband was equally disgusted. "After all his mother has done for him, how can he do this to her?"

Whenever Ron had tried to present his side of his disputes with his mother, his father would angrily cut him off by saying, "I don't want to hear it. You've got to respect your mother."

Convinced that any attempts to reason with his father would only elicit more denunciation, Ron began keeping his complaints to himself. The result was that the father heard only one side of the dispute between his wife and son. Since her complaints coincided with his own views, he naturally sided with her, thus confirming her in the erroneous course she was following.

How can we change such a mother's attitudes without provoking antagonism? Mothers who ordinarily react angrily to criticism are more apt to cooperate if shown how a change in their attitudes will benefit their child. While Ron's mother defended her attitudes at first, she gradually came to understand wherein she had erred. Both parents recognized that Ron's H could be reduced only by nourishing his self-respect. This newly acquired understanding was reflected in the changed tone of their communications with him. Ron's mother began omitting her moralizing sermons, "child guidance" advice, and nagging criticism. When Ron found fault with her, she readily acknowledged it; when he talked about quitting college, she didn't become provoked and remonstrate with him as she had before, but replied that there was a lot to what he said.

I advised both parents to involve Ron in conversations in which, instead of subjecting him to their views, they asked questions that would elicit his own. When he did express opinions, they let him know that he had clarified some points they hadn't previously understood. Instead of the rebuttals with which they had formerly responded, they gave him credit wherever possible. For example: Ron would complain, "The trouble is that your generation is only interested in its own selfish aims and doesn't give a hoot about young people." Prior to treatment, his father would answer, "There's nothing selfish about providing you with a car, allowance, and financing your guitar lessons." Although this statement was true, it antagonized Ron since it made him out to be wrong. Instead, after treatment, his father replied, "What you've been saying has caused me to take a long hard look at my generation and I must admit there's been selfishness and lack of appreciation of the younger generation."

This answer was not only true, but it gave credit and validation to Ron, a form of nourishment he hadn't previously received. You might think this would cause him to disrespect his father because of the admission of selfishness. On the contrary, by respecting Ron's opinion, his father earned respect in return, not only for himself, but for the parent generation.

To be sure, Ron had a field day in ridiculing his parents' views and style of living. Why, you might ask, should they put up with this? Because actually, they realized, they weren't putting up with a thing. On the contrary, they took pride that in not contradicting Ron they were building up his self-esteem and his respect for them.

Tranquilizing drugs, including marijuana and alcohol, have little addictive effect on a person who is relatively free of H and anxiety. As Ron's H decreased, he no longer felt the urge to defy his parents, and marijuana lost its hold on him.

In my experience, more can be done to help youngsters quit drugs by means of this kind of therapy with their parents than by any other route. Otherwise much of what a youngster accomplishes with a therapist may be negated by parents. As illustrated in Ron's case, the aim of therapy is to instruct parents in Anti-H and how to use it to defuse the hostile atmosphere between parents and child.

Along with these changed feelings and attitudes, the following rules will be helpful:

1. Let your youngster finish what he's talking about without interruption.

2. Don't counter his opinions with your own opposite viewpoint. Remember that your primary concern is not the topic under discussion but rather how it can be used to nurture your child's self-respect.

3. Maneuver the conversation occasionally so that he can show you where you are wrong. This maneuver is the equivalent of feeding your teammate the ball so that he can carry it for the touchdown. Not only do you make him a winner, but you get the credit for it.

4. When he blames you, don't show him that he is wrong, martyr it up, or offer an alibi. Simply acknowledge that you're wrong. If you're certain that you're right, you still shouldn't tell him he's wrong; instead ask him his reasons for blaming you. Then listen attentively. For example, suppose he tells you that there's nothing wrong with his use of marijuana. Even though you're convinced that he's wrong, how do you handle this situation so as to bring him over to your point of view? The natural inclination is to interrupt his argument with contradictions, such as citing medical reports on marijuana's harmful effects. Remember that this only lowers his Respect Level and turns him against you all the more. Your most valuable advice is worthless if you fail to get the listener's Receptivity.

Nothing you say will work unless you acknowledge and rid yourself of your H and S, and then listen attentively to his argument in favor of marijuana. Must you agree with him? Yes, as much as you honestly can. For example, he may point out that alcohol is harmful and yet its use is not illegal. Instead of trying to point out that "that's the way it is," agree that overdoing alcohol is ruinous. Only after you have accomplished the essential step of reducing H can you go on the logical offense and gradually insert some of your own opinions. At this point, when you show him why he's harming himself by using drugs, there's a good chance he'll be receptive enough to try to give it serious consideration.

Problems will, of course, continue to arise throughout your child's life, just as they do in all our lives. But now that you have built an affectionate and respectful relationship, he'll find it natural and easy to discuss his problems with you. Since you've lived a lot longer, the experience you've gained should be a valuable asset in helping him.

In most cases, it is preferable that parents and youngsters continue to live together during treatment. This way, their changed attitudes and emotions have the opportunity to react on one another. But in some cases, even though every effort is made to achieve understanding in the parents, one or both are still unable to divest themselves of their harmful attitudes. I've had parents admit these attitudes in my office, but the habits were so ingrained that they were hard to shed. Some adults are so emotionally bankrupt that in spite of a therapist's efforts, they continue their domineering, martyring, and preaching to their children. In such cases, a therapist must rely mainly on his own treatment of the drug-using youngster.

What Makes Youngsters Use Heroin?
Most heroin addicts begin the habit in their teens. The principal reason for starting on heroin is a state of mental depression resulting from the individual's dissatisfaction with himself. But that social factors outside the individual also play a part is attested to by the prevalence of heroin addiction in city slums, where lack of parental care results in a loss of confidence and defiance of adult authority. Shop windows scintillate with goods that the deprived youngster cannot buy. The movies that he longs to attend are out of bounds, because of the admission fee. Recreational centers are virtually nonexistent. Schools are too crowded to provide any individual guidance. When a youngster quits school and seeks employment, his inability to find work—plus the sight of well-dressed people who have jobs, cars, and money—increases his bitterness toward authority. When he does have access to TV, this vicarious glimpse of the affluent life-style only aggravates his resentment. Whenever hostile defiance toward authority has no outlet (for example, in drafted U.S. soldiers in Vietnam), susceptibility to drug addiction increases.

Undoubtedly, the miseries of daily existence contribute to the mental distress that forms the basis of addiction. Nevertheless, the fact remains that most depressed people are able to refrain from using such an injurious drug. Why, then, do so many youngsters start on heroin in spite of having been warned of its harmfulness?

A Typical Case of Heroin Addiction in an Adolescent Boy
Addiction is also found in the more affluent social classes. When Gary, a lanky eighteen-year-old, came to my office with his parents, he had been addicted to heroin for two years. He had started sniffing glue when he was thirteen and switched to marijuana at fifteen. He used Seconal, a barbiturate, for a year, and then started on heroin. The father was angry and the mother was unable to control her tears as she told of her efforts to help Gary break the habit.

Gary had consented to see a psychiatrist only because his father had told him that otherwise he was going to be delivered to the police. His attitude toward me was one of sullen defiance. Only after I told him that I felt his parents were blaming him unfairly did he show some interest in discussing his troubles. Before long, he admitted that he supported his habit by shoplifting. Then he quickly launched into a bitter attack on his father. "He's always yelling at me. Nothing I do ever pleases him. He has to be right about everything. Whatever opinion I have, he tries to show me how I'm wrong. So now I just keep my opinions to myself and try to avoid him."

I asked about his mother. "I really do care for Mom," he said. "She's tried to help me in every way, but she's always on my back, giving me lectures on what I should or shouldn't do. She keeps saying how much she's sacrificed for me and that I'll be the death of her.

"My folks are good people," Gary told me, "but I've never liked being at home. Mother'd always get on the soapbox and Dad would run me down. So I started coming home later and later. That didn't help much because Mother would sit up and wait for me. She'd tell me how she couldn't sleep until I came in, but the truth is she can't sleep anyway. The only reason I haven't run away is that she looks after me when I get sick from withdrawal symptoms."

Gary's description of his parents proved to be quite accurate. When I interviewed them, the mother continually interrupted her husband and me with lectures on the cause of addiction. She rattled on like a broken record about her sacrifices for Gary. Only when we were alone did she tell of her husband's violent temper: "I'm used to it, but Gary can't take it. His father has yelled at him and belittled him since he was a little boy."

When I saw the father alone, he complained that Gary had lied since early childhood. "He's always been lazy and getting his mother to do everything for him. From the time he was a child, she pampered and protected him. When he defied me, I'd give him a good whipping. If it weren't for her, I'd have turned him over to the police long ago. We've given him a decent home, but he doesn't appreciate it."

Investigate the background of most young addicts and you'll find that they have been subjected to hostile, know-it-all, and martyred attitudes. With few exceptions, the individual who tries heroin for the first time is in a highly disturbed mental state. Lacking confidence in his own judgment, he is an easy prey to another's suggestion to try the drug. When their anxiety level is high, not only youngsters, but adults, too, are extremely susceptible to suggestion.

Gary had taken his first injection after coaxing by one of his chums. But more than his friend's assurance that "nobody'll ever notice the needle marks," it was the overwhelming urge to defy his parents that prompted Gary to sample the drug. And it takes only a few such samplings to cause addiction.

Gary's parents sincerely tried to do the best they knew how for him. Unfortunately, it had never occurred to them that their attitudes toward Gary were the product of their frustrations with each other. The father avoided his wife because he couldn't tolerate her long-winded sermons and incessant complaints. The more he avoided her, the more inferior she felt. As her attempts to express herself were ignored or met by outbursts of temper, she looked to Gary for appreciation and intimacy and became possessive, spoiling, bribing, and overprotective, completely unmindful that she was using Gary to satisfy her craving for the importance and power she lacked with her husband.

Gary, however, had been unable to escape from his mother, as his father had done, until he tried heroin. He reacted to her possessiveness and domineering with increasing contrariness and defiance, but he lacked self-confidence since he had not been given the opportunity to work out his own problems.

His mother's affection and indulgence toward Gary were in sharp contrast to her resentment and disregard for her husband. You can see from the I → H + S Reaction how this goaded Gary's father into blame and arrogance toward Gary, which, in turn, intensified Gary's hatred and defiance of his father and the authority that such fathers symbolize. Since the only authority he had ever known —parental—had been accompanied by sermons, know-it-all, and reproachful attitudes, he anticipated the same demeaning response from all authority figures: teachers, ministers, employers, and police. While he was too frightened to defy his father openly, he could do it secretly—by using a forbidden drug. Unless this hostile defiance could be dissipated, there would be little chance of breaking Gary's addiction.

How Parents Can Help the Heroin Addict

Gary's case will be used as an example of what parents need to know in order to help a youngster addicted to heroin. The same knowledge is applicable to cases of addiction to any drug.

Gary's mother said that she knew how restless and agitated he had become, but she had thought he just needed to settle down. She made the invariable claim: "I've always given him lots of love and everything he's ever wanted."

Mother-love is one of the most wonderful bounties bestowed on a child. But it can't prevent the emotional damage of spoiling, bribing, overprotectiveness, and possessiveness. I explained that Gary's anxiety was caused by his low Respect Level and his excessive amount of suppressed H. His mother had to learn that her "everything" had not included approval, credit, a sincere listening ear, and the humble acknowledgment that she was occasionally mistaken. If she had deprived him of food to the extent that she had deprived him of credit, he would have been emaciated.

Although Gary's mother was shocked by this interpretation, she came around very quickly because she dearly loved her boy and desperately wanted to help him. Gary's father, on the other hand, couldn't see any need to participate in therapy. "After all," he said flatly, "Gary's the addict, not me." When I explained that I needed his help in applying the treatment to Gary, he consented, although reluctantly. He had become so hostile toward Gary that he was poorly disposed to admitting any mistakes. I pointed out that he had never been much of a pal to Gary and had often terrified him with his temper. The father maintained that he had been unable to spend time with the boy because of his work, and that he yelled only when the boy did something wrong.

It wasn't the father's fault that he used work as an escape. Listening to his wife sound off did little for his self-esteem, whereas his accomplishments on the job gave him a feeling of pride. His temper would explode when he saw his wife giving in to Gary's whining demands and ignoring his pleas to stop spoiling the boy.

When I let Gary's father know that I sympathized with what he had to contend with at home, he felt that, for the first time, he had an ally. My appreciation of his side of the matter earned his respect. I capitalized on the Receptivity I had earned by getting him to recognize that his wife would do a better job with Gary if he would find ways to give her credit instead of blame.

You can see why it was so essential to get all three family

members to understand why none of them was to blame. An addict's wife, parents, employer, and society too often condemn him because they believe he is responsible for his addiction. Once they realize that addiction is an illness resulting from injurious attitudes that the addict has absorbed from those around him, they feel a lot less blame toward him.

The sharp drop in H in Gary's family resulted in a distinct improvement of the atmosphere in the home. The effect on Gary of being understood and respected had the impact of food on a starving man. Gary was, at long last, getting the emotional nourishment he so urgently needed. Instead of lecturing him, his parents asked Gary questions, thus allowing him to enlighten them. Instead of finding fault, they acknowledged their own mistakes. The father cut down on his hours of work so that he could supply this kind of nourishment to Gary.

For the first time in their marriage, Gary's parents realized how much they had been violating each other's need for appreciation and respect. The fulfillment of their own needs for respect relieved them of the compulsion to manifest H and S toward their son; instead, he received the respect he too so urgently needed.

Gary was put on methadone, a drug that substantially diminishes an addict's craving for heroin. Although in itself addictive, it does not produce heroin's harmful effects; indeed, it has been helpful in weaning addicts from it and in eliciting their cooperation in psychotherapy. As Gary improved, so did his job motivation and performance. At the clinic, the methadone dosage was gradually reduced, and within a year Gary was able to get along without it.

While this may be considered a successful treatment of heroin addiction, the unfortunate truth is that the large majority of addicts are not cured. Very few addicts' parents have access to the techniques that Gary's parents learned. Since the pamphlets on drugs fail to provide this vital information, addicts' parents and spouses continue the same emotional mishandling that caused the addiction in the first place.

Most of us agree on the importance of providing jobs and recreational facilities for young people, and getting them involved in useful community activities. However, heroin addicts who are provided with interesting, well-paying jobs, new cars, wardrobes, and every social advantage show that they rarely overcome their addiction unless the emotional factors that caused it are corrected.

I do not know of any program of drug addiction treatment that employs the method of overcoming H described here, but my own experience with addicts has convinced me that the craving for drugs decreases as their H decreases. For this reason, it is of the greatest help to enlist the cooperation of the parents, as in Gary's case. (The family physician should also be brought into the case, since he is likely to have more knowledge of family relationships than anyone else.) Emotional help can also be provided by ex-addicts living with addicts in a community setting, and indeed the Synanon organization has helped many addicts by their own methods of restoring the addicts' self-respect.

12.
For Young People With Parent Problems

Most of us, young and old, agree on the need for progress through change, so that the underprivileged may be helped, racial tensions reduced, the public schools and universities reformed, and faulty parental attitudes changed. It is a tribute to the idealism and intellectual sharpness of a sizable segment of modern youth that they have striven conscientiously to bring about such changes. Many of us have been impressed with your high-minded principles and accomplishments. Yet for every one of us won over, ten have turned against you. Why?

The reason is that you have too often employed the same mistaken emotional attitudes as your parents and many other members of the Establishment.

A typical example of this was seen in the Democratic Convention of 1968. Thousands of youngsters, dedicated to the cause of ending the war in Southeast Asia, came to Chicago to persuade the Democratic delegates and the public of the worthiness of their cause. However, the forthright assertion of their views was accompanied by so much holier-than-thou arrogance and hostility that they turned most of the delegates and the public against them. The sneering contempt, the vulgar ridicule, and the violence had the specific effect of "turning off" the very people that they had wanted to "turn on."

In order to win anyone over to your viewpoint, you must first cleanse yourself of antagonizing attitudes.

HOW TO PERSUADE YOUR PARENTS

Suppose you want to persuade your parents to let you move out of the house into your own apartment. They've been against it, not because they can't afford to help you with the rent on the apartment, but because they're afraid you'll get into trouble. Insisting that they're wrong will cause them to view your request adversely. Any H and S that accompany your opinion will evoke their opposition. Even if your opinion is presented properly, your parents won't go along with you if these self-defeating attitudes have been manifested too often in previous discussions. To make matters worse, they may be in a state of irritability from their own frustrations. You can hardly expect your father to agree to your proposal after a month of business reverses that have lowered his self-esteem.

Persuasion requires know-how, just as operating a motor- cycle does. I recall a college senior who replied that it would take a loaded gun to persuade his parents. If you think about it, you'll realize that by resorting to intimidation to get your way, you don't end up winning at all. Although you condemn your parents for forcing their way on you, you'd now be doing the same thing to them. You may get the particular item you seek, but not the under- standing, affection, and respect so vital to you above and beyond that.

On the other hand, if you win them over by means of genuinely respectful feelings, they'll be easier to persuade on future issues. This is because you've earned their Receptivity—the key to persuasion. A mind that is unlocked by this key is the most suscepti- ble of all to your ideas and projects. Your parents' approval of any proposal you make depends primarily on their approval of *you*. This, in turn, depends entirely on your sincere approval of *them*. Perhaps you're annoyed with their belittling and moralizing attitudes. They came by these attitudes as innocently and naturally as you did. If you've read the previous chapters, then you already know that the I → H + S Reaction operates in all of us. With this understand- ing, you'll find a new sympathy for your parents rather than the former H.

Now, back to that apartment you want. Sure, they're going to be afraid that you'll be having marijuana parties and be vulnerable to other temptations there; that's why they're opposed to it. Never- theless, your changed feelings will weigh heavily in persuading them. The following example of how parents can be persuaded is based on the application of the knowledge of how to raise their self-esteem Respect Level. It can work only when you have first cleared your feelings of hostility, as described above.

Dad: *What do you need an apartment for? Girls living alone aren't safe these days.*

Instead of contradicting him by telling him that it's perfectly safe to live alone, say something that props up his Respect Level: "*A person has to be careful with all that crime going on.*"

Mother: *I'd worry if you were in an apartment by yourself.*
You: *Gee, Mom, I should have thought of that.*
Dad: *Don't we always have most of the things you need right here at*
home?

You: *"Well, I admit it's been a swell place to live."*

Everything that you've said is true. Best of all, by validating
your parents' opinions, you've raised their Respect Levels. Even
though they don't agree to the apartment *at the moment*, be patient
and use the same approach on all issues. For example, if your father
ridicules your boyfriend by saying "Who was that orangutan you
went out with last night?" don't reply "Why do you have to refer to
my boyfriend as an orangutan?" That would only contradict him
and lead to some jeering answer such as "Well if he's not, what are
those hairy bushes on his jaws?" Use the subject to raise his Respect
Level: "Gosh, with all that hair, I guess he could be mistaken for
some kind of an ape."

Don't be afraid to give the folks an abundance of this kind of
tonic. You'll find a few months of it will make them much more
receptive to your views and requests.

So many young people feel that they are cast adrift in a society
that offers them little hope of successful living. They complain
that the older generation doesn't care about them. True, many
adults are so obsessed with their own problems that they become
quite oblivious to the problems of youth, and conforming to this
description expressed by a college senior in 1969: "Everybody
hasn't read the books we've read. They earn $8,000 a year and have
their home, their car, and their job, and they don't really care about
anything else."

Yet most youngsters can learn how to understand their
fellowmen and, thereby, like and respect them. It's clear that the
$8,000-a-year man wasn't the only one who didn't care. The senior
who made the accusation should have included himself, since his
statement implied inferiority of the workingman and the superiority
of the student class. You know that the better-than-thou attitude can
never elicit an appreciative and caring response. But when young
people learn how the attitudes and emotions of the parent generation
were formed, they can attain the understanding that is the indispensable basis of caring.

The workingman has seen a great deal of arrogance, know-
it-all, holier-than-thou, disdainful, and defiant attitudes perpetrated
against the institutions he cherishes. As a result of the marches of the
fifties and sixties, he has come to feel that he is being blamed in a
contemptuous manner by a group whose message is "We're more
moral than you." Therefore, when a march is staged now, the first

thing that pops up in his mind is, "What am I being put down for now?" His reaction to this is contempt for the protesters and, consequently, a contrary response.

How can protesters win the public over to their cause? Concerned young people must learn not to wait for things to come to them. With the right kind of digging, they can unearth the gold themselves. The fact is that the potential for caring exists in all of us. It only requires a knowledge of emotional reactions to bring it out.

HOW TO GET PEOPLE TO CARE

You get people to care for you simply by caring for them. Understanding that no one is to blame for the mechanisms that shaped his or her attitudes and feelings should generate warm, compassionate, and respectful feelings in any student toward the so-called Establishment. These feelings are as transmissible as hostile feelings, but have a diametrically opposite effect. It is only by showing respect for the other person's opinions that you can earn *his* respect for yours.

In order to prevent negative results, protests must not be accompanied by antagonizing attitudes. A practical method is to formulate the protest in writing and try to get as many signatures as possible—from fellow students, faculty, administration, parents, relatives, and friends. In this way, the protest is not being forced on the public in the form of a traffic-disrupting, window-breaking march. The public responds to intimidation as antagonistically as you do. Approach groups respectfully and request the opportunity to present your views. In this way your representatives can speak at Chamber of Commerce meetings, women's clubs, churches, synagogues, union halls, universities, and many other organizations.

To win any group's respect, your most valuable asset is your own respect for the group. Health, happiness, and social progress are attainable only by nourishing your fellowman's self-respect. You are his chief source of this vital need. You can help your audience feel respected by finding ways to reflect credit on them. Admit in all humility your own past mistakes. Help them understand that you're not arrogant and defiant. (An untidy appearance is interpreted as a sign of disrespect.) This is the best way of acquiring their respect and affection.

Having earned this response, you can change arrogant, bigoted, and selfish attitudes to more humble, unbiased, unselfish ones. Flood the newspapers and magazines with statements of your views. Write to our elected representatives. Ask for time on radio and TV. While you'll be refused some forums, you'll find others. One student who felt that the Establishment didn't care had his views published in *The New York Times*. Freeing yourself of H and S not only increases your self-respect and self-confidence—it will also reduce hostility in others and motivate them to work constructively with you to improve our society.

13.
The Physical Effects of H: Insomnia, Fatigue, Headache, and Ulcer

Hostility exacts a terrible price emotionally and physically. Consider the plight of air traffic controllers—those men in the airport towers responsible for keeping many planes at a time on their correct courses. They have an unusually high rate of stomach and duodenal ulcers, coronary heart attacks, and other stress-related illnesses. Dr. Sidney Cobb of the University of Michigan and Dr. Robert M. Rose of Boston University Medical School recently compared 4,325 air traffic controllers with a matching group of 8,435 second-class workers at the airports. They found that high blood pressure was four times as prevalent in the air traffic controllers. They also show a high incidence of marital conflict, alcoholism, and mental breakdown.

At first glance it would appear that their critical responsibility is the problem. Since the instructions they communicate to the pilots are crucial to air safety, they work under conditions fraught with tension. However, tension alone does not cause men to break down. For example, military commanders, in the thick of war under extreme responsibility, hold up well physically and mentally. The actual factor underlying the production of so much physical and mental illness is something else.

You can well imagine the panic a controller undergoes when he witnesses a near miss between two airliners. Yet, when he reports a recent near miss to a superior, he may be told that the public mustn't be frightened. Since pilots are charged with such great responsibility, the air controllers are under strict orders to show them the greatest deference in the course of their communications. Thus, while the pilots are under no restriction against expressing their anger, the controllers must, in order to avoid reprimand, swallow their angry feelings. Small wonder that this repeated daily suppression of H might create a thirst for relief by alcohol. You can also understand why a man returning home after such a day's work would be so charged with H that he would be likely to take it out on his wife and children. After all, there are no F.A.A. (Federal Aviation Authority) rules prohibiting the display of emotion at home.

The tragedy of this needless exposure to disease is compounded by the increased danger to the flying public. A board of inquiry blamed Britain's worst air disaster—a crash occurring on June 18, 1972, and killing all 118 persons on board—on the pilot, who had suffered a heart attack just before the crash. The report stated: "The heart attack stemmed from a heated argument in the airline's crew room just before the flight. It is clear that he was very angry indeed. It is likely that the blood vessels of the heart had already been weakened by the stress from previous bouts of hostility."

How many more such disasters must occur before flight crews, air controllers, and supervisory personnel are given training in how to manage H—not only so that airplane accidents may be prevented, but so that the mental and physical health of air personnel may be preserved.

THE TRANQUILIZER TRAP

A considerable number of psychiatrists maintain that the nervous patient should be given tranquilizers. This practice is based on the erroneous theory that if the patient feels less anxious, he will be more inclined to discuss his problems. Actually, it's the other way around: Diminution of symptoms usually prompts patients to avoid discussing their critical personal problems with a psychotherapist or any other doctor. Any doctor or dentist will tell you that patients seek him out and cooperate most when they're suffering. When anxiety, depression, or physical symptoms such as headache, spasm, or fatigue actually are relieved by a tranquilizing drug, the personal problems at the root of the symptoms remain and continue to generate H and anxiety. Since these emotions are suppressed, the patient is a prime candidate for heart attack, high blood pressure, stroke, stomach ulcer, diabetes, and virus illness. Because of his lowered resistance to disease, he may, according to reputable researchers, be more susceptible to cancer than the person who faces and resolves his emotional problems.

The most effective way to get the patient to face his problems lies within the doctor himself. Let me quote from an editorial in the

January 15, 1975, issue of *Modern Medicine,* in which its editor, Dr. Irvine H. Page, an eminent heart specialist and one of the most respected of American medical leaders, wrote: "Most important of all, physicians are almost constantly faced with dealing with patients' emotional problems. If they are not, then there is something missing in their ministrations. It is the necessity for decency, warmth, common sense and equanimity, combined with knowledge, that make medicine . . . highly demanding of emotional energy and satisfying. . . . I would therefore suggest to our health professionals that they take a more careful and sympathetic look at the subject of their well-meant intentions before they pre- or proscribe."

Dr. Page recognizes that many patients insist on a prescription before they leave the doctor's office. In some of these cases, the doctor may be justified in prescribing a tranquilizer, lest the patient dispense with his services. For example, consider the difficult position of the doctor confronted with an insomniac's plea for relief. Unless he prescribes a drug, in most cases the patient will become angry, regard him as incompetent, and seek out another doctor; and he'll have no trouble finding one who will comply with his demand for medication.

INSOMNIA

What's wrong with the common practice of prescribing drugs for sleep? Let's assume that the doctor has taken a history and performed a careful physical examination without uncovering any sign of disease. Not infrequently, he tells the insomniac, "Stop worrying, there's nothing wrong with you. Take one of these pills at bedtime and you'll be able to sleep." This advice is much like that given in an October 10, 1975, Associated Press article advising insomniacs to "banish the day's cares and worries from your mind and think of something pleasant."

The flaw in this advice is that it actually aggravates sleeplessness, since most insomnia is caused by anxiety and the suppression of H. Whether or not a drug is prescribed, the patient should be told that it cannot remove his anxiety and H, which will continue to exert their sleep-inhibiting and disease-producing effects. While doctors are vigilant in warning against the most rare harmful side effects of prescribed drugs, they rarely mention that tranquilizers and sleep medications may increase the patient's vulnerability to diseases since the suppressed H is ignored.

The anxiety associated with quizzes and exams is often so

intense that it interferes with sleep. As the burden of studies increases, students with low Respect Levels are liable to self-doubt and overanxiety. The increase in I results in H toward teachers as well as classmates. This is especially so in the case of students who have already been subjected to arbitrary parents. In the last two decades, many of these students have resorted to marijuana and other drugs to combat insomnia. This expedient can result in a lifelong habit of using a drug or alcohol for sleep. The trap in this practice is that the drug user is conditioned to avoid facing the H and anxiety underlying his problems.

The Old Brain interprets any more than a small presence of H as involvement with an enemy. Therefore, it tries to protect you by generating fear. Provided you're resolved to deal with the object of your hostility, the fear is bearable. But when, instead, you give in or try some other escape route (such as physical exercise, busying yourself with a hobby, going on a vacation, thinking positively, or following some ritual such as repeating your own special mantra) whenever your brain tries to remind you of your problem, then the H and anxiety associated with the problem are suppressed. A morbid uneasiness soon asserts itself, since anyone who has hidden his problems from himself has maneuvered himself into the position of fighting an enemy he can't see. Such a patient should be warned that unless he takes the treatment needed actually to free himself from these emotions, he is headed for increasing emotional disturbance and physical disease.

Most insomniacs have over a considerable period of time been suppressing H toward a close associate: marital partner, another family member, boss, or co-worker. Since the H remains unresolved, the brain continues to generate anxiety. It is because the anxiety is constantly present at an abnormally high level that sleep becomes so difficult.

A CASE OF INSOMNIA

When Lil, a waitress who worked in a restaurant near my office, waited on me it was obvious that she was in a state of extreme despondency. When I asked what was wrong, she responded by bursting into tears. I suggested that she come by my office later.

She then told me that she had put up $2500 bail for a recently acquired boyfriend, and he had promptly skipped town. The humiliation of having been used by a man she thought was in love with her was accompanied by intense hatred. She felt so distressed that she was determined to "forget it." But instead of feeling better, she became more tense and jittery, dropped dishes at work, became despondent and unable to sleep.

I explained that the mind can't rid itself of feelings of humiliation and hostility simply by ignoring them. It was these feelings that were the cause of her anxiety, depression, lack of coordination on her job, and inability to sleep. She had felt inferior for years because she seldom had any dates and had remained single. Such extreme I invariably leads to a belief in the reality of the wish that is so desperately desired. This was why she had responded with the Mirage of "romance at last" when the bail jumper courted her; because of this Mirage she put up $2500 for a man she hardly knew. The more she condemned herself for her gullibility, the more hatred she felt for the man who had deceived her. She was now blaming the boyfriend when in fact the actual culprit was her Mirage.

"But why shouldn't I blame that crook?" she asked. Prior to swindling her, he had been apprehended for burglary. But a person commits such crimes only when his I becomes so extreme that it produces a Mirage that promises the realization of his wants. He's the hapless victim of a mental phenomenon that occurs in all human beings under such circumstances.

Lil's understanding of why neither she nor her boyfriend was to blame gave her some relief from her oppressive feelings. But I hastened to caution her that H that has reached such a high level can't be permanently relieved by a single flush of understanding. Unless one repeats "thinking through" procedures at least once a day for about a week, much of the H returns. This should be done even if there is no further consciousness of blame, inasmuch as a considerable amount is still suppressed. Usually, after the first week, it is only necessary to carry out the "thinking through" every other day.

As a result of following these instructions faithfully, Lil recovered her ability to sleep, and her good spirits—although, sad to relate, not her $2500.

Mrs. S., a forty-one-year-old housewife, had been an insomniac for five years. She was also extremely depressed and withdrawn. Her anxiety was so great that she feared contacts with everyone except her husband, parents, and two children.

In the early years of marriage, her angry rebuttals to her husband's complaints and accusations had proved unavailing. He rarely gave in, so she felt defeated after every argument. Gradually she perceived that she could turn the tables by telling him that she had lost her desire for sex. The more infuriated this made him, the more satisfaction she derived.

Many couples proudly proclaim that, no matter how much bitterness builds up in their day, they always kiss and tell each other

"I love you" at bedtime. This has no more remedial value than trying to repair a motor by polishing the exterior of the car. Since the unresolved differences aren't resolved, they continue to generate H and anxiety. Nevertheless, a woman who finds that she can't sleep because of a problem with her husband shouldn't insist on discussing it at bedtime when he is fatigued and wants to get to sleep.

Mrs. S. also found that she could inflict additional hurt by frequent complaints of illness. She woke her husband up at all hours of the night to inform him that she couldn't sleep because of gas pains or some other symptom. Of course she shouldn't have done this, since preventing him from getting his sleep only antagonized him and thus made him more unreceptive.

When he got up in the morning she regaled him with a recitation of symptoms: "Head's splitting, dizzy, pain in my liver, can't make it through the day." This evoked his medical advice, which she would immediately contradict. He would leave for work angry and disgusted, only to have her phone to let him know that all the symptoms were worse. When he returned from work, he was greeted with uncared-for children, a messy house, and a rehash of his wife's complaints.

Any doctor will tell you that the suffering of the husband in such cases equals or surpasses that of his sick wife. After years of enjoying what had appeared to be the upper hand, Mrs. S.'s husband was confronted by a counteroffensive which seemed utterly to defeat him. After a year of such round-the-clock punishment, he acquired a girl friend. What's more, he informed his wife so that she would realize that she had only herself to blame for this turn of events. Soon Mrs. S. noted a return of her sexual desire, only to have him say that her repeated refusals had killed his affection for her.

This rejection aggravated her symptoms. She developed pain in the chest and feared that she was going to have a fatal heart attack. Even though there was an unconsciously directed purpose underlying her symptoms, she wasn't faking them. Her abandonment of angry argument in favor of frigidity and harping on symptoms had resulted in an increasing suppression of H, which had finally reached a concentration high enough to produce physical symptoms as well as severe anxiety and depression.

After six interviews in which she perceived my genuine sympathy for her distress and received credit for many of her opinions, she became receptive to my explanation of why she had become so sick: She was inflicting her own veiled brand of hostility and domination on her husband, while complaining of his more open use of the same tactics. As she learned that she and her husband were the victims of insidious emotional forces, (I → H and vying for S) her H dwindled. She was encouraged to acknowledge his criticism, give him credit for his opinions, and desist from her former interruptions (mostly prefaced by "But"). Since her feelings were now those of sympathy and appreciation, her changed behavior proved effective. (Fortunately, he was not in love with the other woman; he had only taken up with her to punish his wife.) The reduction in H and anxiety was attended by a gradual easing of her symptoms, and for the first time Mrs. S. found happiness with her husband.

I'm aware that it takes less than a minute to prescribe a pill, while it takes many hours to employ the Anti-H therapy. But the expense of a patient's individual visits to a therapist can be considerably reduced by referral to a group therapy class, just as other patients are referred for group instruction in physical fitness and nutrition.

Although suppressed H is the usual cause of persistent insomnia, other factors may be involved. Some individuals appear to be light sleepers from birth. Others are sensitive to coffee and tea. (Some have learned to use sleep as an escape from their worries; thus, despite large concentrations of H and anxiety, they can sleep for long hours.) Therefore every patient with chronic insomnia should have a thorough medical investigation.

If anxiety-producing problems are keeping you from falling asleep, make it a practice to deal with them. It's unhealthy to go to bed with H eating at you. Why allow it to remain in your brain when you can learn to remove it? Remember that nobody's to blame, and that includes yourself and whomever you're feeling hostile toward at bedtime. It isn't always necessary to think through your problems before falling asleep. But you should at least apply Anti-H and assure yourself that you *will deal* with them at a convenient time the next day.

FATIGUE

Most fatigue is also caused by a combination of H and anxiety. These two emotions are generally found together, although in varying degrees. Fatigue is much greater when H is suppressed. In such cases a person often wakes up fatigued after a night's sleep. When you come home from work exhausted, the most likely cause is the H and anxiety generated by the day's aggravations. When fatigue persists, it is imperative to consult your doctor. If he rules out any organic basis for the fatigue, apply Anti-H. Getting rid of H consistently relieves any physical fatigue not caused by organic disease. Suppressed H is also a frequent significant causative factor in such physical symptoms as nausea, dizziness, pain, and headache (including migraine), and in diseases such as coronary heart disease, high blood pressure, stroke, asthma, ulcer of the stomach and duodenum, ulcerative colitis, gall bladder disease, diabetes, arthritis, skin diseases such as giant hives and eczema, pain in any part of the body, infections—including virus diseases—and frequent colds and sore throats. When a cold, case of "flu," or other infectious illness lasts longer than usual, you should check yourself for suppressed H, in addition to consulting your doctor.

SUPPRESSED H AND HEADACHE

It is estimated that about ten million patients a year seek medical help for persistent headaches. Although no known drugs can cure chronic headache, most headache patients are treated by drugs alone. Recently, the president of the American Association for the Study of Headache stated: "Too often, headache patients are treated symptomatically—with pain-killers for the headache, but with no attempt to find the underlying cause. One of the biggest problems with the patients referred to our headache clinic—we get about two thousand new ones a year—is that many of them have become drug abusers, even drug addicts. They've been treated for so many years with a variety of drugs for their symptoms." While these drugs may provide some relief, the headache nearly always recurs since nothing has been done about its underlying cause.

Although our knowledge of migraine is far from complete, I found that 90 percent of a group of migraine patients I treated at Johns Hopkins Hospital were relieved of their excruciating headaches by learning to rid themselves of H; headaches recurred only when a patient failed to continue applying Anti-H. (All cases were treated under the direction of internists whose specialized knowledge of migraine was indispensable in the medical management.) Most of the chronic headache patients I have investigated and treated in the past thirty years were habitual H suppressors. When the patient learns how to keep himself free of H, the headaches disappear or at least greatly diminish in most cases.

A Typical Case of Headache
Ann, a thirty-year-old housewife, had been suffering from migraine headaches for ten years. The medication that had initially helped no longer gave her any relief. The first thing I noticed about this lady was that she went out of her way to be congenial and compliant. In our talk, her head nodded agreement and she'd murmur "Uh-huh"

even before she knew what I was going to say. She couldn't understand why she had been sent to a psychiatrist: "I really don't have any problems, I'm married to a fine man, and I'd be happy if it weren't for these darn headaches."

Unless they are engaged in espionage, shoot-outs, or embezzling, most persons feel that their problems are insignificant. However, the chronic headache victim almost always does have very serious *personal* problems, and Ann was no exception. Her problems were so upsetting that she had been telling herself they were really trivial as a way of avoiding the overwhelming anxiety of facing them. Having been repeatedly punished since childhood for speaking up when criticized, Ann had become conditioned to keep her complaints to herself. She acknowledged that her feelings were often hurt by her mother, but she added, "It's only over the most trivial things."

The incidents that she referred to as trivial were actually of crucial emotional import, since they lowered her self-respect. One of the "trivial" things she alluded to was her mother criticizing her for being too lenient with her eight-year-old son. Although she tried to tell her mother that she wasn't spoiling the boy, the mother persisted with her criticism. Reluctantly, Ann admitted that her mother found fault with just about everything she did. Ann suffered even more from her mother's blame because she had always wanted her approval and affection. Ann's habitual suppression of H was the principal cause of her headaches. No matter how angry she felt at her mother, Ann didn't dare express this feeling. Instead, she would reply to her mother's every criticism with an alibi.

Ann was aghast when she found out that her hostility was perfectly apparent and was constantly prodding her mother into *more* criticism. It wasn't the various items her mother had been criticizing her about that were causing the H. The heart of the matter was that she and her mother were unwittingly depriving each other of respect.

Of course two individuals will often react differently to the same emotional stimulus. However, this is the case only if each has been subjected to different emotional *backgrounds*. Where backgrounds are alike, the response will be similar. Ann's mother had been up against martyred, know-it-all, and blaming attitudes from her own mother. She habitually voiced her complaints to Ann's father. He regularly avoided any discussion of personal problems by simply agreeing with his wife. The frustration of living with such a husband is maddening. The poor man paid the price of suppressing his H by a premature exit from this world.

In therapy Ann learned that the carping criticisms and martyred attitudes of her mother didn't reflect any discredit whatsoever on Ann. Such attitudes are an invariable reaction to the individual's low concept of his own worth. When Ann learned this, she was able to understand that her mother's criticisms, which she had always interpreted as demeaning, actually didn't reflect on her at all and she no longer reacted to them with I → H. Instead of alibiing when her mother accused her of being too lenient with the boy, she would reply, "Maybe I *have* been too easy with him." When her mother blamed her for allowing him too much time for watching TV and not enough for his homework, she asked, "What do you think would be a good balance?" These responses gradually elevated her mother's esteem to a healthier level. Consequently, her criticisms decreased and she began showing genuine approval of Ann.

Ann's habitual suppression of hostility had caused similar problems with her husband and son. Now she applied her knowledge to them. In addition, her husband was invited to accompany Ann to her therapy sessions, which facilitated his cooperation. As Ann's H decreased, so did her headaches.

Ann's case is typical in that her suppressed H was felt toward close associates. The hostility toward someone with whom you're not closely associated does not cause headache.

Able investigators have carried out a tremendous amount of research attempting to correlate individuals' personalities with their diseases. It is this causal connection between personality and disease which prompted William Osler, the renowned head of Johns Hopkins Hospital, to say in the early part of this century, "It is more important to know what sort of patient has a disease than what sort of disease a patient has." I do not believe that we can reliably *predict* that an individual with a certain personality type is more likely to come down with some specific disease. But the individual who regularly suppresses H has a much greater chance of being afflicted with serious illness of any kind than the nonsuppressor.

Medical science can't make any exact correlation between your personality and a specific kind of disease. From the standpoint of staying well it really doesn't matter, since you'll have a better chance to escape any psychosomatic disease by regularly practicing Anti-H.

ULCER

Ulcers constitute one of the serious diseases in which suppressed H is a significant factor. The question is often asked, "Why treat the patient's head when the ulcer is in his stomach or small intestine?" (The great majority of ulcers are not in the stomach, but actually located in the upper part of the small intestine, known as the duodenum.) You can tell that your stomach is reacting to emotion if you experience what feels like butterflies or a knot in it. That the knot really exists was illustrated in an experiment carried out by an X ray professor who wanted to demonstrate to his students how the stomach reacts to suppressed H. For this purpose he had a dispensary patient stand in front of a fluoroscope. The patient obediently remained rigid in the position in which he had been placed by the professor. In order to get him into a state of suppressed H, the professor yelled, "Can't you stay in the position I told you to, you idiot?"

Of course, this verbal abuse was only done for the purpose of medical education. But the patient was in so much awe of the white-coated professor that he could not come out with the anger he felt. Before the students' eyes, the stomach knotted and the patient said that he felt a knot in his stomach.

A Typical Case of Stomach Ulcer (Often Referred to as Peptic Ulcer)
John was referred for psychiatric treatment of an ulcer. He was a handsome, personable man of thirty-seven who appeared to be on his way up the executive ladder. His anxiety had grown with his responsibilities at work, showing up especially just prior to and during staff conferences. His duodenal ulcer had developed after two years of treatment with a variety of tranquilizers. During those two years John had resisted his doctor's advice to see a psychiatrist, and consented to do so only when the anxiety and stomach pain had become intolerable.

He insisted that he was very happy with his wife and two children, a seven-year-old boy and a four-year-old girl. From the way John told his story you would have thought that he really was a happy, successful person, devoid of personal problems. Beneath this facade he was constantly fearful of disapproval from his wife, boss, and other business associates. Although the ulcer patient typically strives to give the appearance of outward calm and relaxation, he is actually often in a state of intense anxiety, based on his fear that he is not sufficiently appreciated. Frequently, he was raised by parents who stressed that he was expected to out-achieve others and blamed him for anything less than outstanding achievement. The result of this conditioning is that such a person grows up fearing that he'll be blamed unless he does things to perfection, and is thus in a constant fear that he is not performing well, despite long hours of work. Apprehensive that his anxiety will expose him as an insecure, weak, nervous person, he strives to conceal it under a facade of outward calm, and his fear of censure is so great that he bends over backwards to pass himself off as a friendly, likeable person.

As you know, the more an individual fears that he is insufficiently appreciated, the more H and S he develops. The trouble is that his H isn't lessened one iota by an outward show of friendliness; it is merely suppressed. Since H signifies the threat of danger to the individual, an equivalent amount of anxiety is generated. As the H and anxiety increase, they exert pressure on the brain center, which, through its nerve connections, regulates stomach functions. The resulting overstimulation causes spasm of the stomach and duodenal wall and oversecretion of hydrochloric acid, leading to erosion and ulcer of the stomach or duodenum.

John's pattern of concealing H was formed in his childhood. His mother was a domineering woman who cowed his father into acquiescing to her control of family matters. The father suppressed his anger toward his wife, but he had no fear of letting it out on John. Although the boy did well in school, his father would scold him for not doing better. The expression of opinions contrary to those of his parents was met with stern disapproval and punishment. Since any display of anger on his part would not be tolerated, John learned early in childhood to keep his opinions and angry feelings to himself.

Having been deprived of approval, he craved it all the more. In order to get it he strove to be friendly and compliant and would smile on the slightest pretext. Since he actually believed that he was incompetent and resentful, he regarded himself as a fraud. Consequently, he became increasingly fearful of being unmasked. Because of his great fear of disapproval, John would give in to his wife rather than argue with her. But his wife perceived that although she was getting her way, she wasn't getting John's sincere approval. Instead, she sensed his underlying hostile opposition and reacted to it with outbursts of rage. Since John was totally unaware that his H was transmitting, he resented his wife's outbursts all the more. His constant suppression of H led to an ever-increasing concentration of it, which was frequently expressed toward his children, especially John—just as his father had done to him.

John complained bitterly that his wife and fellow workers didn't appreciate his effort to build up their egos. "I praise my wife's cooking, tell her how attractive her new hairdo is, and agree with her complaints about the kids. But still she contradicts my opinions and doesn't give me credit for what I do."

John didn't take into account that insincere praise is soon recognized for what it is. For many years he had relied on his display of smiling friendliness, profusion of compliments, and ready agreeableness to convince people that he felt very well disposed toward them. The last thing such a person wants to admit is that he is feeling resentful. This is the principal reason that he often reacts with H when advised that he should learn the method of overcoming H.

The source of John's H was his own fear of inadequacy. He learned that his greatest mistake was in blaming others when his real goal had been to attain their respect.

John's next step was to learn why he *wasn't* inferior. He had simply been deprived of the emotional nourishment every child requires for the development of a healthy concept of self-worth. Any child subjected, as he had been, to the domineering of a frustrated mother and the belittling of an angry father grows up with an inferior self-image. Recognizing that his own craving for approval had blinded him to the fact that his family and fellow workers had the same needs helped relieve him of H toward them. His smile, compliance, and appreciation of his family and co-workers became more genuine. His self-respect increased as he realized how much his understanding and approval were needed by his wife and children.

Since he now had an honest belief in his self-worth and in what he was doing, he no longer conceived of himself as a fraud, and felt at ease at conferences where he had formerly experienced panic. As he ceased transmitting H toward others, their H gradually waned and was replaced with the respect and warmth he had craved for so long. As the result of the sharp drop in H and anxiety, his ulcer healed.

No matter how expertly the doctor treats stomach (or duodenal) ulcers, he must to a large extent depend on the patient's willingness to face and resolve his suppressed H.

"Psychosomatic" Illnesses

Stomach specialists maintain that most abdominal ailments result from emotional factors; in fact, no matter what the physical illness under investigation, the doctor should evaluate the patient's emotional condition. Unfortunately, many patients resent a doctor's inquiries into their personal lives. Very often, these investigative efforts result in the loss of the patient to another doctor who makes no attempt to explore the patient's emotional state. Some patients would rather undergo surgery than be told that their illness is caused by their emotions.

A psychosomatic disease is one in which one of the significant causative factors is emotional. Almost always the emotional factor is suppressed H and the accompanying anxiety. The significance of this factor was recognized even in ancient times. In 500 B.C. Socrates stated, "The barbaric Thracians knew that the body could not be cured without the mind." And Hippocrates, the Father of Medicine, said, "In order to cure the body, it is necessary to have a knowledge of the whole of things." But despite the wealth of medical research since World War II supporting the psychosomatic concept, it is sometimes ignored in medical practice. Instead of helping the patient understand his emotional conflicts some doctors merely prescribe a tranquilizer.

THE HYPOCHONDRIAC

One reason for ignoring the psychiatric component of illness is to avoid antagonizing the patient. Many patients become indignant with a doctor for implying that the origin of their symptoms is emotional, because they think it means that they are not really sick. Such patients may have received very little sympathy from their family and friends, who may have dismissed them as hypochondriacs. Not infrequently even a doctor becomes so exasperated at a patient's insistence that he has some serious organic disease that he angrily tells him, "I've examined you thoroughly. All the laboratory studies are negative. There's nothing wrong with you. It's all in your head." But the symptoms the patient is complaining of do really exist and do constitute genuine physical illness.

It is only natural, when you are suffering, to become angry at someone who doubts that your suffering is real. The superior and belittling manner in which a husband says, "There's nothing wrong with you; you're just imagining it" only increases a wife's resentment. Since her illness is largely based on H, such H-producing behavior on the part of the husband only aggravates her symptoms. But once a patient's family understand that hypochondriasis and psychosomatic illness are just as real and insidious as physical illness, they feel a genuine sympathy for these patients. The psychosomatic patient and the hypochondriac respond appreciatively when we acknowledge the genuineness of their symptoms.

Are You Being Aggravated By a Hypochondriac?

Peg, a 29-year-old secretary, said that she had moved out of her parents' home because she had become fed up with her mother's constant complaints of illness.

"Really, I don't think there's a blessed thing wrong with her, but she's always complaining. Whether I visit or phone her it's either an aching back, heart pains, dizziness, stomachache, or exhaustion. The way she complains makes me feel that she's blaming me for her ailments. But what can I do for her when all the doctors she's seen say that she's in excellent health?"

Peg said that she had always loved her mother. "I couldn't stand my father because he yelled at Mother and me so much. I sympathized with her for having to put up with Dad's temper. Mother never yelled at me."

The underlying cause of hypochondriasis is a low Respect

Level. After thirty years of marriage with a man who habitually vented his wrath on her, Peg's mother's self-respect had reached a precarious low. Her only source of love had been from Peg. When Peg became involved in social life at college, her mother missed the affection and appreciation she had gotten from Peg. Her loneliness drove her to become increasingly possessive of Peg, causing Peg to avoid her mother in favor of her college chums.

It was only after Peg resisted her possessiveness that her mother began complaining of bodily ailments. The more she complained the more resentful Peg became. Although Peg expressed sympathy, her mother could feel the resentment that Peg tried to conceal. Of course, the transmission of Peg's H made her mother feel increasingly inferior. This increased her need to exonerate herself from blame by conceiving that she was a sick person and therefore deserving the sympathy of her daughter.

Peg was astonished at this interpretation of her mother's complaints. It was only with great reluctance that she admitted feeling resentful to her. When she learned that hidden resentment is soon perceived, she could understand how she had been aggravating her mother's hypochondriasis by her steady stream of H. The realization that she had been blaming her mother for a condition that she herself had unwittingly helped bring about evoked a feeling of understanding and genuine sympathy for her mother.

Hypochondriacs cling to their symptoms with extreme tenacity and Peg's mother was no exception. However, with real sympathy instead of the former phony variety from Peg, the mother's need to be cared about by her daughter was fulfilled. There was no longer any necessity for illness as a device to get sympathy. The result was not only a loving relationship, uncontaminated by the former silent H, but a gradual decrease in the hypochondriacal symptoms.

PAIN CAUSED BY SUPPRESSED H

A sixty-eight-year-old woman was in the hospital for investigation of agonizing pain that she felt deep within her body, as well as on the surface. The pain often awakened her at night. For six years prior to this hospitalization she had been treated by many doctors, to no avail. Even strong pain-killing drugs were ineffectual in relieving her suffering. Detailed physical examination, X rays, and other laboratory tests failed to uncover any physical basis for her pain. In fact, her physical condition was found to be excellent. She was depressed, but how could she feel cheerful with such severe symptoms?

When I first interviewed her, she was convinced that her pain was caused by some organic lesion. This was only to be expected since, for six years, doctors had been searching her body for signs of organic disease. Yet her own daughter-in-law had told her in a disparaging tone that she was imagining the pain. When I interviewed her son, he said that his mother was exaggerating her pain to get sympathy.

My repeated observation has been that very few patients who complain of symptoms are faking. The feeling of fatigue, nausea, or pain is real. Suppressed H is a key factor not only in most headaches but, not infrequently, in pain in any part of the body: the eye, face, back, limbs, chest, or abdomen. You might wonder how an emotion can cause pain in the body right down to the toes. The exact mechanism of how pain is distributed is not definitely known. But it is my theory that suppressed H, and the anxiety that accompanies it, causes electrical disturbance in the limbic system (a part of the brain). When the limbic system is subjected to suppressed H for a period of months, it transmits a message to the brain's pain center, causing the individual to feel intense pain in some part of the body. Little is known as to why such pain is felt in one part of the body rather than another. This pain may be as excruciating as the pain of a heart attack or cancer. Such patients don't wish to be ill and have little real knowledge of what has made them ill. Careful examination may show spasm in the stomach, gall bladder, blood vessels, or other parts of the body. Since the patient whose sickness is caused by his emotions *is* genuinely ill, the reality of his symptoms should be explained to his family, who can then respond with genuine sympathy.

There is one key question that I always ask of patients whose symptoms I suspect are being caused by suppressed H: "Has anyone hurt your feelings?" After some reflection, this lady had a vivid recollection that this indeed had happened at her husband's funeral. Out of the blue, her daughter-in-law had said to her, "Don't get any ideas about moving in with us." The pain had first appeared immediately following this remark. For forty-six years this woman's life had centered around her love for her only son and her husband. Since her pain had begun shortly after her husband's death, one physician had advised her to go away on a long vacation. Her son, other relatives, and friends urged her to keep busy so that she would be diverted from her grief. Neither the vacation nor keeping busy had resulted in any relief.

Was her pain due to the loss of her husband? Many psychiatrists theorize that loss of a loved one is the chief emotional factor in causing physical illness. I have found this to be so only where the factor of suppressed H is also present. It is a pity that a mourner is generally bombarded with the wrong kind of advice—he is to forget, keep busy, or take a trip. When he is invited for dinner, his lost one is seldom mentioned. Should the bereaved one give vent to his emotion by suddenly bursting into tears and moaning, "Oh, my poor dear Mary," everyone tries to change the subject. Such attitudes on the part of relatives and friends often influence mourners to suppress their emotions.

Most of us are not eager to be around a weeping, moaning person. Nevertheless, mourners are much worse off when their tears are suppressed. If, in addition, they were suppressors who tried to hide their H toward the deceased, they would be much more likely to develop depression and some type of physical disease. If you want to help a mourner, don't tell him to forget his sorrow; and don't try to restrain him. It's better that he pour it out. Your sympathetic listening will help him get some relief by releasing anxious feelings to a person who cares.

Loss of a loved one seldom causes physical illness except when there has been suppressed H. In this case, there had been very little suppressed H toward the woman's husband, but a great deal toward her son. Although he had always been very close to her, he had become increasingly distant after her husband's demise. Even though he lived nearby, his visits dwindled and finally ceased entirely. She was so ashamed of this that she did not mention it to anyone. At first she endeavored to break the ice by phoning, but she received only short answers and got the impression that her calls were unwelcome. Whenever she asked her son and his wife to come to dinner, there was always some excuse why they couldn't. The only time that she saw them was every other Christmas.

She readily admitted that her feelings had been badly hurt by her son's indifference over the past six years. She had kept these feelings within herself for fear that if she told her son how she felt, he would shut her out of his life completely. When I asked the patient why her son and his wife had taken such a mean attitude, she said, "I just can't understand it. We've always been so close." This poor lady was telling the truth. She had no idea why anyone, much less her only child, should resent her.

Why had her son cut her off? It's a familiar story. I learned from him that his mother had been critical of every girl he had ever dated; he also resented her attitude toward his wife: "I feel that she has never wanted to lose me to any other woman. My wife has been frequently hurt by her domineering, resentful, and critical attitudes."

His wife knew that her husband had been a "mama's boy."

Although she believed that she had finally won him away from his mother, she feared that the old woman might move in and get him in her clutches again.

After their marriage, the wife had fought with her husband over his solicitous attentions toward his mother. Unable to face the arguments, the son adopted a "peace at any price" attitude. The price he paid was the elimination of his mother from his life—"heartless," you might call him, but it was his mother who had made him allergic to arguments with females.

When I asked him why he was so cold to his mother I learned that she had not always been as sweet and agreeable to him as she had portrayed herself. Not infrequently she had made martyred, sarcastic comments about his neglect of her, and belittling references to his wife. He unhesitatingly admitted that he was fed up with her.

In order to rid this lady of her pain, it was essential to rid her of her suppressed H. I felt that this could be facilitated by enlisting the aid of her son and daughter-in-law. Their cooperation was accelerated when I told them that the mother was rapidly dissipating her money on hospitals, doctors, laboratory tests, and cure-seeking trips. I made them aware of the circle of H and its damaging consequences. The wife could see that there was no danger of losing her husband to his mother if she overcame her H to him. While she had blamed her mother-in-law for interfering in her marriage, she had overlooked her own H to her husband.

Getting the mother to acknowledge her H was like pulling teeth. Only when she understood that it was keeping her son away from her did she finally admit its presence. All three were taught Anti-H. The result was that communication was resumed between mother, son, and daughter-in-law, and the woman's pain gradually eased.

Although psychiatrists are medical doctors, most of us don't have the knowledge and expertise in medical diagnosis and treatment possessed by the non-psychiatric physician. For this reason, I never treat a psychosomatic illness unless the medical treatment is directed by a physician.

You'll find that your regular doctor will welcome your efforts to learn how to keep your H and anxiety at a minimum. Without this teamwork, the patient would be the loser. How can you work with him to get rid of an ulcer or other psychosomatic disease and keep it from recurring? The doctor is doing everything that's required medically. The drugs he prescribes should help relieve your pain. But with the large number of cases that he must take care of, he is seldom able to find the time to help you remedy the conflicts in your personal relationships.

Provided that your physician has ruled out any organic basis for your illness, you must check yourself carefully for suppressed H toward your close associates: husband, wife, child, parent, in-law, boss, or fellow workers. Are you trying to hide your resentment toward them? Do you feel that they take advantage of you? Do they hurt your feelings? Are you afraid to express your hostile feelings for fear that you won't be liked? If any of this applies to you, it is vital that you learn how to change these feelings.

You can't do this merely by cutting down on your work, since hard work doesn't cause illness. What does cause sickness is suppression of H and anxiety generated from your manner of relating to those close to you. Anti-H is not only a major factor in the healing of psychosomatic illnesses, but is also of outstanding importance in preventing disease from developing. Along with better health, it provides the key to happy, fulfilling relationships and career success.

14.
High Blood Pressure and Heart Attacks

High blood pressure is a widespread and serious ailment which, if not properly treated, leads to heart disease, stroke, and kidney damage. Medically it is known as hypertension, since it is characterized by tension of the arterial blood vessels. This potentially crippling and sometimes fatal disease is easily overlooked since symptoms are not usually apparent. It is estimated that there are about twenty-three million cases in the United States.

The medical profession has done a great deal to alert the public to a number of factors predisposing one to high blood pressure. In newspapers, magazines, medical journals, and on radio and TV, doctors warn against overweight, too much salt in the diet, and smoking. Yet suppressed H, a significant factor predisposing to high blood pressure, is usually not mentioned.

A Typical Case of High Blood Pressure
You'd never believe that Lex was an angry man, and he wasn't—on the surface. He bent over backwards to be friendly and agree with everyone. He always seemed to be smiling or laughing. Yet the sad truth was that he was inwardly angry a good bit of the time. In his work as a bus driver Lex was constantly exposed to the complaints and irritations of the public. Although he became progressively more bitter, he avoided arguments with irate passengers and motorists. After twelve years of suppressing his anger, Lex began getting violent headaches and one morning had to pull his bus over to the side of the road. He was taken to the company clinic, where it was determined that his blood pressure was dangerously high. The

171

doctor soon found out that Lex had been suffering from extreme nervous tension for years; in addition to prescribing medication to lower his blood pressure, the doctor also referred him for psychiatric treatment, stating that unless the nervous tension was reduced, Lex's life would be threatened by hardening of the arteries, heart attack, stroke, or kidney failure.

His friends felt that he was indeed fortunate in having a lovely wife, a pretty fourteen-year-old daughter, and a well-behaved twelve-year-old son. But Lex wasn't as fortunate as they thought, and neither was his wife.

Early in the marriage she had learned that she would have to face most of their problems without Lex's help. For example, if she asked where they could get money for needed house repairs, he'd reply, "Something is bound to turn up soon." If she complained that she feared their daughter was having sexual relations, he'd say, "Don't worry yourself about it." As a result of his aversion to any discussion of their problems, his wife reacted with increasing outbursts of rage, which Lex simply attributed to her nervous disposition. The truth was that Lex was just as angry and worried as his wife was, but he attempted to rid himself of these feelings by denying their existence.

Fortunately for Lex, his high blood pressure had been discovered before it did him irreparable damage. Since suppressed H may be the most important contributing cause of high blood pressure, the doctor should search for it as assiduously as he does for other causes of disease. Only a very small percentage of high blood pressure is caused by organic conditions such as tumors of the adrenal gland or disease of the arteries leading to the kidneys.

The treatment for Lex was the same as for any other patient whose physical disease seems to have its origin in suppressed H: removal of his H. Most doctors will tell you that there's no difficulty in getting their hypertension patients to take their advice on dietary restrictions. Their greatest problem is in getting them to do something about their stressful close relationships. Typically, in cases of high blood pressure as in other psychosomatic illnesses such as coronary heart disease, ulcer, and migraine, the patient is extremely reluctant to admit his H toward his close associates. To the doctor's question, "Do you have any anger toward your wife?" the usual reply is "No, I'm just hurt" or "Goodness, no, we talk over all our problems." However, after careful investigation, the doctor finds that despite frequent discussion of problems, the patient is either blind to his H or conceals it.

In Lex's case, as in most cases of high blood pressure, the marital partners were involved in a circle of H. Therefore, it was of the greatest importance to involve the wife in the therapy so that she could learn, along with her husband, how to deal with the H between them. Lex's improvement was expedited by his wife's willingness to work jointly with him, and as they learned how to apply Anti-H, his blood pressure gradually dropped and within six months was down to normal.

High Blood Pressure in Blacks

Black Americans have a much greater likelihood of developing many of the diseases in which suppressed H is a significant causative factor. In an editorial in the *Journal of the American Medical Association* Dr. Frank Finnerty called attention to the recent alarming increase in high blood pressure in young blacks. He pointed out that 88 percent of deaths from this disease in Washington, D.C. occurred in blacks. Some authorities have attributed this to heredity. However, blacks in the all-black countries of Africa don't have this high incidence of hypertension. In the United States, social and economic discrimination against blacks have generated a high level of counter hostility. Blacks don't have workers under them to vent their anger on since they're more likely to be in lower-echelon jobs; and few workers are brash enough to blow their tops at higher-ups. Also, since blacks socialize with blacks for the most part, they don't have the opportunity to express their anger directly to the whites they resent. This frustration at not being able to reach the target of their angry complaints is a prime cause of suppressed H. The alarming increase in high blood pressure in young blacks is not surprising, since their H level is higher than that of older blacks.

My observation has been that those blacks who can either overcome their H or express their gripes without inhibition are much less prone to develop hypertension. Thus, I wouldn't expect a black who openly and honestly expresses his feelings about discrimination, such as the columnist and commentator Carl Rowan, to develop high blood pressure.

I would advise people with high blood pressure to take heed of the experts in this field who urge them not to keep their hostility inside. Blowing our tops only turns our families and other close associates against us. Moreover, a person who habitually vents anger is likely to soon become angry again. What makes a lot more sense is the practice of Anti-H and using reason and resolution aggressively to attain one's rights.

H AND HEART ATTACKS

It doesn't make any sense to be robbed of the fruits of hard work by a heart attack or stroke in the prime of life. Yet this is the tragic price that so many families have had to pay. More persons die of heart and circulatory disease than of any other illness; many die without having had previous symptoms. By far the most frequent form of serious heart disease is that involving the coronary arteries that nourish the heart muscle. Since the sedentary and obese are more prone to heart disease, doctors stress the need for diet and exercise. Because of evidence that smoking is a factor, the medical profession strongly opposes smoking. But despite these preventive measures, deaths from this dread disease continue at an alarming rate.

According to many specialists in heart disease, the greatest factor of all is stress—anything that puts a strain on or overtaxes the system. The menace of hostility in stressful jobs is borne out by an increasing number of medical investigations. Some heart specialists maintain that the busy, overactive person who tries to crowd more and more events into his shrinking reserves of time is the type most apt to succumb to a coronary. They refer to this as Type A Behavior or "hurry disease." However, there are no harmful effects upon the heart from hurrying alone. For example, no group hurries more than my fellow doctors, most of whom have been putting in eighty-hour work weeks since they began premedical training. Nevertheless, they live as long as nonhurriers, and often longer.

Heart specialists who believe that hurry is in itself stressful recommend cutting down: allowing more time for rest, making fewer appointments, and rising earlier so as to allow more time for dawdling over the newspaper and chatting with a neighbor. But rest doesn't relieve the severe stress caused by suppressed H and anxiety. Moreover, this advice overlooks the self-blame and anxiety that often arise from frittering away time in aimless activities rather than spending it in ego-filling accomplishment. It isn't the hurry but the H that is the critical emotional factor; it can't be dissolved if it is overlooked, and the H carrier is in even more danger of a heart attack than the sedentary, obese, cholesterol-consuming, cigarette-smoking person.

It may very well be that, in advising people to give up smoking in order to avoid heart and other physical diseases, doctors may be falling into the error of treating the symptom while the cause continues to wreak havoc under the surface. A sizable majority of heavy smokers use cigarettes to relieve excessive anxiety, usually due to suppressed H and frustration. Since it is a well-established medical fact that the emotionally disturbed are more apt to develop disease than the stable, it's not unreasonable to theorize that a smoker may develop heart disease, high blood pressure, and lung cancer not only because of his disease-producing habit of smoking, but because the heavier the smoker the greater the degree of emotional stress.

I subscribe to the prevalent opinion in modern medicine that overweight, lack of exercise, and smoking increase the probability of a heart attack, but the public is being led into a dangerous trap by well-meaning physicians and public health agencies who warn them to give up smoking while ignoring the chief reason why they are heavy smokers in the first place.

A Typical Case of Coronary Heart Disease

Chet had been raised by a father who insisted that his word was law. As a child, Chet was punished severely for any disagreement with his father's orders. He soon learned, along with his mother, that he could avoid punishment by doing what he was told and not talking back. You can easily understand how, as a result of his father's tyranny, he developed a lifelong pattern of suppressing hostility.

At the age of thirty-five, Chet was well on the road to having a brilliant career. He was chief research metallurgist for a large organization and worked closely with the president, Mr. K. Unfortunately, despite his success on previous research projects, he was constantly running into opposition from Mr. K, who drove his men unmercifully, with no concern for the frightful toll in mental and physical breakdown wreaked by his vicious temper. In working under Mr. K, Chet was being subjected to arbitrary, dogmatic, arrogant domination similar to that which his father had meted out. He reacted as he had been conditioned to do: he kept his resentful feelings to himself.

Finally, after ten years of bitterness, he determined that he would get even with Mr. K by quitting and starting his own metallurgical firm. He had made many good contacts in his former position and resolved that he would pry them away from Mr. K.'s firm.

As a consequence of Chet's ability, his new business grew rapidly. There was just one problem: His hostility toward Mr. K. spurred him into working long hours in his effort to outdo him. The H that was goading him into herculean efforts to destroy Mr. K.'s business was also taking its toll on his coronary arteries. After three years of hard work, he built up a healthy business, but one afternoon, Chet slumped over, dead of a coronary heart attack.

Most persons who have worked for a cutthroat tyrant scoff at the idea that they could learn to genuinely like and respect such a person, since they believe that he is inherently evil. Almost invariably, the adamant refusal to relinquish H toward such a boss is the result of the employee's own compulsion to visualize himself as superior.

Suppose the company that insured Chet's life had sent him a pamphlet containing information on H's disease-producing effects and a simple explanation of how to keep oneself free of this poison. My experience has shown that even a brief explanation often stimulates a man of Chet's intelligence into finding out more. Let's consider what Chet would have been able to do had he been thoroughly trained in Anti-H.

First of all he would have recognized that he was condemning Mr. K. for something that Chet himself was actually inciting; at the very least, Chet was actively aggravating Mr. K., since the H that Chet thought he was concealing from Mr. K. was perfectly apparent. How can we blame someone for becoming hostile to us when we are infecting him with our own feelings?

I would have asked Chet, "How can you expect Mr. K. to understand the nature of H and how to manage it when a man of your Ph.D. education has no understanding of it?" He would have felt some sympathy for Mr. K. had he learned that he had acquired I feelings as innocently as Chet had: from exposure to the attitudes and feelings of his parents, wife, and others—and more recently, from exposure to Chet himself. Had Chet been familiar with the I → H + S reaction, Mr. K.'s H and domineering wouldn't have bothered him since he would have understood its true meaning: Mr. K. was simply reacting to his own I.

Once you understand why the other fellow is blameless, whatever you say or do to him is free of hostile contamination. He then reacts appreciatively to you because he isn't getting the antagonistic response that his arrogance evokes in his other associates.

No matter what the other person is angry, resentful, derogatory, arrogant, or martyred about, you need only apply one uniform maneuver: elevating the other person's Respect Level. Suppose Mr. K., in his own inimitably obnoxious style, said to Chet, "I'm sick and tired of your taking a month to do a job that shouldn't take more than a week. I want this done by the end of this week."

Chet knew he was a fast worker. If he replied indignantly, "Look, Mr. K., you have no right to accuse me of dilly-dallying. I work faster than most people. It's impossible to get this job done in that time," it would serve only to make Mr. K. out as wrong and thus increase his anger—the very thing that was responsible for his unreasonable demands. By first dissolving his H and then adhering to the principle of elevating the other person's Respect Level, Chet could have answered: "I'll get on it immediately and work as fast as I know how."

Such a reply contains nothing that is disrespectful—it is a far cry from a hostile, contradictory reply. The propping up of Mr. K.'s Respect Level would effect a reduction in his H. Under these circumstances, even if Mr. K. complained the following day about the job not being completed, Chet would only have to say, "I know how important it is to finish this job; I'll give it everything I have."

One reason that Chet was so embittered was Mr. K.'s accusation that he was wasting the company's money for unproductive chemical experiments. Chet had replied in an indignant tone that the experiments happened to be productive. This was the worst possible reply, since it implied that Mr. K. was wrong, and the tone served only to intensify Mr. K.'s opposition to his projects. Had Chet first dissolved his own H and then replied to Mr. K, "I'll go over the experiments carefully to see if they're worth continuing," he would have shown that he was giving Mr. K.'s opinion every consideration. Since this would have elevated Mr. K.'s Respect Level, it would have elicited a respectful response. Not only would Chet have attained Mr. K.'s Receptivity, but also the nourishment Chet needed so badly for his own self-esteem. As one *regularly* handles all issues in this uniform manner, the respect and therefore the cooperation between employee and boss increase. More importantly, with his H reduced, it is unlikely that Chet would have suffered his fatal heart attack.

"So what?" commented one patient. "I can follow this advice and still get killed in an accident." Not likely, for most accidents—at home, at work, and on the road—happen to individuals carrying too great a load of H or anxiety. So if the H suppressor doesn't suffer a heart attack or some other serious disease, he is likely to wind up in the emergency room as an "accident" victim.

15.
Skipped Heartbeat and Cardiophobia

*WHAT HOSTILITY AND ANXIETY CAN DO
TO YOUR HEART*

There is a condition known in medical terminology as Premature Contraction, in which one heartbeat "jumps the gun," and there is a pause before the next, naturally frightening anyone not medically trained.

Although the heart normally reacts to anger and fear with more rapid and forceful beats, suppressed H may disrupt the normal flow of synchronized nervous transmission from the brain centers to the heart. This may cause such unpleasant symptoms as rapid heartbeat, pounding of the heart, skipped beats, gasping, sighing, and flushing of the face.

Most people are reassured after their doctor examines them and informs them that there is no heart disease. However, some fail to respond to their doctor's reassurance. Not infrequently, they become panic-stricken because they interpret these symptoms as a heart attack and fear they are about to die.

Howard, a forty-year-old electronics engineer, had become increasingly alarmed because for six months he had experienced skipped heartbeats. His family doctor assured him that examination and tests had demonstrated that there was nothing wrong with his heart, and referred him to a psychiatrist with a diagnosis of cardiophobia (fear of a heart attack). Howard indignantly stated that he couldn't see how the doctor could say that there was nothing wrong with his heart when it had been skipping beats for six months.

Since Howard was an electronics engineer, I presumed that

he could easily understand my explanation of the transmission of electrical impulses from the brain centers. But the blank expression on his face indicated that my explanation wasn't getting through to him. It soon became apparent from his facial expression and voice that he was feeling resentful toward me.

You might think it strange that a patient who had pleaded that he urgently wanted a doctor's help would turn on me with H. However, when it became clear to me what extreme feelings of I Howard was laboring under, I could understand why he had been so quick to react to me in such a resentful manner. Since early childhood he had resented persons in authority—a consequence of having been raised by a father who forced his opinions on him. The result was that Howard reacted to those in authority with an uncontrollable urge to contradict their opinions. Without any conscious intention he would set a trap to lay the blame on such a person, whether it was his boss, wife (when she wanted her way), or doctor. When I asked him why he seemed resentful of me, after some hesitation he blurted out, "Because you're forcing your opinion on me and not hearing me out."

I knew that his H was not basically a reaction to me, but primarily a reaction to his inferior concept of himself. I had no need to blame myself for my authoritative approach; I had as much right to it as the doctor who is called upon to treat a surgical emergency. Nevertheless, I had erred in presenting an authoritative explanation without securing my patient's receptivity to me. Accordingly I acknowledged to Howard that he had me dead to rights, that I had thoughtlessly deprived him of his right to express himself. He responded by the usual detailed description of his symptoms and statement of his conviction that his doctor and wife were treating him as a mental case instead of recognizing that he had a bad heart.

Knowing that his extreme fear was generated by the I → H Reaction, a prime aim of therapy was to elevate his self-respect. This was already taking place, since the H he had anticipated in response to his own was not forthcoming.

Rather than try to convince Howard that his doctor knew a lot more about his condition than he did, I again acknowledged that he was right—something *was* indeed wrong with his heart. Now that I had raised his Respect Level by honestly validating his opinion, I was rewarded by a receptive response. This time, when I drew a diagram showing how his heartbeats were being disrupted by the disordered impulses from the brain center, his mind opened up to my explanation of his trouble.

When I asked him about his H, he admitted that he had been feeling extremely bitter toward his wife and his boss. An important project that Howard felt should have been assigned to him had instead been given to another engineer, and he had been left with very little to work on in recent months.

Crushed because of his belief that the boss was deliberately slighting him, he felt all the more need for his wife's sympathy. When he returned home from work in this depressed and bitter state, he said to her: "The boss had no right to assign that project to Murphy. I just can't go on this way anymore."

His wife replied in a know-it-all and disparaging tone: "Why don't you speak up to the boss and tell him how you feel?"

This, of course, infuriated him. "I realized that she just didn't understand. She lacked sympathy for me, and all she wanted to do was force her opinion down my throat. That's why I had nothing further to say to her."

Howard hadn't answered at the time, but his black look intensified the circle of H between him and his wife. While she complained loudly, he persisted in remaining silent. The result was an enormous increase in suppressed H toward his wife, plus the anger he did not dare express to his boss. Howard had no trouble now in understanding how this had caused his skipped beats and other heart symptoms. I instructed him in Anti-H and he applied it to his wife and boss. The reduction in H caused an equivalent reduction in anxiety, leading to a rapid reduction in his symptoms. Consequently, instead of his former anticipatory fear that his symptoms were coming on again, he now had sound evidence for anticipating that they were instead decreasing. This altered anticipation further reduced his anxiety, and within five days his symptoms were entirely gone.

It is only natural for any of us to have a moderate degree of fear of heart attack. Most adults know of some friend, relative, or neighbor who died suddenly of a coronary occlusion (clotting in one of the small arteries of the heart). Newspapers, magazines, doctors, medical societies, and health clubs warn us of heart disease, thus creating fear in persons who may have been previously ignorant of the danger. Most people react by trying to follow their doctor's advice on diet, exercise, and the reduction of stress and tension.

Fear in moderation is valuable, since it may prod us into taking better care of ourselves. However, H suppressors generate so much anxiety that they become more vulnerable to ordinary fear-producing situations and aggravation. It is this group that is more prone to obsessive fear of sudden death from a heart attack.

This syndrome was described in soldiers during the Civil War, but came into increased prominence in World Wars I and II, when it began to be referred to as "soldier's heart." Many cases occurred in soldiers who doubted that they would take risks for fellow soldiers they resented. The feelings of guilt generated by the suppression of this H, added to the fearful climate of combat, produced the "Soldier's Heart Syndrome." That this condition does not have to occur from combat service in war is obvious from the great increase in the number of cases in nonmilitary individuals since World War II.

The typical patient is tormented by the fear that he may die of a heart attack at any minute. His symptoms consist of pounding and rapid rate of heartbeat, gasping breathing with frequent sighs, pain in the region of the heart, exhaustion, dizziness, flushed or pale face, sweating, tremor, and extreme anxiety. In spite of being told by the doctor that he is free of disease and that no one ever dies of this syndrome, he is not reassured and remains panic-stricken.

Walter, a fifty-year-old man, had been living for a year tormented by the fear that he was on the verge of a fatal heart attack. His symptoms consisted of sharp pain in the front of his chest, accompanied by frequent gasping respiration, gagging, and extreme anxiety and tension. Frequently he felt that he was smothering to death. He had been hospitalized several times, but no signs of disease of the heart or any other organ could be found. After treating him for a year with a variety of tranquilizers, his doctor persuaded Walter to see a psychiatrist.

The basic cause of this phobia is an *extreme* degree of suppressed H. We have already seen that H always generates anxiety; the greater the H, the more anxiety is produced. The individual hasn't the slightest idea that H is the source of his fear, and not knowing the cause, he undergoes a feeling of helplessness and impending doom that generates the most intense and unbearable anxiety.

This abnormally high level of fear precipitates sudden attacks of pounding and runaway heart rate, pain in the heart region, and labored breathing. Such symptoms naturally make the person suffering them fearful of a heart attack. The intensification of the fear stimulates the heart symptoms even more. Now, more than ever, the anticipation of a heart attack is increased, forming a vicious circle of heart symptoms and anticipatory fear.

Afraid that he is about to die of a heart attack, he frantically pleads with the doctor to do something immediately to save him from imminent death. In many instances, the doctor responds by rushing the patient to a hospital for a battery of laboratory tests including an electrocardiogram and X ray of the chest.

You might think that when the most reliable tests of the heart all show that it is free of any disease the patient will be reassured and therefore relieved of his agonizing fear. But such is seldom the case. Instead, as the result of being rushed to the hospital and having his heart tested, the patient is apt to become even more fearful. Since nothing has been done about the suppressed H at the root of his fear, the symptoms continue unabated. A typical response to the doctor's assurance that the examinations reveal nothing wrong with the heart is "No one can tell me there's nothing wrong with my heart when I can feel it pounding and racing; it never used to do that."

The patient's conclusion is that the doctor is either concealing the truth or mistaken in his diagnosis. Consequently, he becomes resentful toward his doctor or any consultant brought into the case. If the consultant also reassures him that there's nothing wrong with his heart, he's liable to go from one doctor to another until he can find one who will go along with his conviction that he's having a heart attack. Most of these patients are treated by an assortment of tranquilizers, none of which has the slightest effect on their fear.

In therapy, it's senseless to listen too long to a patient with such symptoms. If you do, he'll waste valuable time repeating the reasons why he fears he's about to die of a heart attack. Instead, the therapist should recognize that this condition is caused by suppressed H and get straight to the point. I knew I had Walter's confidence after I told him his heart symptoms were real. I then discussed the hidden H factor and urged him to tell me about it so that I could show him how to get rid of it.

Walter finally admitted that he hated his boss's guts. He had worked at a large plumbing and heating firm for twenty years and had advanced to a managerial position. For the past fifteen years, however, he had worked under the supervision of the owner of the business. "It's impossible to reason with him. He's extremely domineering and opinionated; he thinks nothing of telling me off in front of employees or customers. Recently, at the office Christmas party, he shook hands with everyone but me. But there's nothing I can do about it, because I'm in no position to look for another job."

Most people are unwilling to acknowledge that their H is a factor in their inability to get along with another person, but anyone who suffers from the fear of imminent death will give the doctor his fullest cooperation. While Walter at first complained that the boss didn't give him credit, he began to realize that he didn't give the boss any either—he had only pretended to go along with him because he felt that he was forced to. Walter came to see that the boss was just as human as he was and bound to become hostile and slighting in response to the disrespectful feelings that Walter believed he had concealed.

With his newly acquired understanding, Walter was no

longer afraid to look the boss in the eye when they conversed. His look and tone of voice reflected his changed feelings. He found many ways of giving the boss genuine credit. Instead of shrinking from the boss' harsh criticism, he readily acknowledged his own mistakes. If he didn't think he was mistaken, he told the boss that he would check into the matter. What had been a bitter relationship turned into one of mutual respect.

Of course you can't get rid of fifteen years of H in a few days. Fortunately, that isn't necessary; enough H is dissolved in a few days to bring about a sharp drop in anxiety. Since Walter's heart symptoms were specifically due to his abnormally elevated level of H and anxiety, they were relieved within three days after Walter's initial visit to me. Besides, for the first time he clearly understood the *reason* for his fear, and was therefore relieved of his agonizing terror of the unknown.

If you are in fear of a heart attack you should consult your doctor. Most likely you don't have any heart disease, but it's up to him to determine this. He'll also advise you on preventive measures. These will include taking regular exercise, keeping your diet low in fat and cholesterol, and avoiding cigarettes and stress. But your doctor's advice on avoiding stress won't help you unless you implement it by learning exactly how to go about this. You must ascertain the cause of the stress, and counter it by making Anti-H a way of life.

The patients with heart conditions described above overcame their symptoms by the specialized knowledge obtained in their treatment. They learned that the most disease-producing form of emotional stress is that caused by suppressed H. The gratitude these patients feel is so great that they are only too happy to appear before any medical society or therapy group and explain how they conquered their fear. And in making Anti-H an unfailing daily practice, they are far *less* likely to fall victim to heart attacks than the rest of the population.

16.
Between Doctor and Patient

H is just as prevalent among physicians as among the rest of the population. Far too many competent practitioners are incapacitated by diseases in which suppressed H is a significant factor. The usual opinion is that they worked too hard. This isn't logical, inasmuch as there are few doctors who *don't* work too hard.

Dr. R., after fifteen years of successful medical practice, took in a younger partner to lighten his heavy load. Dr. R. was a kindly, gentle man who had an aversion to arguments. He became increasingly resentful toward his partner because of the partner's frequent angry scolding of their patients. His partner also made demands on their sharing of duties and profits that Dr. R. felt were grossly unfair. When Dr. R. attempted to discuss these matters, the partner went into tirades of rage. Dr. R. thereafter reacted by avoiding these angry disputes. Although fifteen years of day and night work had not impaired his health, after four years of suppressing H he came down with an almost fatal heart attack. Unfortunately, doctors aren't trained in Anti-H at medical school. Many a time, when I am discussing an intern's H with him, his comment is, "What am I supposed to do about that?"

In medical school, endless hours are devoted to the study of diphtheria, smallpox, and even hypertrophic cervical pachymeningitis, but most of us never see a single case of these diseases in a lifetime of practice. In my Anatomy course, the instructor castigated me for my failure to find the sphenopalatine ganglion. Perhaps his hostility served a purpose, because it struck such terror in me that I've never forgotten this minute structure, although I have never once found an occasion to make use of this piece of anatomical knowledge.

184

Early in my training it became apparent that even learned professors of psychiatry were subject to vying for superiority. Once, each of us interns had been assigned to give a report on a technical work of psychiatry. My assignment was *Selected Papers of Karl Abraham*. Although I had had six months notice, I still hadn't glanced at this book when the day arrived for my report before the staff.

In previous meetings, we interns had been so anxious to show how well we had studied our assignments that we ignored the erudite faculty's eagerness to display *their* abundant knowledge. Now, instead of hogging the limelight, I showed the utmost consideration in allowing the faculty to participate. A slight nod of my head and one of them would take over, until interrupted by yet another encyclopedic brain. With admirable reticence and scrupulous impartiality, I permitted the faculty members to vie with one another until the two-hour period was up. On the way out, the chief of staff congratulated me for an outstanding presentation!

The medical student soon learns that he'll be expelled or severely disciplined if he or she expresses any H toward a teacher. Doctors are taught that they must be kind, gentle, and pleasant to patients and nurses. It's not uncommon for a physician whose skills are badly needed to be dropped from a hospital staff because he or she has incurred the H of a higher ranking member. A doctor may be punished by the local medical society, not because of infractions of the rules, but because of the H of several of the officers of the society. With such a background, it is no wonder that so many doctors become habitually soft-spoken and smiling, no matter how resentful they feel.

It was only after many years of medical practice that I realized that patients and nurses weren't fooled when I tried to conceal my H beneath a veneer of gentility. It's especially provoking to a patient when his doctor tells him in dulcet tones to control his anger and yet the patient can perceive that the doctor himself is hostile.

AGGRAVATING A PATIENT'S ILLNESS BY HOSTILITY

Sometimes a patient fails to get well not because the treatment isn't correct, but because the doctor is infecting him with H. The doctor's H is often due to provocation by the patient. For example:

Doctor: *Where in your head is the pain located?*

Patient: *I believe I must have eaten something that disagreed with me.*

Doctor: *Will you please answer the questions I ask?*

Or a mother calls to ask the doctor to phone the drugstore for something for her little boy's skin rash.

Doctor: *I can't prescribe for it unless you bring him in so I can see the rash.*

Mother: *I can't disturb him now; he's doing his homework.*

The doctor may be so preoccupied with the technical aspects of his work—studying the patient's skin, heart, lungs, X rays, and electrocardiogram—that he fails to recognize the effect of his own feelings, attitudes, and actions on the patient. In spite of escalating the treatments, the symptoms may stubbornly persist and sometimes become worse.

Mrs. W., a sixty-two-year-old woman, was hospitalized for asthma. The lengthy duration of the asthma had given rise to emphysema, a serious lung disease. It was imperative to control the asthma in order to arrest the progression of the emphysema. The doctor in charge of the case, a specialist in internal medicine, was assisted by a number of attending doctors, including the medical resident, assistant resident, two interns, and a specialist in allergy. The patient also received round-the-clock care from six nurses.

During the first week in the hospital Mrs. W. improved under medication, but in the second week she became progressively worse. The doctor in charge became alarmed because the asthma had worsened in spite of extraordinary amounts of medication. Knowing that asthma is a disease in which emotional factors are important, he called for a psychiatric consultation.

In my interview with Mrs. W., I soon perceived that she was attempting to hide the hostility she had developed toward the staff, including the nurses, during her eleven days in the hospital. I then discussed the case individually with each of the doctors and nurses in attendance. Every one of them had taken a dislike to the patient, mostly for the same reasons. They said that Mrs. W. would ask for their opinions and then contradict them. She took the nurses to task for what she believed was carelessness. She developed a running battle with one of the nurses over the position of a chair. No sooner would the nurse move the chair to the location she preferred than Mrs. W. would move it back to where she wanted it—a tug-of-war that had been going on for a week. A similar battle went on over the air conditioning, with the nurse taking an uncalled-for, bossy attitude. Mrs. W. accused each doctor in turn of contradictions with the other doctors. The result was that she was looked upon as a pain in the neck. But true to their training, the doctors and nurses attempted to conceal their hostility toward Mrs. W. behind an outward facade of friendliness; and so the hostility between patient and staff mounted by leaps and bounds.

Mrs. W.'s asthma had become so critical that I felt Anti-H therapy must be applied immediately, to the staff as well as herself. I called an emergency meeting for the nurses on duty at the time and all the doctors on the case. The meeting with the remaining nurses took place on their duty shifts. I told them all that the most likely reason for the failure of the medication was the high concentration of suppressed H in the patient. Each of the medical personnel freely admitted his or her own H and saw the urgency of getting rid of it. The method of accomplishing this was explained and they did remarkably well in putting it into practice, considering that their training in Anti-H was brief.

It was much more difficult to teach the patient how to rid herself of H in such a short time. However, each staff member helped through frequent visits with her. Within forty-eight hours of these contacts, the patient began responding favorably to the same medication that had been ineffectual all during the past week. The patient's husband stated that she had been miraculously cured. Of course, there wasn't anything miraculous about it. The patient recovered because the suppressed H, which had been blocking the anti-asthma medication, was substantially reduced. She was warned that there was every likelihood of a flare-up of her illness if she did not continue to practice the Anti-H therapy.

At a meeting of psychiatrists in 1948, the subject of extreme provocation by psychiatric patients was under discussion. Dr. Franz Alexander, one of the world's outstanding psychiatrists, described one of the most irritating patients he had ever treated. As he lay on the couch, criticizing Dr. Alexander for not curing him, the patient would pick pieces out of it, flick cigar ashes on the floor, and rub his dirty fingers on the wall. This kind of behavior began to prove annoying to the good doctor. After some eight months of daily analysis, the patient for the first time verbalized his H with the remark, "I have a feeling you don't like me."

The usually kindly doctor replied, with some exasperation, "*Who* could like you?"

THE H FACTOR IN MALPRACTICE SUITS

A sword that hangs over the head of every doctor is the threat of a lawsuit for malpractice. These suits have become so prevalent that in order to safeguard themselves, doctors often order tests that rarely have any bearing on a case, so that they won't be held liable for overlooking even the remotest possibilities. In the large majority of these suits the doctor is cleared of blame. Yet the number of suits continues to rise. Why?

An important reason that is often overlooked is the doctor's H. Its unconscious effect on the patient may prod him into a malpractice suit. And when the doctor develops antagonism toward a patient, the presence of the H in his mind may cause blunders in judgment and surgical procedures despite his technical competence when not provoked.

There's no reason why a patient shouldn't express an opinion about his case to his doctor. But the doctor who takes a patient's suggestion as a mark of disrespect for his own expertise is apt to react with H. On one occasion, a doctor ordered a laboratory analysis of the stool of a patient who had passed a small amount of blood-streaked feces. The patient then said he thought his bowel should be X-rayed. It's annoying for a man with years of training in the complexities of medical science to have his patient tell him what to do for his illness. The doctor replied sharply that he'd X-ray him when *he* thought it was necessary.

H often causes even the most intelligent people to act in a contrary fashion. Why else would a doctor who knew that blood-streaked feces may be a symptom of cancer fail to order an X ray? It wasn't until five months later, when the patient reported the presence of blood again, that an X ray was ordered. The cancer of the bowel that was found had grown larger in the five-month interval.

On the face of it, it would seem ridiculous for either doctor or patient to exact vengeance, since each needs the other. However, revenge is frequently unconsciously motivated. Thus, it may be the insidious presence of H that causes the doctor's scalpel to slip; or the hidden H in a patient's brain may cause symptoms to persist that otherwise would have long since disappeared.

AN APPEAL TO THE MEDICAL PROFESSION

I can never fully repay the medical profession for the education it has given me. Not a day passes on the medical wards and clinics that I don't learn something from my fellow doctors. Just as they persuaded me to exercise, shed fat, and give up smoking, so I beseech them to give as much priority to the management of H.

Daily and often nightly exposure to the justifiable anxiety, impatience, and irritability of the sick and their loved ones imposes considerable emotional strain on doctors. Yet they are trained to hide irritations and manifest a friendly, cheerful disposition. The consequences of this suppression may be exhaustion, heart attacks, strokes, and other serious diseases. At the very least, such suppression robs them of the energy they need for their loved ones, and may cause them to lose their practiced control and snap at their patients.

Some of the attitudes that arouse resentment in patients are listed below. I confess that in thirty-eight years as a doctor I have committed *every single one* of these errors, with resultant setbacks to the treatment and loss of the patient's respect. Let's consider some of the most common gripes of patients and see how they could have been avoided.

1. *My doctor gets annoyed with me whenever I attempt to express my opinion. I know I'm not trained in medicine, but he should show me the common courtesy of hearing me out.*

It's not unusual for a patient to quote opinions gleaned from newspapers, magazines, radio, TV—or even from mother—much to the doctor's annoyance. While it makes no sense to let a patient dictate his own diagnosis and treatment, there is no harm in listening respectfully while he expresses his opinions on these technical matters. When the doctor fails to take the time to listen to the patient's opinions, the patient's resentment may cause him to resist following the prescribed treatment. Furthermore, his H may reduce the effectiveness of the treatment because of an unconscious need to prove the doctor wrong.

2. *My doctor never admits that he's wrong about anything. He always has a ready alibi for his mistakes.*

Patients, like everyone else, resent being contradicted when they offer a criticism. All of us frequently err; by admitting this, we raise the patient's respect.

3. *My doctor's a know-it-all. When I asked for a referral to a specialist, he said a specialist couldn't do anything for me that he couldn't himself.*

The patient doesn't resent his doctor's superiority in medical science, but naturally distrusts his insistence on infallibility. The enormous advances in medical science make it impossible for even the most expert physician to know it all. If the doctor has exhausted his own diagnosis and treatments he should call in a consultant.

4. *I resent my doctor yelling at me.*

Since yelling damages the patient's self-respect and arouses his H, the doctor should try to scrupulously avoid doing so.

5. *I resent being told there's nothing wrong with me when I know that the pain I feel is real.*

Whether it's pain, nausea, or any other symptom felt by the patient, the doctor should recognize that it signifies a malfunction of his system. How can a patient trust the doctor's diagnostic ability when the doctor denies the existence of something the patient knows to be real? Why not simply say, "So far, I haven't been able to find the cause. I know you're suffering pain and I'll keep investigating to find out what's causing it."

6. *He expects me to overcome worry by merely telling me, "Don't worry; it's not good for you."*

This is a useless prescription. The patient should be told that there are adequate causes for worry, just as there are for dizziness or headache. We can't rid anyone of a symptom by telling him that he shouldn't have it, or that it's not good for him. Symptoms require investigation and treatment.

7. *My doctor comes by my hospital room and asks, "How are you doing?" When I begin to answer, he waves, smiles, says "Fine," and takes off.*

Failing to take time with a patient doesn't save time for the doctor. The resentment it arouses in the patient harms the treatment process and thus delays recovery. The great masters of medicine recognize the importance of taking the time to be thorough. Tragic mistakes and accidents are more apt to occur when we try to rush through what we're doing.

8. *I resent being treated like a machine. My doctor doesn't seem to recognize that I'm a creature with sensitive feelings.*

What a pity that, in some cases, the doctor's secretary, attending nurses, medical technicians, and nurse's aides treat the patient with more warmth than the doctor himself does. The patient's feelings are a vital part of his functioning. He can't relax and cooperate with the doctor unless he is shown the consideration that every human being deserves.

The pioneers in psychiatry learned a great deal by dint of long hours of listening to their patients. Such research helped pave the way for modern psychiatric treatment. However, we mustn't lose sight of the fact that the patient comes to the therapist for the best available treatment, not to be a guinea pig for research purposes. The most widely practiced technique of psychotherapy—listening while the patient talks—not only fails to reduce the patient's H, but sometimes makes the psychiatrist hostile as well. To listen with a poker face or an occasional "Oh?" is no help to a patient.

By virtue of his understanding of emotional problems the therapist should know that the patient is the victim, not the cause, of his problems. This should arouse sympathy and respect for the patient. Far from being concealed behind an impassive expression, these feelings should be openly displayed. Since feelings can't be hidden for very long, a therapist's attempt to conceal his feelings is interpreted by the patient as a form of insincerity. The result is that he becomes resentful and loses trust in the therapist. Without trust, treatment is a lost cause. On the other hand, the patient who feels liked and respected by the therapist is less inhibited about asking questions, disagreeing, or expressing his real feelings.

9. *My doctor becomes irritated with me when his treatment doesn't work.*

Every doctor is faced with the immense complexities involved in illness. No matter how competent he is, his treatments may not do the job. There's no loss of face in admitting this and then starting a new treatment.

10. *When I ask my doctor to explain what's wrong with me, he gives me a disdainful look as if to say, "You'd never understand it, so why should I bother."*

Although, in some cases, the patient is not helped medically by being given a long, technical explanation, he's bound to resent the doctor for not giving him credit for the capacity to understand a simple one. When the doctor answers questions in nontechnical language the patient is gratified because it indicates the doctor's respect for his common sense. Moreover, without an adequate explanation the patient may fear the worst and suffer much unnecessary anxiety.

HOW THE DOCTOR CAN MANAGE THE AGGRAVATING PATIENT

A frequent source of aggravation is the know-it-all patient who insists that he has an organic disease despite the doctor's repeated assurance that there is none present. Such cases are among the most puzzling and difficult that the doctor is called upon to treat.

Patient: *I can still feel the fluid from my brain trickling down my neck into my shoulder.*

Doctor: *My examination, laboratory tests, and X rays haven't revealed any fluid.*

Patient: *How can you tell there's no fluid when you refuse to operate?*

Doctor (becoming so irritated that he's beginning to feel fluid trickling in his own brain): *No surgeon would operate for such a complaint.*

Patient: *Oh, so you think I'm imagining the fluid. Maybe I should go to a doctor who takes my symptoms seriously?*

Of course, patients occasionally make disrespectful remarks. Yet a knowledge of the real source of the patient's attitude and behavior would free the doctor of H in a matter of seconds. The absence of H in his response would then have an agreeable effect on the patient, and the doctor would then be in an excellent position to reduce still further the patient's disrespect toward him by a respectful attitude toward his opinions. For instance:

Doctor: *I'm sure that you're feeling a flow of fluid from your brain.*

There's nothing insincere about this statement, since the patient actually *does* feel what he interprets as fluid. Although the doctor knows that there is no known disease entity conforming to the patient's description, he recognizes and acknowledges the patient's honesty by concluding:

"So far the laboratory tests and X rays haven't revealed the presence of fluid, but I'll keep checking for it in every way I know."

No matter how skilled a doctor is, he cannot expect to overcome every patient's H. Occasionally, for example, a patient insists on being given a drug that I cannot prescribe because it would be harmful to him. The patient may become so angry that he declares that he's never coming back and proceeds to leave the office. My policy is to declare in a firm tone, "Just a minute! I just want you to know that if you ever decide to come back, my door is always open to you." This statement, made *without any feeling of H* usually results in the patient's return—at a later date, if not at the moment.

HOW TO KEEP FROM PROVOKING YOUR DOCTOR

Your recovery from illness and, at times, your very life depend on your doctor's skill and judgment. It doesn't make sense for you to consult him and then presume to tell him your diagnosis and what treatment should be prescribed. Despite his medical competence, your doctor, like the rest of us, may be easily angered. As the pressure of H increases, so does the likelihood of error, even in the most brilliant physicians, so antagonizing your doctor is as foolhardy as pushing his arm when he's operating.

As a patient, you can minimize accidents and blunders in diagnosis and treatment on the part of your doctor by attention to your own H. A lady who had taken Anti-H training told me how she had applied it to her doctor. When she phoned his office, the doctor's secretary told her that she would get the doctor as soon as he was available. After ten minutes of waiting on the phone, the patient became aware of a feeling of mounting resentment since she felt the doctor didn't respect her enough to get to the phone sooner. She wasted no time in applying the I → H Reaction.

First, she recognized that her own frustrations and problems had already lowered her Respect Level before she had phoned the doctor. Her system was endeavoring to relieve her of this I feeling by the formation of a Mirage in which the doctor was seen as the one who was at fault. After recognizing that her own I needed correcting, she considered the doctor's side. She reasoned that he simply hadn't been able to come to the phone because of the many demands made on him and not because of lack of respect for her. (She soon learned from the doctor that he had been tied up with a patient who had unexpectedly begun to hemorrhage.)

Had the woman retained her H, it would have been transmitted to the doctor. Antagonizing her doctor might have unconsciously turned him against her, despite his conscious dedication to do his best. Not only did she prevent this complication, but she also averted the damaging effects of H on her own mental and physical processes. By maintaining a hostile-free atmosphere, *both* doctor and patient can avoid these pitfalls.

Doctors are required by their medical societies to take continuing medical education courses to keep themselves abreast of the latest medical developments. Although the most diverse phases of medical science are covered, there is not yet to my knowledge a single course offered on how the doctor can keep his H down to a harmless level and how he can reduce H in his patients. Over a hundred years have elapsed since Professor-In-Charge Joseph Klein fired Ignaz Semmelweis from the Vienna General Hospital for recommending that doctors cleanse their hands before entering the maternity ward. How long will it be before doctors are taught to cleanse their feelings as well?

17.

Overcoming Depression

Almost always, the close relative of an individual with a behavior disorder focuses on the *symptoms*, rather than on the cause of the symptoms. Thus, a father will state of his son, in a matter-of-fact manner, "His trouble is that he's lazy," or "He thinks everybody owes him a living," while the boy's mother will point to such symptoms as her son's not eating when he should, or refusing to get up in the morning. A lady frantically pleaded for help for her husband: "Doctor, he won't leave the house. I told him that if he'd go out with me his spirits would improve. I've begged him to go back to work, but he won't budge."

The "lazy" son and the "stubborn" husband weren't trying to give their families a hard time; they were the victims of an illness that few people understand: depression.

Everyone is subject to occasional feelings of depression, lasting for short periods of time. However, when these feelings persist, they constitute a mental disorder that blights the individual's entire existence. A depressed person is anxiety-ridden, tense, feels guilty and worthless. He is overwhelmed by daily tasks and social contacts and, consequently, avoids them. He feels lethargic and fatigued, and often complains of headache and an assortment of other pains. Pessimism is profound, often reaching the point of hopelessness. His negative response to advice from family and friends, and his disinclination to speech and activity make him a burden to his family, evoking a reaction of anxiety, exasperation and, not infrequently, depression of their own. It is estimated that about one out of every eight Americans will be victims of this illness at one time or another. Depression is a life-threatening illness, since

194

the incidence of suicide is twenty-five times greater in depressed persons. Even when it abates for months or years, depression is likely to return.

What causes this widespread mental affliction? The experts disagree. One group believes that some malfunction of chemicals in the brain makes certain individuals unduly susceptible to stress and strain. Other psychiatrists believe that depression is entirely due to the stresses and strains themselves. I believe it is likelier that chemical changes in the depressive's brain are produced by stress and strain, and not the other way around, since anyone conditioned to suppress H reacts with depression to disrespect.

True, depression is more apt to occur in persons, one or both of whose parents were depressives. However, this does not prove a hereditary chemical defect, since whenever a parent is depressed, the children become victims of his or her emotional state, and this has nothing to do with heredity.

WHY WE BECOME DEPRESSED

A depressed feeling is a natural response to the belief that one is disrespected. As with virtually all emotional disorders, depression has its roots in parental attitudes that lower the child's self-respect. By the time such a child begins school, he is convinced that he is not on a par with his schoolmates in worthiness, likeableness, capability, and therefore acceptability. Lacking self-confidence, he is fearful of social participation. Schoolmates tend to ignore a child who shies away, thus helping confirm his fear that he is inferior. When criticized by teachers, his feelings are badly hurt and he becomes increasingly fearful.

Many persons who appear to be living successfully actually feel dissatisfied with their achievements. This can occur, for example, if they were raised by fathers who constantly expressed dissatisfaction with their accomplishments. As adults, such people may develop depressive illness out of the belief that they rate as poorly with their current associates as they did with their fathers.

A common symptom of depression is guilt. The depressed person feels that he has failed to measure up to his end of the bargain—with his wife, children, boss, or other close associates. Guilt kindles a need to atone. Since the depressed person feels incapable of redeeming himself, his atonement doesn't bring relief and he condemns himself all the more. On the other hand, the normal, undepressed person has little difficulty in carrying out his need to make amends.

Depressive illness seldom occurs in those who habitually fight back with uninhibited anger. However, if a child is punished whenever he speaks up for himself or expresses his anger, he becomes conditioned to keep these feelings to himself. Habitual suppression of H may also arise from other forms of emotional conditioning—as when, after ten years of arguments with her husband, a woman decides that harmony can be achieved only by giving in and keeping her feelings to herself. No matter how the habit has been formed, suppressed H is a basic factor in depression.

When I first saw Frank R., he looked about as depressed as a human being can get. Like most men, Frank had opposed consulting a psychiatrist. He had come only because his boss had told him that otherwise he would be fired. He was accompanied by his wife, who said, "He's lost interest in everyone and everything. He seldom talks to me or the children. I've tried to get him to participate with us, but it's no use. The more I try to help him snap out of it, the worse he gets. I can't take it anymore."

Because of the retardation of speech which occurs in severe depression, it was hard to get Frank to talk. He frequently failed to answer my questions, and when he did, his replies were limited to expressions of despair. However, he reacted to my compassion and respect for him by gradually opening up about his problems.

Before the onset of his depression he had been a very capable foreman, partly because of his compulsion to do jobs to perfection. This trait was also his undoing, inasmuch as he condemned himself even for small mistakes. When such a mistake was criticized by his supervisor, Frank would react with extreme self-blame and H. He wasn't aware that this H which he thought he had concealed, was nevertheless perceived by his boss. This, of course, led to a circle of H between them.

Frank didn't believe in taking work problems home with him. Nevertheless, his preoccupation with his own troubles made him so withdrawn that his wife felt he'd lost interest in her. She had been raised in an atmosphere of openness, in which, unlike Frank, she hadn't been punished for speaking out. Frank responded to her carping criticism with sullenness and withdrawal. She had no idea that in reaction to his mother he had developed an allergy to any form of criticism and domineering. The inevitable result of these repeated blows to his self-respect was a feeling of utter futility, and since he couldn't give vent to his H, his depression increased.

Almost invariably, those in close association with the depressive try to bolster his spirits through encouragement, optimism, and reassurance. For example, when he says, "It's no use, I just can't make it," his wife, employer, and sometimes his doctor attempt to act optimistically and reply along these lines: "Nonsense, you're coming along fine; you'll be your old self in short order." But when we counter with optimistic reassurance we are, in effect, contradicting him. He becomes even more convinced that we don't respect his opinions, and his depression deepens.

It's a waste of time trying to advise a person in this condition about the issues at home and work. His trouble is not due to the particular issues themselves, but to his conviction that, no matter what, he is the loser. What the depressed person needs and craves is validation and crediting of his opinions. You can do this and still be truthful. Thus, when he moans about feeling hopeless, you can honestly credit his opinion by saying, "Well, you've been through a lot. No wonder you feel so hopeless." No matter how trivial the issue, every effort should be made to *corroborate* his viewpoint. Suppose a wife is trying to persuade her depressed husband to take a drive with her, and he says he's too tired. His wife can boost his respect by saying, "Well, with all you've had on your shoulders, it's no wonder you're so tired."

In therapy, I saw to it that Frank's opinions were not contradicted. When he corrected me, I was quick to acknowledge my mistakes. After several weeks of such respect-elevating tactics, I was able to earn Frank's Receptivity to my views. He learned that he wasn't inferior at all; rather, he was the victim of attitudes that would have caused anyone to doubt his self-worth. He realized that he had been transmitting to his wife, children, and boss hostile and superior feelings, the very attitudes and emotions to which he himself had been subjected—initially from his parents and then from his wife. Such knowledge has the same effect as finding out that the athletic contest you lost was due to a virus infection you had at the time; it helps restore your belief in your true potential. Frank's recognition that no one can resist respectful feelings and attitudes gave him a surge of self-confidence.

This newly acquired knowledge gave him the understanding he needed to respect his family and boss. He returned to home and work, eager to apply what he had learned.

Several months later I received a letter from his boss: "We are happy to report that Frank's progress is excellent. He is bright and cheery. As a result of his improved work, he has been promoted and given increased responsibility. Since his visit with you he has changed entirely."

A few weeks of reconditioning therapy can't counteract a lifetime of emotional conditioning any more than a few weeks of exercise can counteract a lifetime of sedentary habits. I therefore advised Frank to return three times a year for the next two years, in order to reinforce the initial short period of therapy.

When he returned, he brought his wife along to participate

in the treatment. The know-it-all way in which she had prescribed what he should do had made him feel more inferior and, consequently, more depressed. When she understood the cause of his illness she could see why she had to cease pounding him with her can't-be-wrong opinions. She reversed her tactics and, with sincere respect, listened to his opinions. In this way, she furnished nourishment for his depleted self-respect. Her reward was the respect she received in return and a truly loving mate.

WHEN THE DEPRESSED PERSON REFUSES COUNSELING

Suppose a member of your family or a co-worker is suffering from depression and refuses to see a doctor. With an understanding of the nature of depressive illness, you can help him.

Willard, a fifty-four-year-old business executive, wanted to know if I knew of some means of persuading his wife to see a psychiatrist. She had become increasingly depressed over the past two years. On coming home from work, he would find her in bed in a despondent state. When he asked what was wrong, she would reply with a reproachful "Leave me alone." The poor fellow also had to fix his own meals and do the housework and shopping, since she would not leave her bed. Despite his pleas, she adamantly refused to see a therapist. He was rather puzzled when I advised that he himself visit a psychiatrist but, out of desperation, he was willing to do anything that might help. He said, "I've told her she'd feel better if she kept busy, but she says it would only make her feel worse. I've always made it a point to talk over any complaints she had, but the more I try to talk to her, the more sullen and withdrawn she becomes. I've pleaded with her to go for a ride, out to dinner, or to visit friends, but she won't budge." I asked Willard whether she had been resenting anyone.

"Yes. About five years ago she accused our minister of being money-minded and she's disliked him ever since. In the last few years, she's been on the outs with her two sisters; she said they were cool to her. Our son's been married for eight years and, a few years ago, she began referring to our daughter-in-law as 'that fat pig.' Now she won't even talk to her. To cap it all, she claims that her mother's always criticizing her."

Willard said that his wife had often told him of being picked on by her mother. As a child, she had been punished if she did not strictly obey the rules her mother set down. The mother would not tolerate her attempts to speak up in her own defense. When she brought her complaints to her father, his reply was "A good girl obeys her mother" or "You mustn't talk back to your mother."

A child who is punished for speaking up is certain to develop suppressed H. Early in their marriage, Willard came to realize that even the slightest criticism would hurt his wife's feelings. Accordingly, he avoided criticism and tried instead to reason with her—to show her gently that she was wrong and that everything would be peachy if she'd just do it *his* way. But this had the same effect on his wife that her mother's criticisms had had. The more her self-respect was lowered, the more depressed she became.

"Have you been resentful toward your wife?" I asked.

"Believe me, I'm always nice to her. I've been very patient and listened to her complaints. I told her, 'Because you find something you don't like about a person doesn't mean that you should harbor a grudge.' Her reply to this was, 'You're against me too; it's no use.' "

It's easy to see the operation of the $I \rightarrow H + S$ Reaction in this lady, unconsciously acting to extricate her from the pit of Inferiority by the Mirage-like conception that her troubles were the fault of others. The hostile feelings generated in this way transmitted, of course, and insured a hostile return from all sides. With so much hostility rebounding on her from her closest associates, you can see why she felt so inferior.

Willard learned that his wife's depression wasn't the result of the many issues they discussed; rather, it was because he had been using these issues to show her she was wrong. When, for instance, she would express her dislike of one of their friends, in his "nice" way he would tell her that one has to overlook some faults, unwittingly showing her how wrong she was.

As in almost all emotional problems, the basic trouble is the individual's deficiency in self-respect and "blissful" ignorance of the contagiousness of his feelings of Superiority and H. To help the depressive, it is imperative that you learn to be aware of these attitudes in yourself as well. Willard could now understand what he must do; *no matter what the issue, he must use it to elevate his wife's Respect Level.* He began applying this technique to every issue under discussion. Thus, when she condemned her sisters for their coolness, he replied, "I know how badly that must have hurt your feelings." When she told him how disgusted she was with her daughter-in-law's "big rear end," his response was: "She shouldn't eat so much."

It took only a month of this method to lift the woman's depression. What had hurt her most was being constantly put down by the man whose respect she wanted most. After gaining her

Receptivity, he was able gradually to persuade her to reestablish friendly relationships with her family and friends.

DOES THE MENOPAUSE CAUSE DEPRESSION AND OTHER NERVOUS SYMPTOMS?

You can't go through medical school without being taught that nervous symptoms of all kinds in the female, and particularly depression, are due to the menopause. This is a dubious concept at best. But some doctors are so awed by traditional authority that they don't bother to investigate the facts—which are that nervous symptoms occurring at this time are unrelated to the menopause.

The most frequent cause of nervous trouble in a woman at this time of life is her hopeless expectation of finding love. If she is unmarried, she is apt to have given up hope; if married, she has arrived at the conviction that she is trapped in a loveless relationship.

For example, a girl whose respect has been beaten down by one or both parents would enter marriage with a Mirage of finding happiness there. She is soon faced with the reality of a man whom she had overestimated because of her Mirage. Due to her low Respect Level, as well as his, a circle of H develops, leading to progressively increasing incompatibility. The only reason she remains in the marriage is because of her fear of being on her own and the guilt resulting from her H. In such cases, she may be able to maintain a tolerable level of self-respect by means of her devotion to her children, job, or social activities. But by the time she's reached menopause, her children are on their own, and she's found that job and social activities are seldom a satisfactory substitute for a satisfying love relationship. The Mirage of hope that she had in her younger years has faded. Hope does not spring eternal when a woman whose self-respect has been crushed in childhood and again in marriage must live without love—from a man, from her children, friends, or associates at work. She becomes increasingly anxious, martyred, bitter, and depressed and suffers mental and physical symptoms produced by this emotional syndrome, increasing her difficulties in making a new workable relationship.

In the mind of a woman who feels so unwanted, a Mirage of Superiority may impel her to tell her daughters and daughters-in-law how to manage their children or how their living rooms should be arranged. She incites H in one of the grown children by implying that she is treated better by one of her other children. Her conversation often consists exclusively of symptoms and complaints. In addition to her know-it-all attitude, her deprecating remarks relegate others to the inferior status. If her associates are so condemnable, then, by comparison, she's superior. Inevitably, friends and relatives come to treat her with increasing avoidance and disdain. Since her attitudes evoke a hostile reaction in her family and friends it is no wonder that she becomes more nervous and depressed, and develops new aches and pains.

Some husbands are only too eager to latch on to the menopause as the cause of their wives' nervous and psychosomatic symptoms. Husbands may be prompted to do this by the guilt they feel for having been selfish and unfair to their wives for so long. Their need to exonerate themselves as the cause of their wives' illness is manifested when they bring their wives in to me and remark knowingly "It's the change of life, isn't it, Doctor?"

Besides looking for scapegoats such as the menopause or the fact that "she worries too much," such a husband seeks additional exoneration by blaming his wife for not appreciating that he's given her everything any woman could ever desire—it turns out that what he means is everything *material*. But her depressive illness isn't caused by a lack of material comforts.

Not only her husband, but her grown children and not infrequently her doctor advise her to keep busy. She may become an accomplished housekeeper and cook, devote herself to activities with children, cultivate golf or bowling, busy herself with women's organizations, take her mother shopping; but meanwhile, since she is still being ignored by her husband, and is the unwilling recipient of her children's know-it-all advice, she only becomes more worried and depressed. Often she is told by her parents and best friends, and sometimes by her doctor, that she should count her blessings. So she tries to grin and bear it, while her H remains suppressed. In this form, it becomes the basis of depression and physical disease.

If your wife is suffering from anxiety and depression at this time of life, take a reading of your own attitudes and feelings toward her. If you find that they include blame, disgust, resentment, hurt, or martyrdom, then you are making her worse, since such feelings can't be hidden. To overcome her depression, she needs understanding and compassion. Belief in her potential will help provide relief from her nervous symptoms and from your own—relief that can't be obtained with the help of a female sex hormone (estrogen).

Full-page ads in many medical journals recommend that doctors prescribe estrogen for menopausal women with symptoms of nervousness, anxiety, irritability, depression, fatigue, and insomnia. Estrogen, however, has little effect on nervous symptoms. Moreover, in studies published in the December 4, 1975, issue of *New England Journal of Medicine*, a group headed by Dr. Donald C.

Smith of the University of Washington found that the risk of cancer of the uterus was 4½ times greater in women exposed to estrogen therapy; Drs. Harry F. Ziel and William D. Finkle of the Kaiser-Permanente Medical Center in Los Angeles found that the risk in their series of cases was 7.6 times as great. In addition, for patients exposed to estrogen for seven or more years, the risk was 14 times as great. These two studies were stimulated by the alarming fact that the incidence of endometrial (inner lining of the uterus) cancer has doubled in the last few years.

SIR, ARE YOU GOING THROUGH THE CHANGE?

Another common misconception is that men go through a menopause that produces nervous upset, depression, sexual disturbances, and impotence. As in the case of the female, such symptoms occur at this time of life as the result of repeated blows to a man's self-respect. Male sex hormones are worthless in treating these conditions, since they fail to correct the real cause of the symptoms.

What can a woman do about a husband who demeans her and their children with his arrogance and vicious temper? It seldom occurs to such a man that he bears any responsibility for his wife's nervous condition. Such men almost always refuse to see a counselor. Much can be accomplished, however, by therapy with the wife. She can become aware that she is unwittingly provoking his temper with her own H, which she has been cowed into suppressing. She'll also find that she's just as arrogant as her husband, but doesn't come out with it openly. By learning Anti-H she will transmit far less H. Not only will this reduce his temper and arrogance, but also her excessive worrying; for worry is simply a manifestation of anxiety, and her anxiety is a natural reaction to her H.

While the treatment of a depressed person should be adapted to his individual characteristics, you can help most by seeing to it that he is a consistent winner in the contest for respect *and that you follow this up by honestly giving him the credit for winning.*

Inferiority is the principal cause of depression, as is shown by the quick rise in spirits when the patient's Respect Level is raised. But since a depressive's Inferiority feelings have accumulated and been reinforced over many years, the relief from one dose of respect is only temporary. An example is the baseball player who becomes depressed because he is batting poorly. Then one day he knocks out two home runs, and for the next day or two his spirits rise. Unless he continues to hit, however, he'll soon return to his depressed state.

You must use the leverage principle to elevate the depressed person's concept of his worth over a period of time. This doesn't make you the loser; on the contrary. In fulfilling his need, you eventually win his respect and achieve your goal of overcoming his depression.

When the depression is extreme, there is a real danger of insanity or suicide. Under these circumstances, the depressed person can be committed to a mental institution by law. If he is extremely agitated, has delusions of guilt, and doesn't respond to psychotherapy or antidepressant drugs, electroshock therapy should be instituted, since it usually brings relief within a week and can be repeated if symptoms recur. A disadvantage of electroshock is that the patient's memory may become impaired for several months after the treatment. As soon as the memory returns to normal, the patient should have a course of psychotherapy, as described above, in order to build up his self-respect and reduce his H. Unless this is done, the depression is very apt to recur.

However, institutional confinement should be resorted to only when all other efforts have failed, because a patient's low Respect Level is lowered even more when placed in a mental institution.

Mr. Z. was a slight, sixty-year-old man who had for several years been refusing his family's pleas to see a doctor. He had performed capably in a bookkeeping job until he became too depressed to work. However, when he began having delusions of worthlessness and became emaciated, his family committed him to a mental hospital. After eighteen months of stubborn resistance to treatment by a succession of three doctors, he was assigned by the merciless Chief Resident to me.

A lifelong bachelor, Mr. Z. had led a lonely existence, coming home to a solitary apartment each night after work. The contrast between the brilliant careers of his two brothers and his own lackluster job accentuated his feeling of Inferiority. His spinster sister offered unrestrained and unsolicited prescriptions as to how he should live his life. When I interviewed her, she complained, "He's as stubborn as a mule. He won't do anything I tell him to do, even though it's for his own good." In earlier years, he had listened with little protestation, but after some forty years of meek compliance, he had begun to balk.

Mr. Z. insisted on staying in his hospital bed most of the time. In our first interview, he let me know that even being brought to my office in a wheelchair put too much strain on his weak heart. (Examination had shown nothing wrong with it.) His feeling of humiliation was so pronounced that when he saw me coming, he would try to turn his body into a position where it would be least visible. He felt so sure that everyone looked down on him that he had the delusion that he was infested with lice.

After going through the therapy notes of each of the three doctors who had treated Mr. Z. previously, I was struck by one outstanding pattern: His doctors constantly countered his expressions of hopelessness with the most cheery optimism. Mr. Z. never failed to respond pessimistically to their reassurance, thus luring his doctors into being even more positive. No matter how dismal his complaints, they would insist that he would soon be well. "Why, we've checked your heart thoroughly; there's absolutely nothing wrong with it," and "If you walk around, you'll see for yourself that you're not too weak," and "You look in better spirits."

I realized that all of his life Mr. Z. had been told what to do; on her visits to the hospital his sister was still doing so. This poor fellow had always been on the lower end of the totem pole—and here we were doing the same thing. But he had finally resolved to put up a fight. Since reassurance made him out to be wrong, it automatically prodded him into a response that would show that he was right: contrariness. This compulsion to superiority over his doctors necessitated the conviction that his heart was bad, that he was weak, down in the dumps, and getting progressively worse. The more he was reassured, the more contrary would be his response. "It's no use," he would reply dolefully. "I can't do anything because of my weak heart."

In my experience, any treatment that succeeds in raising the patient's Respect Level is justified. Suppose, I conjectured, that he was told that we were going to limit his activities because of his bad heart and generalized weakness. Wouldn't he go all out to prove we were wrong?

The next day, when I saw him walking to the bathroom, I admonished him sternly that he was much too weak to be up and around, and ordered him back to bed. At the next interview, I told him that he was a hopeless invalid who simply didn't have what it took to get well. I knew that in spite of the coaxing of the ward nurses he had been eating very little. I explained my plan to them; he was not to be coaxed to eat. Instead, they were to tell him that my orders were for a restricted diet and confinement in bed.

I believe that the nursing staff probably thought I should have a bed on the ward myself. But as usual, Mr. Z. adamantly opposed what he was told to do. He indignantly demanded more food and would not stay in bed. In fact, he told me in his squeaky voice that he should be permitted to eat more and to walk the halls. I replied in no uncertain terms that as long as he was my responsibility, he'd have to follow my orders: "With your weak heart you might drop dead in the hall!"

He protested vehemently, and I was "forced" to give him permission to go out in the hall. But, "Don't go out in the courtyard or you might have a heart attack," I "warned" him.

Soon he went out to the courtyard and couldn't wait to tell me that I had been wrong again. A week later, he demanded permission to join the daily athletic programs in the yard. I really blew my top then: "What, you, a cardiac invalid, a weakling, out with those healthy fellows? Not while I'm running this ward." Nevertheless, after much argument, I threw up my hands in exasperation and yelled, "All right, but if they carry you back in, you'll be confined to bed again."

All I got for this was a sneer. The next day, he defied me by doing a lot of base-running in the afternoon ball game.

What had happened?

For most of his life he had been the loser in the quest for status with his sister and his two brothers. In therapy, he won the contest for Superiority for the first time, and won it again and again. Moreover, his Respect Level was raised even more because I acknowledged, albeit indirectly, that he won, thus giving him the validation denied him in the past. The energy he had wasted in self-condemnation and suppressed hostility was now being used for successful achievement. When the need for respect is fulfilled it becomes the human mind's most powerful energy catalyst.

Within a few weeks, Mr. Z. demanded permission to spend evenings at home. And after a week of overnight passes, he demanded to be discharged.

"But, what could you do?" I asked. "I'm sure that you can't make it back on the job. You'll soon be brought back on a stretcher." He did come back to the hospital the following year—to let me know that he was doing well on the job and feeling strong and chipper. Oh well, wrong again!

18.
The I of Alcoholism

According to some authorities, biochemical and hereditary factors predispose certain individuals to susceptibility to alcohol. If this is true, then it gives weight to the insistence of temperance crusaders that persons predisposed by heredity are doomed when they take the first drink. However, this statement appears to be based more on a need to deny a "sinful" pleasure to fellow human beings than on any valid evidence. Thus far, investigation of the role of biochemical, hereditary, and metabolic disturbances (malfunction in the formation and breakdown of the substances that maintain vital functions) has not yielded any satisfactory explanation of or treatment for alcoholism.

Why can some people drink in moderation while others become alcoholics? I believe that the critical difference lies in the extreme emotional pressure an alcoholic feels himself to be under. My own experience in treating alcoholics has pointed to a typical pattern of concealment and avoidance of the most intimate personal problems. With rare exceptions, this pattern has its root in feelings of I acquired by the patient in reaction to the superior and hostile attitudes of parents or other persons who raised him. Despite indignant denials by his parents, the complexes at the root of the alcoholic's problem were inflicted by them during his childhood and adolescence. These denials themselves are an indication of the parents' "can't be wrong" attitude.

As a result of his dissatisfaction with his status, the alcoholic resorts to lies and pretense in order to present the picture of a worthwhile, likable person. The trouble with this approach is that its insincerity is soon detected; his associates perceive the superior, resentful, contemptuous feelings lurking beneath the surface. Thus, while he strives to pass himself off as self-assured, happy, and successful, he suffers not only the oppressive burden of suppressed H, but also the ever-present fear of being unmasked and exposed as a fake. In fact, his humiliation is so great that he cannot bear to admit it. The pressure of suppressed H and anxiety from the constant effort to conceal his low self-esteem is so unbearable that the craving for any form of immediate relief, however temporary, is well-nigh irresistible. Alcohol is a commonly used agent. Its only effect, however, is to deaden the oppressive sensation of these emotions, just as morphine deadens the pain of an acute appendicitis without curing the disease itself. Since the relief is of such brief duration, the craving for more soon returns.

Paradoxically, alcohol's most treacherous effect is the relief it provides from suppressed anxiety and H. The drinker can then ignore his personal problems without being troubled by any perception of his anxiety. The problems that he ignores are specifically those involving conflict with close associates, at home and at work. Since the drinker habitually avoids them, he becomes increasingly inept at working them out. As a result, his fear is heightened and he makes even more of an effort to avoid confronting them. The more the lack of confidence (Inferiority), the more the H. Since the presence of H is interpreted by the nervous system as a sign that danger is present, the system reacts with the production of more anxiety and therefore an increased compulsion to drink.

While lamenting your unhappy fate as the victim of an alcoholic marriage partner, you may be unwittingly driving him or her to drink. Preaching to an alcoholic on the pitfalls of alcohol is usually interpreted as an implication of superiority on the part of the one doing the preaching and therefore causes the drinker to react with I $\rightarrow$ H. Regaling him or her with the heroic story of how you overcame alcoholism has the same derogatory effect.

Take the case of a lady brought in by her distressed husband for treatment of alcoholism. The husband indicated that he considered himself an authority on alcoholism: "I've told her the way to stop drinking, but she doesn't pay any attention to me. She's ruining my life as well as her own." At this point his wife tried to speak. After all, she was the patient. Without even looking at her, he gestured with his hand for her to shut up while he went on with his lecture to me on how she should be treated. A look of complete futility spread over her face. The long-suffering husband was quite unaware that his belittling and superior attitudes were battering away at his wife's self-respect, day in and day out, increasing her suppressed H and thus her craving for alcohol.

Few persons are equipped with the knowledge needed to help an alcoholic marriage partner. Many believe that they can get the individual to cut down on alcohol by persuading him or her to eat more. However, what is really needed is more nourishment for the drinker's depleted self-respect.

How can we raise the alcoholic's Respect Level? Consider the case of Mr. S. His wife desired with all her heart to help him overcome his addiction. However, in not being aware of the humiliating effect on him of her resentful, belittling, and know-it-all attitudes, she had literally been driving him to drink. When I pointed out the damage these attitudes were causing, she protested, "But I love him." But her love couldn't counteract her deprecatory attitudes.

Knowing the importance of looking her best for her husband, Mrs. S. spent a lot of time fixing her hair, applying cosmetics, and dressing attractively. But no amount of grooming can disguise the resentment conveyed by facial expression and tone of voice. She tried to hide the H that enveloped her when he came home reeking of liquor, but she only became more indignant at her husband's resentful response to her "friendly" manner. Like most alcoholics, he habitually attempted to conceal his resentment beneath a veneer of agreeableness. Since it transmitted nonetheless, his H served to increase his wife's.

"How badly is he hurt by my blaming look?" she asked.

"As badly as you are by his," I replied.

"Well, then," she asked, "why doesn't he consider *my* feelings?"

Like anyone else with deficient self-respect, the alcoholic is so obsessed with anxiety about himself that he fails to supply his wife, children, and others with the understanding, sympathy, respect, appreciation, and encouragement they require. They react to this in kind, so that he doesn't receive the emotional nourishment he requires from them.

I asked her *why* she was feeling inferior. Mrs. S. had undergone a steady barrage of domineering, belittling, and can't-be-wrong attitudes at the hands of her parents. The low Respect Level resulting from these attitudes generated superior, blaming, and martyred attitudes toward her husband and children. Mrs. S. felt that she was the victim of an inconsiderate and resentful husband. For one thing, her husband didn't seem to think enough of her to come home on time, giving her the impression that he would rather be with his cronies than with her. I reminded Mrs. S. that she had greeted him repeatedly with withering looks and tones when he had come home late. The more she had made him feel unappreciated, the more she had driven him toward those who were more appreciative.

Inasmuch as the alcoholic reacts with extreme sensitivity to your attitudes and feelings, it is of prime importance that you learn how to understand and manage them. You already know the futility of attempts to conceal them; the only way to protect someone else from the damage inflicted by your negative feelings is by ridding yourself of them. If you have harbored H and contempt for an alcoholic for a long time, you will have to think through your new understanding many times in order to thoroughly flush out these feelings.

In order to elevate a person's self-respect, you must first use Anti-H on yourself. The next step is to use yourself as a prop. Simply utilize the subject under discussion as a vehicle to give credit to the other fellow, rather than as a forum for your own opinion. You can almost always find something in what he says that you can validate. For example, suppose Mr. and Mrs. S.'s little girl lacerated her foot as a result of playing barefoot.

Mr. S.: "I told you to see that she wore shoes out in that backyard." A reply from Mrs. S. like "If you had cleaned up the yard when I asked you to, then she wouldn't have cut herself" would only put the blame on her husband and thus produce more hostility. On the other hand, any form of humility in which she admitted her own mistake would be helpful. Suppose Mrs. S. replied, "Well, I've finally got it through my skull that she won't hurt her feet if I see to it that she wears her shoes." This statement would indirectly validate her husband's opinion and, therefore, elevate his Respect Level. The most valuable technique of all is that of making use of the issue under discussion so that the alcoholic, not yourself, gets the credit. For example, suppose he complains that the dirty so-and-sos have unfairly denied him a promotion. Instead of reminding him that it's his own fault, mention some accomplishment on the job for which he should have received credit. The elevation of his Respect Level will lessen his compulsion to blame.

HELPING THE ALCOHOLIC IN INDUSTRY

About four and a half million Americans currently employed in industry and government have problems with alcohol. The resulting cost in absenteeism, sick pay, high accident rates, decreased productivity, poor executive decisions, and friction with fellow employees is estimated at eight billion dollars annually, or thirty-two million dollars each working day. Despite this staggering toll, supervisory personnel are seldom aware of the kinds of attitudes that aggravate an employee's drinking problem.

The connection between the alcoholic's work and home life

is the same as described for other workers. When frustrated and antagonized at home, he becomes more irritable and know-it-all at work. The increase in H from his vicious circle between work and home aggravates his susceptibility to alcohol.

The underlying cause of alcoholism in industry is the same as in the family setting. It isn't the complexity of the job, or the long hours of work, but the extreme anxiety resulting from habitual concealment of anger and feelings of failure. Many a boss looks on the alcoholic as a weakling, unmindful that this disdainful attitude causes hurt feelings and, therefore, a craving for relief through more drinking.

The following case is typical of how a manager of a large firm unwittingly contributed to the alcoholism of one of his key employees.

George, solely on the basis of ability and hard work, had risen from the ranks to district manager of a firm that made fine crystal. He believed in being soft-spoken and friendly with his men. Above all, he prided himself on the fact that he never displayed anger, always endeavored to avoid quarrels. George's work came under the close supervision of Fred, the general manager of the company. Fearing face-to-face arguments with anyone in authority, George would express his gripes in mild language via notes to Fred.

Had Fred understood that the sensitivities of human beings merit as much consideration as the sensitivities of the firm's fine crystal, he would have handled George with equal care. Unfortunately, when Fred did not go along with George's gripes, he simply made no reply.

George interpreted this as meaning that Fred did not value him enough to give consideration to his complaints. Because of his poor opinion of himself the alcoholic reacts with hostility to criticism, indifference, and fancied slights, especially when they occur in close personal contacts—as between a boss and secretary, a manager and an assistant. Neither Fred nor George had any knowledge of the operation of feeling transmission. Thus, although they made it a practice to be pleasant when together, each was, nevertheless, fully aware of the other's resentment. Because of George's inability to voice his resentment to anyone in authority, he kept it within himself. The load of suppressed H and anxiety became so unbearable that he would frequently avoid meetings with Fred. The only relief he got from his miserable feelings was through cocktails at the company's luncheons and after-work drinking with his staff.

As you have learned, a person becomes an alcoholic as a result of insidious forces that none of us can resist. Does this mean that you don't have the right to blame an employee for repeated drunkenness? Fire him, yes. Blame him, no. For every alcoholic is the victim of other persons in his background. His personality disorder is a reaction to the way he was treated by his parents, and, to a lesser extent, by his brothers, sisters, relatives, teachers, friends, and neighbors. The personality traits of even the brightest individuals are determined by the attitudes and feelings to which they were conditioned in early life. There is every reason to deal with the victim of such difficulties firmly, but no justification for condemning him.

I explained to Fred why George's resentful, disrespectful attitude toward him did not at all mean that he felt Fred was unworthy of respect. Its true meaning was that *George* felt inferior, and a portion of this inferiority had been produced in response to Fred's resentment.

Fred asked, "How can I respect a person who resents me?"

I replied, "How can George respect a person who resents him? You've been doing to him the very thing you condemn him for doing to you."

Fred asked with some exasperation, "Why doesn't George speak up and tell me what his gripes are, instead of hinting at them in those cute little notes he sends me?"

"Because of George's fear of complaining to anyone in authority over him. This fear was formed in childhood when he was repeatedly made out as wrong and scolded any time he attempted to voice his gripes to his father. In duplicating his father's response, you've hit him smack where he'd already been hurt before."

What George needed was an authority figure who would listen respectfully and give him credit for whatever portion of his criticism was valid. By doing this, Fred could overcome George's fear of being humiliated and of voicing his criticisms to Fred personally.

Fred and George, as well as the company, would benefit from their freedom to criticize each other without antagonism. The flow of mutual respect and affection would produce a steady reduction in the H and anxiety of both, resulting in a gradual lessening of George's craving for alcohol—and thus improve his efficiency—and also preserve Fred's own mental and physical health.

A widespread misconception is that the only one who can help an alcoholic is the alcoholic himself. Actually, he can seldom help himself since he lacks the knowledge of alcoholism's underlying basis. He needs sympathy rather than moralizing. An alcoholic isn't cured simply by openly admitting that he is an alcoholic. However, the elevation of his Respect Level through association with a group of persons who admit their own problems often enables him to bring to the surface and begin to deal with the personal problems that he had previously been unable to admit, even to himself. I believe this is the reason why many alcoholics have been helped by Alcoholics Anonymous.

The wife, husband, parent, child, employer, or co-worker who learns to apply the respect-building measures described above will furnish invaluable assistance not only to the doctor, but to any other therapist or organization, such as Alcoholics Anonymous, engaged in treatment of the alcoholic. In addition to this instruction, every effort should be made to get him involved in activities that help him feel needed.

Anyone who can't control his drinking should apply to himself the same understanding and techniques the alcoholic's family and fellow workers are instructed to apply to him. It is essential that the alcoholic understand that the attitudes and emotions of his parents were formed in the same manner as his own. Like himself, they were the innocent victims of a chain reaction from parent to child. This knowledge will enable him to understand why he is inferior to no one in self-worth. Furthermore, as a result of elevating the respect of others, he will earn the respect from close associates essential to bringing his own self-respect up to a healthy normal level.

I am keenly aware that much remains to be learned about the cause and treatment of alcoholism. Nevertheless, despite many disappointments, I have found that the method recommended here is effective, provided the patient doesn't drop out of treatment. If all those involved—his family, employer, physician, therapist, and fellow members of Alcoholics Anonymous—add the principles and techniques based on I $\rightarrow$ A + Ob + H + S + Mar. to their efforts, they can contribute much to the conquest of alcoholism.

19.
Gambling

The prospect of a huge payoff for a small wager has made gambling a popular pastime since time immemorial. I wouldn't try to deny that gambling is pleasurable, and as a doctor I'm eager to promote, not restrict pleasure. The trouble is that, for those who overdo it, the momentary pleasure of the gamble is replaced by long periods of misery.

Why, then, do millions of Americans pay the painful price of gambling way beyond their means? Why do businessmen who know better risk bankruptcy by speculative policies?

Almost always, the answer is to be found in an excessive amount of I → H + S. The excessive I is the result of malnourishment of the child's vital need for respect. Investigate the emotional background of a compulsive gambler and you'll find that being a loser is nothing new to him—he was a consistent loser throughout his childhood and adolescence in the quest for respect. Since he was reared by know-it-all parents who regularly made him out to be wrong, he developed a craving to be right—to be a big winner.

Such a person can't take rejection or defeat. His fragile self-respect can't withstand even ordinary buffets—from his family, co-workers, and other associates—and he is particularly likely to fall victim to the S Mirage.

As a businessman, he reacts to reverses with undue self-blame and H, which prods him into practices based on vengeance rather than profit. For example, H may prompt him to fire or reassign a key member of his firm. While he has the satisfaction of revenge, the loss to the firm may be considerable. Under these circumstances, he falls victim to the S Mirage. This produces fantasies of achieving superior gains by the use of risky policies that he would have rejected when his self-respect was at a higher level.

A businessman whose self-esteem has been fortified by years of success is much less affected by respect-lowering factors such as family problems or periods of business recession. This is exemplified by J. P. Morgan, who seldom yielded to the temptation to take risks. Bernard Baruch, another giant of business, discovered this when he accidentally made the wrong choice of words in regard to a joint venture with Morgan. Merely intending to convey that he had studied and approved a proposed deal, he said jovially, "I'll gamble a million on this deal." Morgan gave him a frozen glare and replied, "I never gamble."

THE S MIRAGE IN GAMBLING

It is only after repeated blows to his self-respect that an individual becomes a compulsive gambler. For this reason, the incidence of gambling is higher among members of minority groups. As a result of having been relegated to inferior status through social and economic discrimination, they're more apt to become subject to a Mirage that finds its expression in the vision of big winnings.

You can't fail to note specific characteristics of the compulsive gambler when he's at the racetrack, casino, or other gambling site. His superiority complex is readily discernible:

1. When one of his choices finally wins, he deafens his chums with his screams of victory. The skilled professional, on the other hand, though pleased with hitting a winner, makes little noise about it.

2. He belabors the fans adjacent to him with lectures on his supremacy in handicapping. He elaborates on his winners and seldom mentions his losers. His normal competitive drive is heightened by H and S so that competitors are regarded as enemies who must be humiliated. This is seen in the haughty derision he heaps upon his fellow players when his horse or team wins, and his reluctance to give credit for the winners his companions may have picked.

3. Instead of concentrating on handicapping, he is obsessed with showing superiority to his companions. This need is so compelling that it goads him into foolhardy risks based on Mirage rather than reason. For example, after handicapping the number 9 horse, he changes his mind after a companion announces that he, too, has picked number 9. His S Mirage is so powerful that he believes his revised selection will defeat his companion's.

The gambling addict's need for superiority is illustrated by the case of Rick, whose daily schedule began at 1:00 P.M., post time at the local racetrack. His personality and business acuity had enabled him to build up a very successful real estate business. He had more money than he could ever spend; yet his greatest thrill was a mutual ticket on a winner.

When he informed me that he had perfected a system that gave him a winning ticket in every race, I gaped in disbelief. However, Rick proved to be a man of rugged honesty: The system consisted of purchasing a ticket on every horse. He would place each ticket in a separate pocket, and he knew exactly where each was located. When his friends gathered around after each race, he would pluck the winning ticket from the correct pocket and nonchalantly comment, "I didn't see how I could lose." When asked by his friends how he had fared in his day at the track, he would stun them with, "I came home with eleven hundred dollars today." Again, he was telling the truth, merely omitting the trivial detail that he had gone to the track with fifteen hundred dollars.

As his losses pile up, a gambler's I feelings increase and he becomes more hostile toward his companions. Of course, these traits aren't likely to win friends and influence people. The disrespect he evokes increases his I feelings and, accordingly, the urge to gamble. Examine the life of any confirmed gambler and you'll find that he is suffering from the fear that he is a failure—either in love, career, or status with his associates. Rick's explanation for his love of the bangtails was that he was sexually frustrated. "My wife's a cold fish," he said. "She only grants sex once a month and it's like sex with a mannequin. The horses help me keep sex off my mind."

Sexual frustration, however, was merely one consequence of the circle of H between Rick's wife and himself. As a result of his I feelings he had been vying for Superiority with her throughout their marriage. One of her ways of retaliating for his habit of contradicting her was to withhold sex. That his real trouble was his low Respect Level was shown by his compulsion to flaunt winning tickets under the noses of the R.D.G.'s—Rick's abbreviation of the name he'd given his fellow gamblers: "Racehorse Degenerates." I didn't ask him how he classified himself.

WHY THE COMPULSION TO GAMBLE GROWS

The gambler's compulsion is often as overwhelming as that of the drug addict. The sad truth is that the more he gambles, the stronger the compulsion. Instead of seeking the real reason for his losses, he is deceived by his I $\rightarrow$ H into blaming someone else. Thus, when his horse loses, he is prone to condemn the jockey for holding him back or for riding him in a faulty manner. Paradoxically, the *worst* eventuality is for him to win, for the greater the amount he wins, the stronger the reality of actually having won fortifies his Mirage. When he has a winning streak, he has no desire to be cured of this pleasurable way of making "easy" money so fast. Thanks to his Mirage, he conceives of even more fabulous winnings and therefore increases his wagers. Since one can't continue a lucky streak indefinitely, he is soon wiped out.

But losses intensify the urge to gamble as much as winnings do. The more the bettor loses, the more he becomes victimized by I → H into a craving for revenge on the proprietors of the casino or track. Even though he doesn't have the slightest idea who they may be, he must, in the gambler's lingo, "get even." The result is that he doubles his bets, multiplying his losses. You can see from this that the I → H Reaction is the silent partner of racetracks and casinos, increasing their profits many times over.

In games of chance, as in sports, where winning depends in part on skill and knowledge, a player's mistake can pave the way for a losing streak. This is all the more so in the case of a gambler who has a low Respect Level, who because of the I → H Reaction is especially prone to anger and becomes known as a "hard loser." The compulsive gambler is most prone to binges when his Respect Level is at its lowest, as is also true for the compulsive drinker. Thus, the more desperate the gambler's financial plight, the greater his compulsion to gamble. Although he's promised his wife that he'll leave the dice table promptly at 8:30 so that they can have dinner, he won't budge. In fact, because of the overreaction of his balancing mechanism, he is driven to frantic efforts to exceed merely getting even and, instead, to become a big winner. Not only does he continue to play, but he also increases his wagers.

The S Mirage also explains why the gambler rarely keeps his winnings. Even when he's lucky enough to win several consecutive bets, his Mirage causes him to double and triple the amount of his wagers. These visions of victory are so powerful that they suppress such frightening realities as the consequences of losing: no paycheck to give to his wife for food and rent, no money to keep the check from bouncing, or the bill collectors from the door. Instead, his conscious mind contains only the thrilling concept of a big win and *its* consequences: bragging to his friends, and the things he'll buy with it. He truly exists in a make-believe world, the product of his Mirage. It is this illusion of Superiority, the very opposite of his underlying feeling of I, that gives him the intensely exciting thrill that is gambling's magnetic attraction. Instead of the fifty- or one-hundred-dollar investment that he had promised himself not to exceed, he ends up losing five hundred dollars, a thousand, or more. The prospect of coming home without money and having to face the H of his wife and creditors produces overwhelming anxiety and depression. Consumed with his troubles, he loses interest in sex, wife, and children, and is unable to function on the job.

But to make matters even rosier for the casino or the race-track, the addict can't wait until he gets a fresh bankroll so that he can try again. Stimulated only by the anticipatory Mirage of recouping his ever-mounting losses, he is driven to turn over any stone that might yield money. This may include pawning his valuables, borrowing from loan sharks, cashing worthless checks, and stealing from parents, wife, child, or employer. Obsessed with his need for betting money, he's a stingy chiseler on food, clothing, and other necessities. But on the rare times when he's won big, he's a lavish spender. The popular expression, "Most horseplayers die broke," brought out this comment from one turf veteran: "Most horseplayers *live* broke."

WHAT CAN THE GAMBLING ADDICT'S WIFE DO TO HELP HIM?

The wife of a gambler is caught up with him in the dreadful consequences of his gambling. No wonder she becomes so resentful. Unfortunately, because of a lack of knowledge of the emotional causes of gambling she unwittingly aggravates the problem. If she is not disturbed when she marries him, she is bound to become so as a result of the humiliation and hardships she suffers at his hands. The more her Respect Level is lowered, the more intense her I → H + S. Her S is manifested by dictatorial control of the family decisions and the children; and her H by gripes and argumentativeness, frigidity, and not infrequently, infidelity. The inevitable result is a rapidly growing circle of H between husband and wife.

A SUCCESSFUL CURE OF A GAMBLING ADDICT

Investigate the gambler's life and you'll find that his I feelings have been developing since childhood. H, belittling, know-it-all, and better-than-thou attitudes consigned him to the losing side, eternally opposed by the smug winners: his parents, abetted at times by teachers, and, as he grew older, bosses and marital partner. The more he has been made out to be the loser, the greater has become his craving for a rapid and extreme success: the fulfillment of his Mirage of Superiority over the oppressive enemy.

Ted Ramsey, a compulsive gambler from the age of fifteen, was raised in the crowded streets of Brooklyn by eternally bickering parents who had to work long hours to eke out a living for the boy and his three sisters. The constant dissension between the parents inevitably turned the mother's frustrated need for masculine affection to Ted. This evoked jealousy and resentment in his father, whose cruelty, tyranny, and scorn generated in the boy increasing H toward adults, which took the form of wanting to outdo them.

The father brought home presents for the girls, but nothing for Ted. Nor could he get any pennies or nickels from his father as did his sisters. Needless to say, such extreme discrimination kindled an increasing craving in Ted for material wealth. When he began earning money at fifteen, this craving drew him to the gambling games in the neighborhood. To hell with his father and the adult establishment, was Ted's feeling. He wouldn't allow them to keep him down any longer; he'd make it big on his own.

When he lost at dice or cards and was threatened with violence when he couldn't pay off, he always had someone to bail him out: his mother. An overprotective mother and a harsh father comprise a perfect combination for the rearing of a gambling addict. His mother had no idea that she was increasing her son's addiction to gambling by her unfailing constancy in paying his debts. Had she not come to the rescue, he wouldn't have been able to escape the beatings for not paying his debts, and therefore would most likely have been conditioned to renounce gambling while he was still young.

It wasn't long before Ted shifted his gambling to the horses. He developed into a superior handicapper, so that he often won large sums. However, while he consciously went to the track for the sole purpose of making money, his hunger for esteem would cause him to lose valuable time persuading others to bet on his selections. When his advice was disputed, he became so angry that it interfered with his judgment.

Even though experience had taught him the fallacy of betting races in which the payoff was much too small for the risk involved, his craving for superiority led him to bet every race. On one occasion, for example, he had a streak of seventeen consecutive losers. In the next race, the horse he liked was part of a two-horse entry. The odds on the entry were 1 to 4. This meant that if either horse won, he would win twenty-five dollars for his hundred-dollar wager. This would hardly compensate for the twelve hundred dollars he had lost on seventeen straight losers, yet the craving to flaunt a winner prompted him to take a risk that his own experience contradicted.

As luck would have it, one horse in the entry was in the photo for the win. After two minutes of agonizing waiting, while the judges studied the photo, Ted heard one of his horses declared the winner. His Superiority complex was so great that he proceeded to march up and down the aisle, beating his chest as if he had hit a 100 to 1 shot, while screaming over and over again, "Ramsey wins again!"—to the disgust of at least one of his cronies, who commented, "Whadduyuh mean, again?"

When he lost every nickel he would be forced to beg, borrow, lie, and steal to get more money. As the years went by, he reached the point where he could no longer get any credit; his mother had died and his friends finally refused his pleas for loans. Only when he reached this state of hopelessness did he seek help in a psychiatric clinic.

In therapy, he came to understand that his disdain for those who worked for a living originated from his H toward his hardworking father. With an understanding of the conflict between his parents, he was able to see that his father had acquired his H as innocently as Ted and his mother had. Ted came to realize that his father must have resented his invariable siding with his mother, just as he had resented his father for always taking his sisters' side against him. For the first time in his life Ted was now able to feel sympathy for the man he had hated since childhood.

Since the compulsion to gamble often has its roots in an arrogant, tyrannical father, the gambler has an overwhelming urge to outdo authority. Ted was contemptuous of the working man, whom he regarded as a square, lacking his own talent for making easy money. In fact, like so many gamblers, Ted had never realized that his talents could be applied elsewhere. He started in a small job. But, with his changed attitude, he began to taste the dignity and respect he had always longed for and was amazed at how rapidly he progressed. At this writing, he had already been on the job and off gambling for fifteen years. Successive promotions have enabled him to marry and lead a happy, fulfilling existence.

When you participate in any games or any form of gambling, you'll do a lot better to watch carefully for the appearance of any H and S and make sure that you use your Anti-H. What good is it to master the intricacies of bridge, chess, handicapping, or the stock market, only to make a foolish mistake as the result of H and the mirage of S? (Remember, these two saboteurs go together.) The method you've learned will help save you from such blunders. Make it a regular practice to check your H and S before making a critical decision.

Unfortunately, because of their compulsion to use their money almost exclusively for gambling, few gamblers ever take psychological treatment for this destructive addiction. It's futile for a wife to threaten that she'll leave if he doesn't quit gambling, unless she backs it up by leaving and staying away until there is proof that her husband has mended his ways. If she is determined to stay with him, she can help him by applying the instruction for wives given in the earlier chapters on marital problems and alcoholism. But the most important piece of knowledge for the gambler's wife is the recognition that his compulsion is the product of devastating blows to his self-respect. He is as much the victim of what others have inflicted on him as she is the victim of what he has inflicted upon her. Since his Mirage is specifically due to his Inferiority feelings, the logical way to help him is to raise his Respect Level. As in the case of the alcoholic, moralizing sermons and angry recriminations don't work because they imply the superiority of the one doing the lecturing.

If the gambler blows his salary at the racetrack should his wife excuse him and grant his request for a loan? Excuse him, yes; loan him, no. If he insists that he wants her to hand over the rent money for a horse that can't lose, she should not dispute his opinion, but simply refuse to hand over the money. Recognizing that her husband's high degree of inferiority causes him frequently to be irritable and critical, she can counter it with Anti-H.

By humbly admitting her own failings, a wife can help her husband realize that he isn't as far below others as he believes. He's apt to respond with suggestions on how she can remedy these failings and she can indicate her appreciation for his advice. Obsession with her own anxieties should be avoided in conversations with him. Instead, the husband should be encouraged to discuss his *own* interests while she, in all sincerity, asks questions indicating that she is interested in his opinions.

As the gambler's wife rids herself of H, her sexual desire is likely to return. While the compulsion to gamble can't be cured by sex, her improved response will contribute to raising her husband's self-respect. These respect-building measures are the best ways of helping him. If he refuses therapy, the wife should consult a therapist herself—not only to find out why her husband gambles, but to learn which of her own attitudes and emotions may be aggravating the problem. If these measures fail, she may be able to steer him to G.A. (Gamblers Anonymous). She can also learn a great deal by attending G.A. meetings for the wives of members.

20.
Crime, Violence, and War

Our country's rapidly increasing rate of violence has stimulated a flood of research into its causes. Dr. Karl A. Menninger has written: "Violence is getting more conspicuous because there are a lot more of us living closer together. Crowding people as they are now crowded is in itself one of the great aggravations of tension and irritation and proneness to violence."

Some have called Americans a uniquely violent people. Dr. John P. Spiegel, the director of Brandeis University's Lemberg Center for the Study of Violence, disagrees, citing the fact that while we have more crime than, for instance, the Scandinavian countries, England, and Iceland, those are homogeneous societies rather than the melting pot the United States is. ". . . We are full of immigrants and people of different racial origins who have a hard time seeing eye to eye. Also we are an open society. No one would dare to get out of line in Russia."

Until the forties the term "psychopath" was often used as a wastebasket classification. Most psychiatrists now consider it an outmoded classification. Therefore, it is useless in helping us understand the criminal mentality. Violence is seldom the result of an organic lesion of the brain. In the case of the sniper Charles Whitman, who murdered his wife and mother and then continued his killings with a high-powered rifle from a university tower, a brain tumor was found. However, Whitman's diary, which he kept for almost five years before the killings, revealed that the killings were planned, rather than the result of sudden impulse. Few patients with brain tumors become violent, and there is no reason to conclude that Whitman's violence was caused by his tumor.

In 1970, a meeting of eighteen scientists from fourteen countries, representing various life science fields, met in Paris under the auspices of the United Nations Educational, Scientific and Cultural Organization. They concluded that man is not a killer by nature, and does not possess an "aggressive instinct." Konrad Lorenz does not agree. In his book *On Aggression*, he declares that aggression is as innate as hunger and the sexual instinct, and serves purposes essential to the preservation of the species. "Aggression, in the proper and narrower sense of the word," Dr. Lorenz wrote, "is the fighting instinct in beast and man which is directed against members of the same species. It serves that species by balancing the distribution of its members over the available environment and by selecting the most rugged members to do the reproducing of the species."

I also disagree with the conclusions of the scientists at the UNESCO meeting. However, their discussion brought out four major categories or situations that may lead to individual aggressiveness: 1) a clear and present danger to survival; 2) *frustration of self-esteem;* 3) a threat to close personal relationships; 4) *a threat to one's sense of belonging to a larger group.* The italicized factors certainly translate as a lowered Respect Level, and all four qualify as situations that put one in a position of inferiority. Similar findings were brought together under the heading of the "frustration—aggression" theory, by the National Commission on Violence. Summarizing these findings, the commission stated: "We are warned by this theory that 1) all people are likely to be ready to aggress against others, because all people experience frustrations of varying intensity during their lives; and 2) the worse the frustration, the greater the readiness for aggression, and perhaps even for violence."

The H and aggression instincts are as much a part of man as the instinct for self-preservation. They are always there, ready to be triggered by anything that lowers self-respect. In one such case, a woman who had separated from her husband was seriously wounded as the result of a derogatory remark. The husband, coming from his job as a nightwatchman, stopped by to ask her if she had received the letter he had written her. She replied, "The letter's in the garbage can, and that's where you belong." Unfortunately, she hadn't reckoned with his precariously low level of respect. The instant rage reaction to her respect-lowering remark provoked him into shooting her.

We live in a world menaced by the threat of nuclear war. Knowing that a nuclear holocaust could come about through the decision of one man, we should be terrified by national leaders with high concentrations of H. In problems between nations, a leader may make decisions based on his H rather than the welfare of his country. There is ample evidence of this throughout history, most recently in former President Nixon's order to bomb Hanoi—a product of $I \rightarrow H$ following repeated failures to achieve his objectives.

Again and again, the Mirage of Superiority has produced leaders with a messianic complex. Their greatest appeal is to those who because of their own I feelings are prone to identify with the Mirage of the leader—a sort of *folie à deux*. Since there is always a sizable segment of the population of any nation that suffers from respect deficiency, this segment is vulnerable to leaders who appeal to their H and S. Dazzled by their S Mirage, they identify with such leaders and are easily led to believe "Follow me and you'll reach the highest mountain." By portraying his supporters as the martyred victims of an evil group, a leader can easily incite them to make such a group their scapegoat—as happened during the McCarthyism of the fifties. The same pattern of forces is operative in the conflict between differing religious groups and races.

Napoleon was one of those leaders who had a magnetic appeal for those with low Respect Levels. After crushing Tsar Alexander's army at Friedland, he met the young Tsar in Prussia to discuss peace terms. The Tsar's humiliating defeat gave rise to an S Mirage causing him to exclaim to his conqueror, "What is Europe; where is it, if it is not you and I?"

The feeling of superiority that drives a leader to even greater conquests must generate a hostile response of equal intensity: "Upon what meat doth this, our Caesar, feed that he is grown so great?" While Napoleon's S Mirage egged him on to military campaigns of increasing scope, the inevitable reaction to it was an equal force of vengeance from the opposition—a force that led to his final crushing defeat and banishment to the rocky island of St. Helena, and only intensified his I feelings. In his memoirs we find ample evidence of his S and martyr complex. Napoleon depicted himself as the true friend of oppressed nationalities, a lover of peace, who had been driven to war by the wiles of the British and the treachery of despotic European monarchs.

The consequences of excessive feelings of inferiority are glaringly apparent in the rise and fall of Adolph Hitler. His I was a product of a childhood in which he was bullied, beaten, and denounced as a weakling and a worthless idler by his drunkard father. The extreme I accounts for his extreme Ob + H + S + Mar. He was so obsessed with himself that he ranted on and on, oblivious to those with whom he was conversing. His S Mirage caused him to believe that he could direct the strategy of the Nazi armed forces better than his most seasoned generals. His martyr complex was responsible for his conviction that he was the victim of malevolent oppression. The intensity of these forces activated an opposition of equal intensity resulting in his destruction.

The rise and fall of Nazi Germany is typical of the significance of I in influencing the masses. Crushed by the total defeat and humiliating reparations of World War I, the mass inferiority of the German people grew rapidly. It was for this reason that they became so vulnerable to a leader who stood for superiority and hatred.

Ob and H in International Relations

Inattention to the self-defeating quality of Ob and H is often ignored even in the highest diplomatic transactions. This is illustrated by the hostile exchange after the United States declared a military alert during the 1973 Middle East war without consulting its ally, France. Certainly, we can understand why the French foreign minister stated indignantly that the United States had revealed France as a "nonperson." Feeling disrespected by our failure to consult them, it is no surprise that the French responded by failing to consult us when they arranged an oil conference with the Arabs. Sure enough, the U.S. State Department reacted with I → H by blaming the French, thus perpetuating a vicious circle.

The same thing happens when the United States "unselfishly" helps other countries only to have them subsequently thumb their noses at us. Because of inattention to an impoverished country's need for respect, doling out food to their hungry masses has often failed to decrease their H to the United States. We wouldn't complain about their ingratitude if we realized that generous help is negated when it is accompanied by moralizing and demeaning attitudes.

Dr. Marvin E. Wolfgang, Research Director for the National Commission on the Causes and Prevention of Violence, has pointed out that there is a subculture of violence, consisting of the poor, living in crowded ghettos where a set of negative values is transmitted from generation to generation.

Dr. Shervert H. Frazier, Professor of Psychiatry at Harvard University, speculates that persons who were physically brutalized throughout their childhood grow up with a propensity to kill or make homicidal threats. Although muggers and violent criminals quite often do develop from such backgrounds, the record shows that when youngsters receive adequate nourishment of their self-respect they do not become criminals, despite being reared in extreme poverty.

Some sociologists maintain that one of the reasons underprivileged youngsters commit a disproportionate percentage of crime is that chronic hunger causes H. But my observation has been that this causes only a fraction of the H. The major portion is a consequence of the I → H Reaction: feeling a deficiency in self-respect as a result of comparing one's own lot with that of the well-fed segment of society. For this reason, it is a mistaken policy to attempt to gain the affection and respect of the hungry by doling out food and welfare alone. If we overlook the respect factor, the poor are certain to react with H. Underprivileged youngsters should be given opportunities to gain badly needed self-respect; for example, training that would pave the way to get into the higher professions; camps where they would be given instruction in forestry, conservation, carpentry, and other useful vocations. The change in environment from poverty-stricken and crime-infested city slums to camps in the outdoors, supervised by dedicated teachers, could not fail to be a help in itself. The accomplishment of the C.C.C. (Civilian Conservation Corps) along these lines was amply demonstrated during the Depression of the thirties.

I heartily subscribe to any measures that will improve the social and economic conditions of any underprivileged group. Nevertheless, any minority or underprivileged group elicits more genuine concern for its needs as its H to the majority is reduced. The willingness of the middle and upper economic classes to help better the lot of the underprivileged is sharply compromised by any H shown toward them, which only provokes such vengeful responses as the "benign neglect" of economic measures for the benefit of the underprivileged. Unfortunately, despite some helpful measures, not enough has been done to improve the social and economic lot of the underprivileged, whose frustrations often prod them into violence and crime.

Certainly, law officers must give first priority to protection of themselves and the public in dealing with any form of violent public protest. But violence is increased in agitated individuals when the authorities manifest hostile and arrogant attitudes toward them. Dr. John P. Spiegel, one of the country's foremost investigators of violence, stated in August, 1973, that "when the city administration adopted the position of all-out resistance, refused to listen and communicate, then the disorders tended to escalate, particularly when the police and National Guard were used in an infortunate way. . . . That set up unresolvable conflict in which the only solution was war."

Too often, during a political demonstration, for instance, officials put the blame squarely on the demonstrators while ignoring their own attitudes. In all fairness, this is a natural reaction to the protesters' hostile defiance, but highly placed officials increase H and, therefore, rebellious defiance. Wouldn't it be far more preferable for police and National Guard members to learn how to reduce H in demonstrators and in themselves than to unwittingly foment increased H? Wouldn't it be better if our government leaders would learn to refrain from belittling and moralizing behavior toward frustrated and embittered protestors? In doing so, they would be better protected since they'd be provoking less H in the opposition.

Is there any reason why Anti-H measures should not be instituted before resorting to brute force? The H of a mob, like the fury of a hurricane, is the product of its individual components. Since each individual in the mob is susceptible to Anti-H measures, the total H of the mob can be reduced. Rioting students, violent truckdrivers, hijackers, or strikers should be dealt with by officers equipped with an understanding of $I \rightarrow H + S$.

If these officials had a better understanding of emotional factors, they would arrange for more meetings with the young and provide them with every opportunity to express their opinions. This has been done recently in some cities, with encouraging results. Just as young people need humble acknowledgment of mistakes from their parents, so they need this from government officials and policemen. Such an approach to a young gang, for instance, would have a far better chance of enlisting their support than the usual scolding and sermonizing. Instead, they could be told, "You've shown us where we've erred. Your suggestion as to how to correct things makes sense. We'll follow your suggestion. Will you work with us to help it succeed?" While Anti-H doesn't supply the answer to the socio-economic and political problems that lead to protests, riots, hijacking, and gang wars, it is my conviction that the diffusion of this knowledge would contribute to a reduction in the violence associated with them.

Many police departments have learned that conciliatory communication with agitated community groups has resulted in decreased violence. Where college authorities have been willing to listen to the complaints of protesting students and heed their request for removal of antiquated and senseless restrictive regulations there has been a proportional decrease in violent confrontation. The lesson Dr. Spiegel has drawn from his studies at the Lemberg Center is that the disturbances of the sixties were less violent in those cases where city authorities or college administrators recognized the validity of grievances and tried to communicate and negotiate with protesters in a respectful manner.

It might seem that the drug addict's only motivation in resorting to crime is to obtain money for his drug habit. We have seen, however, that it is those with an overload of H who become addicts, and that the H increases as the addiction does. A considerable segment of the criminal population is capable of earning a decent living legitimately. But, with rare exceptions, a person who resorts to violent crime, be it mugging or murder, is carrying an excessive load of H and a Mirage of Superiority. The mental picture of a quick and large gain is perceived as reality, and its duped victim acts upon it. The worst thing that can happen then is for the individual successfully to carry off his initial attempt at crime, for this only confirms his Mirage as reality and thus impels him to try again. You can see that the criminal who "succeeds" is lured into further disaster by his Mirage in the same way as the gambler whose Mirage of winning is followed by an initial success.

Throughout the ages, man has reacted to criminals with H and vengefulness. The effect of these attitudes on the criminal has been to increase his $I \rightarrow H + S$ and, therefore, his urge to crime. Even a law-abiding individual might have few if any compunctions about robbing a hated enemy, so it's only natural that the criminal reacts to society's traditional feelings of vengeance toward him by further criminal acts.

The police officer should be taught that the criminal is mentally disturbed. Does this mean that an officer of the law faced by an armed thug should drop his weapon and employ only Anti-H Therapy? Of course not; the Anti-H approach to the problem of violence and crime is not a cure-all. Since a person becomes violent only as a result of a large number of hurts to his self-respect, he can't be expected to be transformed into a nonviolent person by a single dose of considerate treatment. A law officer should do everything possible to protect himself. This may necessitate incapacitating or even killing a criminal in the line of duty, but it doesn't require H, any more than H is needed by a doctor to protect himself against a patient with a contagious disease.

Authorities on criminality and imprisonment have pointed out that inhuman living conditions in their jails and prisons, and the scarcity of rehabilitation measures, only lead to more criminality when the prisoners are released. Yet releasing a criminal on the basis of a form of therapy that doesn't work is foolhardy. We must quarantine the criminal as we do the contagious-disease patient, not to punish either of them, but only to protect ourselves. Punishment only increases H, the emotion that is the essential basis of criminal behavior. Certainly lawbreakers should be arrested and prosecuted, but not demeaned or berated. On the other hand, in the process of ridding yourself of H you generate an abundance of respect—for yourself and the violent person or persons; and the transmission of this feeling is the vital ingredient in reducing H and, therefore, in ameliorating violent impulses.

Most attempts at psychiatric treatment of criminals in prison have not stopped them from resuming their criminal pursuits once released, and conscientious administrators of the law have become fed up with psychotherapy for prisoners, as this statement (January, 1975) by the Governor of California indicates: "The idea that crime is a sickness—I don't accept it. The idea of putting lawbreakers in a room and talking about how their mother treated them or what society did to them is no good. When you say people don't intentionally do wrong and they're not responsible, you are denying their dignity as human beings."

Since therapy of prisoners has been ineffective, the Governor concludes that criminals aren't sick. It should be obvious, however, that the failure of a treatment doesn't prove the absence of sickness, just proves that the treatment employed wasn't effective. Moreover, it's precisely because they're *not* responsible that individuals become criminals.

I strongly recommend that we make Anti-H instruction available to help reduce their criminal tendencies. Along with improvement of basic living conditions in our prisons, Anti-H therapy could contribute to a reduction of violence between correction officials and convicts if taught to both groups. This would diminish feelings of condemnation and ensure the transmission of more mutually respectful and sympathetic feelings. But since Anti-H therapy has not been tested in prison, I don't recommend that prisoners be released on the basis of exposure to this treatment alone. Vigilance against escape from prison must not be relaxed just because of rehabilitation therapy; and unless there is ironclad evidence that he has been rehabilitated, a criminal should not be released before he has served out of his term.

Society must continue to let criminals know that it will use all the force necessary to protect itself against them, short of H. The same approach should be applied to a violent child, adolescent, rioter, striker, husband, or wife.

Epilogue: Anti-H Therapy

"Only you can do it. . . . Work out your problems yourself. . . . You have only yourself to blame for your troubles." These noble-sounding calls to self-determination have been repeated since time immemorial by parents, brothers and sisters, bosses, clergymen, doctors, judges, political leaders, philosophers and, to be sure, many psychologists and psychiatrists. Apparently it's sensible to consult a surgeon for surgical problems, or a plumber for a leaking pipe, but if you're suffering from nervousness, depression, or marital unhappiness then you must work it out on your own.

A nineteen-year-old youngster whom I treated following a suicide attempt said that when he had told his father that he felt confused and hopeless, he was simply told that he must get a grip on himself. This advice only made him feel more inferior since he had been trying to do that all along and had failed. How can the emotionally disturbed person possibly "get a grip on himself" if he isn't equipped with the knowledge needed to solve the emotional complexes at the root of his troubles? A person can become emotionally ill only as a result of what is done *to* him, not as a result of what he does to himself. It may seem that he often provokes or allows the hurts inflicted on him, but this is not so. He is the victim of forces over which he has no control, so there need be no loss of pride in admitting he is ill. Sure, some people ridicule those they know to be seeing a therapist. Well, some people ridicule others for being black, white, American, or Republican, too. Remember, if you're the one being ridiculed, that it's not your problem—it's the scoffer's problem: specifically, his low opinion of himself. Admittedly, most people can't afford the high cost of professional therapy. However,

229

it's a lot better to spend half your salary on such care than attempt to do it yourself and lose a lot more than money.

In the most prevalent form of psychotherapy the patient does the talking, while the therapist has little to say except for an occasional question or interpretation. I believe that this is because the "listening therapists" have held the power in most of our schools of psychology and psychiatry since this technique was first taught by Sigmund Freud, and have continued to teach the ritualized procedures with which they were indoctrinated in their own training. Of course, the patient may find it gratifying to talk about his problems without interruption, criticism, or explanation. However, it is impossible to learn the knowledge assembled and refined by thousands of behavioral scientists in the course of history by merely having someone listen to you. Fortunately, with the advent of new forms of treatment such as behavior modification and transactional analysis in the last few years, "listening therapy" has begun to be seriously questioned.

Most of my patients are referred to me by their physicians. I advise the patient that it will be to his benefit if his doctor and I can cooperate in the treatment since his doctor may have a considerable knowledge of his personal life. Furthermore, the need for the physician's medical expertise is often essential and I insist that patients be checked by their physician before, during, and following their psychiatric treatment. I also suggest that they consult their physician for advice on exercise, nutrition, and other health matters.

Besides using my relationship with the patient to elevate his self-respect, it is essential that I keep myself free of H and S toward him and the persons he discusses. I must be careful to avoid any obsession with myself and martyred complaints such as "It's hard to get any time off with this load I'm carrying."

I explain to the patient how his treatment may be accelerated if he allows me to see his wife, husband, brother, sister, parents, or even his employer. Working with persons who live or work in close association with the patient provides them with insight into how their attitudes and feelings are aggravating a relationship they're seeking to improve. They are instructed in the technique of raising the patient's self-respect. Family and friends also can supply the therapist with information that the patient may be withholding.

At times, a patient needs advice on his social activities. Thus, after teaching a father how to manage his H, I explain the emotional benefits for his children as well as himself in joint expeditions to the zoo or ball game, or other activities. Lonely patients often need encouragement to go on a vacation, have friends or relatives over for dinner, join an organization, or take up some activity such as bowling or dancing. However, the therapist must be careful in giving advice to patients who may follow it unquestioningly. This occurred in the case of a patient who said that she had refused to have sexual relations with her boyfriend because he was hairy. I replied, "That doesn't make any difference." On her next visit, she remarked, "You were right, it didn't."

THE ADVANTAGES OF THE TEACHING
METHOD IN GROUP THERAPY

One of the advantages of group therapy is that it can be afforded by large numbers of people. In the most widely practiced forms of group therapy, however, much of the time is consumed in listening to the comments of the group, while the therapist limits himself to occasional questions such as "Is there anything else you'd like to tell us?" or "Why do you think so?" or just plain "So?"

The result is that years may go by and the patients learn very little from the therapist. Some relief is provided in learning that others in the group have problems similar to their own, and in having the ears of a sympathetic audience. However, the patients entered therapy and paid their fees in the expectation of receiving help from an expert in the field.

In the teaching method of group therapy, the basic principles elaborated in this book are taught by lecture and discussion with the group. This *teaching* method of therapy includes the basic elements of learning the underlying principles and their application as in any course or apprenticeship—as, for example, in cabinet-making or algebra.

Much can be accomplished in groups of hundreds, except for the disadvantage of having to limit questions and comments from the class. This, however, is not a great disadvantage, since the questions that arise are remarkably alike. For example:

"How can I get my daughter to keep her room neat?"

"What should we tell our kids when they ask why we've separated?"

"Why should I let my mother-in-law run my home?"

"I've been nice to Mary [a fellow worker], why is she so mean to me?"

"How can I get my husband to discuss our problem with me?"

The same techniques of elevating respect and gaining Receptivity from the class are employed as in individual therapy. The therapist's acknowledgment of mistakes, and any other expressions of fallibility, are invaluable. If a pupil asks, for instance, "Do you have problems, too?" the therapist should admit that he does. When I was a medical officer in the army in World War II, I was assigned the task of lecturing on Sex Hygiene to an entire command consisting of several thousand men, from privates to generals. One of the questions was: "Sir, does masturbation affect a fellow any?" My spontaneous reply was, "Well, it never affected me any."

Other than the techniques for attaining Receptivity, the teaching is carried out as it would be in any other course. The students are encouraged to break in with questions and comments at any time, but no one pupil is permitted to hog the discussion. Only typical personal problems are discussed, since it's impractical to discuss problems that most of us don't encounter in a lifetime. Accordingly, if a pupil asks for information on the emotional problems of astronauts or lion tamers, he is told that this material isn't included in the course.

Taking notes is as valuable here as it is in other courses. Some students record each session and use the recordings as a basis for discussion with family, friends, and other students. Simple diagrams on a blackboard are useful to help the student understand how the mind functions and how individuals react emotionally toward one another.

Most of the talking is done by the therapist in setting forth the principles, showing how they are applied in typical cases, answering questions, and correcting errors. The student learns why resentments are formed, why some members talk too much, show off, manifest jealousy, envy, flattery, meekness, sullenness, hurt feelings, martyring, smugness or subserviency. A person's behavior becomes easy to analyze when he learns the underlying principles that explain: $I \rightarrow A + Ob + H + S + Mar$. It becomes increasingly apparent to the class that each student's mode of reaction in any discussion is based on his particular Respect Level.

Once the students have learned how the emotional system operates, they are shown how to apply this knowledge to their own personal problems. When a group member demonstrates that he can do this correctly, he is allowed to assist other members of the group in solving their problems. Each session with the teacher is followed by one in which the teacher is not present. This offers the students an opportunity to discuss the previous session among themselves and formulate questions for the next one with the teacher.

The rest of the course consists of about an hour of homework daily. This includes discussion with family and friends of what the patient has been learning; he practices the technique of using himself as a prop to elevate the other person's respect, applying his new knowledge to such problems as friction between his wife and child or between two of his key employees. An essential part of the homework is to apply this knowledge in freeing himself of superior and hostile attitudes in his personal relationships. Thus, a woman who has been resentful toward her mother thinks over her new understanding of their relationship several times a day. She is also instructed to have more contact with her. This permits her change in feelings to react on her mother and thus reduces her mother's H toward her.

Merely telling a student to do or say thus and so is worthless; he must learn to understand *why* he feels as he does and *how* to change his feelings so that he can cope successfully with the problems he is facing. For example, a mother in the group asked, "If I become angry at my child for misbehaving, what do I do about it?"

The answer given by another member was: "Instead of venting your anger on the child, you should simply state the particular *thing* you're angry about, rather than say you're angry at *him*. For example, if you're angry because the child hasn't heeded your repeated requests not to throw his clothes on the floor, say, 'I feel good and angry about this mess.' "

Now the reader knows that the child is not fooled by this technique; he knows perfectly well that his mother is angry with him, regardless of what she says, since H is always transmitted.

The next step is to ascertain why the child misbehaved. Some acts are simply the result of the child's playful nature, or of his lack of caution due to inexperience. The most likely reason, though, is that the child is hostile toward his mother. If the child misbehaves mostly around his father, on the other hand, then he must be hostile toward him. If he doesn't misbehave when his father is present, that doesn't prove that he isn't hostile to his father; it may merely mean that he's learned from painful experience that he'll be punished for misbehavior when his father is around. These are the children that develop the most severe emotional damage since they are conditioned to become suppressors of H. Children, like adults, become hostile in reaction to the way they've been treated. Therefore, they shouldn't be blamed for bad behavior since it is almost always due to their H.

Practicing what has been learned in class is vital. Thus, in the next session, the difficulties the mother met in applying the method are ironed out with the teacher's help. Nothing is lost if she doesn't get the chance to ask about her particular problems, though. Since the origin and the solution of most of our personal problems are remarkably uniform, she can get her answers when others ask the same or similar questions.

Of course, we can't expect anyone to master the entire field of behavioral science in a few months of teaching therapy, but it is possible to understand and remedy most emotional problems with a working knowledge of $I \rightarrow A + Ob + H + S + Mar$. After applying this technique in a troubled relationship, the path of interaction isn't all sweetness and light forever after, of course. As with other formidable accomplishments, applying Anti-H requires common sense and persistence. In my own experience in teaching Anti-H to individuals and groups, most of those who failed in using my methods did so because they didn't persist long enough, omitted one of the essential steps, or attempted to persuade someone before earning his Receptivity. Some of these folks returned to therapy because their symptoms recurred. After being shown that they weren't continuing to use the knowledge that had previously worked so well, they could easily understand why this had happened.

One patient, for example, had been served very well by his course of instruction but had lost sight of some essential components of it as the years went by.

This man had many excellent personal qualities. He was fair, decent, unselfish, loyal, self-reliant, and truthful. He had finally arrived at a level of success that permitted him to shorten his work hours, take frequent vacations, and enjoy time at home with his wife. He had earned the respect and affection of his employees, customers, and friends; and he had the satisfaction that comes from leading an upright existence and achieving success in his work. But twenty-one years after his original therapy he returned for advice in regard to his son.

Ned, twenty-eight years old, with a master's degree in business administration, had quit a succession of jobs and could not be persuaded to look for another one. The father, motivated by a sincere desire to help his son, was quick to offer him his advice.

Unwittingly, though, he proffered his counsel in a series of moralizing sermons delivered with exaggerated self-importance. He repeatedly told the boy that he had nothing to worry about, that he would "personally" guarantee his success. What the father failed to realize was that his son's anxiety was the direct consequence of his own condescending attitude.

His father's implication that a position could be secured for him through his own high standing in the business world was humiliating to Ned. The lowering of the son's Respect Level inevitably produced a hostile, and therefore contrary, reaction. Ned became so depressed that he spent most of his days in bed, virtually paralyzed by a crushed ego. Thus, in spite of the father's high level of intelligence, he had lost sight of the vital need to maintain his son's self-respect.

In order to divest himself of his H, Ned had to understand that his father was not trying to brand him as inferior, but that he was reacting to his own fear that he had been a failure as a father with a Mirage of S. As son and father received instruction, their H gradually diminished. Ned recognized that he was reacting to his own I with H and the urge to S over his father—precisely the same response to I that occurs in everyone. Freed of the intolerable burden of I and H feelings, Ned was no longer depressed and did well in a job that he obtained without his father's help.

The United States may soon institute national health insurance. Since suppressed H is a major factor in the formation of disease, such a national health program should provide everyone with the knowledge of how to deal with this disease-producing poison. It is my firm conviction that the teaching method of group therapy should be made as easily accessible to the public as are other forms of preventive medicine. Local, state, and federal agencies should make this teaching available to everyone, including employees and inmates of jails and reformatories. Hospital medical staffs could be enlisted for such teaching, using hospital auditoriums, public libraries, and community mental health centers as classrooms. Schools and universities should include this teaching as a standard part of the curriculum.

Blue Cross and other insurance companies could save billions in payments for sickness by instituting centers of teaching in every community. Teaching workers to overcome H would more than pay its cost to industry. As little as one teaching session would pay off in decreasing accidents, illness, alcoholism, absenteeism, and poor cooperation and motivation.

To be realistic, however, I don't believe that a system of therapy has yet been devised that can assure a continuous flow of success in every relationship and endeavor. Nor can everyone achieve equal proficiency. Some of my students and patients were not able to acquire consistency in dissolving their H even after lengthy treatment.

WHEN ANTI-H DOESN'T WORK

The following case illustrates some of the difficulties encountered in the method and how they can be surmounted.

Mrs. F. was a tall thin woman of forty-nine. She had entered group therapy because, as she told us, "I'm depressed and feel lost. Life is a burden. I have migraine headaches, feel tired and run-down." With encouragement, she was able to tell the group of her resentments toward her husband: "He always expects me to listen to his complaints about his boss and co-workers, but he's not interested in the troubles I have at home. He gets peeved whenever I won't go along with what he wants me to do. For instance, even though he knows that I don't like to drink, he often insists that I have a drink with him. Then when I refuse, he sulks."

Mrs. F. was asked to bring her husband to the group. It turned out that he had just as many complaints about her: "She tells me all about her troubles, but doesn't want to hear about mine. I can't even get her to join me in sipping a little wine. She often gets huffy if I make some simple request, like asking her to exchange some article at the store."

This couple was involved in a full-blown circle of hostility that had become progressively worse in their twenty-six years of marriage. I instructed them in Anti-H therapy and, after seven group sessions, they felt that they had learned it well enough to withdraw from treatment. Indeed, they appeared to have done an excellent job. Hostility had taken a sharp drop, they were getting along well, and Mrs. F. was relieved of her symptoms.

I heard from them again five years later. Mrs. F. was more distraught than ever. After eighteen months of feeling better, her symptoms had gradually reappeared. In addition, her husband had become very depressed. For the past three years he had found it increasingly difficult to work because of tension and depression.

One of the mistakes I had made with Mr. and Mrs. F. was that I had failed to emphasize sufficiently the need for a longer period of participation in the course. Most of my students require twelve group sessions. Moreover, the compulsion to Ob + H + S + Mar. behavior is so deep-seated that the knowledge of Anti-H must be maintained by study and practice as an essential discipline. Unless we do so, we lose our mental fitness, just as physical fitness is lost if we don't continue to exercise.

The reason for the breakdown between this couple was the intensity of their vying for S. If Mrs. F. said that there was going to be creamed turkey for dinner, Mr. F. too often would deflate her by a reply such as, "Honey, why can't we have a pot roast?" He spent most of his time in the den, a place where she was not comfortable, yet he would insist that she stay in the den with him. On the few occasions that she didn't comply, he would go into a long-lasting burn. Most of the time she'd switch her dinner plans for him, and stay in the den with him, but despite this apparent agreeableness, she was filled with H. Mr. F.'s uge to S was so great that when their troubles recurred, he told his wife that she needed to return to the class but that he didn't. This superior attitude made her feel more I and, therefore, more hostile to him; accordingly, she opposed his advice. Only when her migraine recurred could he prevail on her to return; and he was able to do this only by admitting that he, too, needed therapy for depression.

When they returned, I reminded them of the destructive pattern that had caused their previous trouble. The trouble really wasn't the issues on which they differed; the heart of the trouble was exactly as before: the vying for S over *any* issue. Mrs. F. recognized that her ready compliance with her husband's wishes wasn't sincere; she had only been going along with him as a ploy to demonstrate that she was really a better person than he. Thus, she was giving him the same S treatment that he was giving her; and he was vividly aware of her martyred air and suppressed H.

Proficiency in Anti-H technique, as in any other, requires repeated searching for and correction of mistakes. With rare exceptions, failure is due to deviation from the principles on which the technique is based. By means of regular participation in the group, Mr. and Mrs. F. learned to recognize their hostile and superior patterns along with the Ob. and Mar. As both applied Anti-H, they overcame their symptoms once again. This time they realized the importance of continuing on a once-a-month basis until they felt a more secure mastery of Anti-H therapy.

The following case is another instance of a breakdown in Anti-H therapy, and how it was remedied by searching for flaws in its application.

Mr. and Mrs. W. were referred because of severe anxiety, tension, and depression. They did not join a class, but came in together for hour-long visits.

Mrs. W.: "We can't stand each other anymore. We've been married for seventeen years and the only happiness we ever had was in the first few years. We argue most of the time. Since my seventy-year-old father came to live with us three years ago, the arguments have been worse than ever. My husband says that if I don't ask my father to leave, he's going to move out. I don't blame him. My father is impossible. He constantly picks on the children, our twelve-year-old girl and ten-year-old boy. He argues with me about everything: the food, furniture arrangement, and my housekeeping. I love my father, but I can't stand the arguments any longer. My children hate him. He's breaking up my marriage, but I can't bring myself to ask him to leave. His memory is poor, so he's often confused and he can't take care of himself."

Mr. W. blamed his wife for being too easy on her father: "I've told her that she's got to lay down the law, tell him to quit picking on the kids; but she always ends up giving in to him. He's afraid to make any demands on me. He knows I'd kick him out in a minute." Mr. W. also complained that his wife had shown a progressive disinclination for sex in the past twelve years.

In the first six hours, I explained the basis of the trouble in their home: the vying for Superiority between husband and wife, the couple and the father, the children and her father, and the parents and the children. I taught them the principles and practice of Anti-H therapy. At this point, they withdrew from treatment, insisting that they wanted to try to manage on their own.

Three years later, the situation had gone from bad to worse. Fortunately, Mrs. W. finally phoned me out of desperation and returned to therapy. Obviously the therapy had failed. What had gone wrong?

Mrs. W. said that the real reason she had quit therapy was that she felt I was siding with her husband against her. After searching my memory, I came to the conclusion that I had moved too fast in criticizing this lady. I had attempted to show her what was wrong with her attitudes before taking the time to secure her Receptivity. Because of a very low Respect Level, she had reacted with hypersensitivity to my criticism, and therefore had quit therapy out of H toward me.

This time I was extremely careful to postpone the necessary corrective criticism until her Receptivity was fortified to a point at which she wouldn't buckle under; this is like postponing the ice skating until the ice is thick enough to take it. I was careful not to interrupt her, and gave her credit whenever I honestly could. When she criticized me for having been too critical of her in the initial round of therapy, I acknowledged it. When she blamed her husband or father, instead of taking their side I told her that I could understand her feeling about them.

I had made another mistake, too. In teaching this couple how to elevate each other's Respect Level, I had not sufficiently emphasized the danger of being too compliant. Mr. W. had misconstrued my teaching; he had ceased arguing with his wife and started agreeing with everything she said. Since he had had only a few weeks of therapy, he couldn't dissolve the large amount of H he had accumulated in twelve years. Nor had he relinquished his self-obsession, S and martyred feelings. These attitudes are certain to make the recipient more hostile. Since Mrs. W. perceived them, she interpreted his quick agreement on every issue as an underhanded means of manipulating her to his own ends.

Having learned my lesson already with Mrs. W., I withheld any criticism of Mr. W.'s mistake in trying to be nice and agreeable with his wife until I had carried out the techniques needed to earn his Receptivity.

When I felt secure about having attained this, I explained

why you can't raise the other fellow's Respect Level merely by agreeing instantly with him. Mr. W. learned that the fundamental basis of attaining receptivity is to *feel* good toward the other person. In order to attain the good feeling, it's essential to figure out why the other person is blameless. For Mr. W., this entailed his recognition of how he had provoked his wife into antagonism and uncooperativeness by transmitting his S and H; and how her father had done the same thing to her; and how, since childhood, her self-respect had been battered by a hostile, domineering mother.

It's a crucial error not to distinguish humility from submissiveness. An example is the girl who is bullied by an arrogant boyfriend. She believes that her submissiveness on one issue will beget his compliance on the next—where to go for dinner. "How about going to Sardi's?" she says.

"Don't be silly," he replies disdainfully. "We're going to Mama Leone's."

On the surface, "Turn the other cheek" would appear to be a noble precept that should gain a spot in heaven for those who follow it. In the case of the sweet little fellow who won't fight back, the spot in heaven may come all too soon. While his wife pours out torrents of abuse, he responds with "Yes, dear," "You're right, sweetheart" or "I should have done it." Meanwhile the H he tries to hide is goading his wife into more rage and churning up his own heart and blood pressure. While he's apt to die prematurely as a result of suppressed H, his wife lives on. Friends and relatives say, "What a pity that this sweet fellow died, instead of that nasty loudmouth." But he was as enraged inwardly as his wife was outwardly.

Submissiveness alone *may* inhibit violence or other vengeful acts of an angry person. But a soft answer doesn't turn away wrath if it's accompanied by suppressed H and presumptuous S.

This is the flaw in turning the other cheek. The recipient of "the other cheek" is not fooled when it is accompanied by H, S, and an air of martyrdom. He knows full well he's being demeaned. For this reason, the person who makes it a practice to give in will only perpetuate the other's H and continue to be despised and used as a doormat.

If "turning the other cheek" evokes such a hostile response, how come an early advocate and practitioner, Jesus Christ, was so successful in applying it? According to my concepts, it would have to be because of his *genuine* humility, dearth of H and S, and unselfish concern for others (rather than obsession with himself). Nevertheless, he did arouse H in some, most likely because his way was so different from theirs and because they *interpreted* his attitude as being "holier than thou."

The way to save ourselves from H is not by pretending that

we're not hostile, but by aggressively taking the measures necessary to liquidate it.

Must you excuse *everyone*, no matter how badly he or she behaves? If you are to be fair about it, you certainly must, since their bad behavior is determined by their emotional state. You've learned that no one is responsible for his emotional state since it is the natural product of the attitudes and feelings to which he has been subjected since birth. The sensible thing to do about bad behavior is to protect yourself from it and apply measures that are corrective, rather than respond with blame, which worsens it.

Returning to Mr. and Mrs. W.'s problem: Because of her guilt formed by years of H to her father, Mrs. W. felt compelled to go to extremes to take his side against her husband and children, and to be overzealous in insisting that he follow a diet, take naps in the afternoon, and make his doctors' appointments. His strenuous objections to her domineering regime had led to bitter arguments. But with the correction of my initial errors, I capitalized on Mr. and Mrs. W.'s Receptivity by proceeding rapidly with instructions in how to apply Anti-H therapy. They soon recognized the pernicious consequences of vying for S—with each other, with their children, and with the father. As their domineering and H abated, the father became more cheerful, friendly, and cooperative, and his memory improved. Mr. and Mrs. W. had attributed her father's depression, crankiness, contrariness, and confusion to senile deterioration. The vast improvement he made showed that his behavior had been caused by resentment, not by organic deterioration. With the sharp drop in H in the home, Mr. and Mrs. W. became a loving couple, and Mr. W. no longer resented having his father-in-law live with them.

They explained to their children that much of their grandfather's H was a reaction to the H and domineering of his daughter and the H he had been receiving from the rest of the family. The children responded by joining with their parents in the Anti-H campaign. Their reward was an affectionate and approving grandfather. For the first time, they had the fulfilling experience of a grandparent's love. Annual checkup visits revealed that Mr. and Mrs. W. were continuing to practice Anti-H therapy, thus maintaining the health and happiness they had achieved.

As one student complained, "If I humbly admit error, the other may perceive that I have buckled under, and continue to bully for further unfair advantage." But that's like saying, "After a few days on a diet, I still haven't lost any weight." The error is in not reckoning with the food consumed in the days immediately preceeding the diet. Like the dehydrated person, the bully has a deficiency syndrome. Just as a dehydrated person's system hoards its water content, so the respect-deficient person hoards every bit of respect. His thoughts and his conversation are about himself and his own importance.

When you dissolve your H and employ humility to elevate the bully's respect, you're doing the equivalent of giving water to a person who is dying of thirst. Just as water is a specific for dehydration, so the transmission of warm and respectful feelings is a specific for the bully's hostility. The fact that he continues to bully only indicates that his respect level is so low that he requires much more of the same—he's not ignoring your warmth, he's "gulping it down."

HOW NOT TO BE ASSERTIVE

I've just started reading one of those assertiveness training books, *Don't Say Yes When You Want To Say No*, by Herbert Fensterheim and Jean Baer. Assertiveness Training is of undoubted help to those individuals who feel so inferior that they're afraid to stand up for their rights for fear of being disliked. Thus, if a person suspects he is being mistakenly blamed, he should take the necessary steps to clear himself. Say you feel that you were taken advantage of by a car that darted into a parking space that you were about to back into. So you tell the driver in no uncertain terms, "I was here before you were. Now you just pull out of there." Since you're a follower of Assertiveness Training, you're supposed to stick up for your rights. But if you accompany your assertiveness with H, S and Mar., it is very likely to provoke a fight when used on a stranger—and generate antagonism when used on family, friends, and co-workers. Is it worth it?

No! Save your fight for issues that matter to you. Besides, you've learned that a person who behaves selfishly is saddled with an over-amount of $I \rightarrow A + Ob + H + S + Mar.$ He's just as innocent of what has been perpetrated on him in life as you are of what he did to you—the three-car accident all over again.

I agree that one shouldn't let others use him as a doormat; and should always protect himself and his rights. But we only provoke retaliation when we assert in a way that humiliates the other person—a serious flaw in Fensterheim's technique.

On page 32 of the paperback edition he gives this example: Sally, who had always let people walk all over her, had just completed her Assertiveness Training. Her boss yelled at her, "You left that Xerox room in an awful mess." Sally started to answer defensively with, "I wasn't in the Xerox room today," but just in time remembered her Assertiveness Training. She told her boss, "Now, you just apologize."

Startled by her change in manner, the boss shot back, "Apologize for what?"

"For yelling at me for something I didn't do," said Sally firmly. This example ends with Sally getting her apology. But her assertive order must have evoked some H too. Sally needs to understand that when the boss blasts her, he's reacting to his I feelings. He isn't any more to blame than she is for reacting in the same way.

It's obvious that Sally too reacted with H when she felt disrespected. But with Anti-H training, her understanding of the true source of the boss' H would be reflected in a sympathetic reply: "It *is* disgusting to see that room in a mess, but I wasn't in that room today. If you can spare me from my typing, I'll tidy it up."

Such a response would not only lessen the boss's H, but would elicit his gratitude for Sally's not taking advantage of his mistake to "rub it in." He would be agreeably surprised, and her display of understanding would increase his respect for her.

Now this is what I teach my trainees. For example, I discussed the case of Sally with a former student. When she began working as secretary to a college administrator, he frequently blamed her for things she hadn't done. Since she's been applying the technique, this formerly irascible boss has developed increasing respect and affection for her, and seldom blames her. She now enjoys working with him and has received a substantial raise.

Admitting error doesn't include "buckling under." In employing humility one should also employ whatever degree of fight and resolution that may be needed to protect oneself. Great animal trainers such as Ivan Tors approach lions, tigers and other wild animals with feelings of respect and affection. But at the same time, they keep themselves in a constant state of readiness to employ force if necessary. The "loser" continues to stick to his guns, but his "guns" include his H-free brain, humility, and genuine transmission of respect.

It takes time to nourish a "starved" Respect Level, just as it does to nourish a starving person back to health. Years of working with the Anti-H method domonstrates that, as in any other treatment (drug, radiation, physiotherapy), it must be repeated often enough as required to attain the desired result. An outstanding characteristic of Anti-H is that the more you practice it, the more evident its validity. That is why the people who have employed it for the longest periods are the ones who believe in it most.

Your personal problems won't vanish just because you've read through this book. Proficiency in applying Anti-H requires that you refer back to this book as often as you do to a cookbook or textbook. Whenever your application of Anti-H doesn't seem to be working, go back to the appropriate chapter; you'll find that with rare exceptions, you've deviated from one or more of the basic principles, applied the recommended techniques incorrectly, or haven't taken the time to win the other person's Receptivity.

As you follow these practices, you'll become increasingly more successful in escaping the H trap, mankind's most insidious and ruinous snare.

Index